From Baylor to Baylor

Competitive Learning Institute

From Baylor to Baylor

1991-2006 ACM-ICPC World Finals

From Baylor to Baylor
1991-2006 ACM-ICPC World Finals

Third Edition

ISBN: 978-84-122380-3-7
DL VA 835-2020

Contents ©2009 by the Competitive Learning Institute
Book concept and design ©2009 by Miguel Ángel Revilla
This edition ©2020 by Miguel Revilla Rodríguez

Formatted with X∃LATEX

Revision date: November 9, 2020

*To all the ACM-ICPC World Finals
staff, judges, volunteers and contestants*

PREFACE

What makes the ACM-ICPC the contest it is today? It's the people. The ACM International Collegiate Programming Contest (ICPC) community spans 1,838 universities in 88 countries. It includes great people at leading IT companies with IBM leading the way. We have tremendous support from Microsoft, AT&T, Apple, Texas Instruments, Sun, Google, Borland, Intel, and the myriad of companies that step forward each year to help our competitors compete on a global stage.

This book is dedicated to great institutional support. The UPE Computer Science Honor Society has supported the contest since its inception in 1970. ACM has provided venues and support since 1977. Baylor University has fostered the contest from the 1982 Championship, through establishing the Baylor Contest Model at the regionals that was adopted by the Finals in 1985, and then in the late 1980's assisting with the first major sponsorship and headquartering the ACM-ICPC to this day.

This book is dedicated to that collegial spirit that quietly provides a major component of the backbone and integrity of the ACM International Collegiate Programming Contest, the spirit that is typified by being there day in and day out to assist and not rule, to shine the spotlight on others, to be content with the outcome of a good deed. At Baylor, we call it the Baylor spirit. But, that spirit permeates humanity if we only tend it a bit and care.

This book is dedicated to people of that spirit drawn from academia and industry, people like Miguel Revilla and his crew who selflessly make the ACM-ICPC Problem Archive available at the Competitive Learning Institute web site for all to try. Their work at the University of Valladolid On-Line Judge system has graded over 7,000,000 solutions to problems since its inception, at no cost to those who would better hone their skills.

At the end of the day, the contest is about challenging the next generation to build their problem-solving prowess to the highest possible levels so that they can be equipped to challenge the problems the current generations cannot solve and the problems that are to come. It takes team work, know how, genius, and committed coaches to make that happen. It takes volunteers to put on the thousands of regionals and commitment to preserve the results decade after decade.

And, it takes a great team of judges to come up with the challenges for these students. So, on behalf of the ICPC Community, I would like to express my appreciation to Dick Rinewalt, Jo

Perry, and the outstanding World Finals Judges from 1991-2006 for contributing these problems for your enjoyment.

In future editions, we will provide insight into the contests from this era and acknowledgement of the many great volunteers who have given thousands of person years to make the ICPC fun and who amplify the opportunities of tens of thousands of students world-wide.

We may tell you about Problem F, about maintenance men blowing rows of computers minutes before a Finals, about using a B-B gun to shoot down errant balloons, about super computers that weighted less on departure than arrival to China, about Naval security in Hawaii, a bomb scare during an Awards Ceremony, too few i-nodes in Unix, heads of state who have helped the ICPC, a parting gift of a 1,000 Microsoft posters, a team from Eastern Europe who, at the fall of Iron Curtain, hitch-hiked to Belgium to compete in a regional, a young man from Mexico who gave me a $1 and told me he would get it back when he qualified for the World Finals and did, another team placing 6th and pledging to return for the Championship Trophy and did.

Maybe I'll share stories about my Baylor colleagues Pat Hynan, Jeff Donahoo, Don Gaitros, Mark Measures, Mike Korpi, Joel Korpi, Jim Nolen, Bill Booth, Sharon Humphrey, David Sturgill, Brian Sitton, and Ben Kelley who regularly give of the time and effort. Or possibly I'll share tales of James Comer and border guards, Joe DeBlasi, Steve Bourne, Henry Bassman, Jim Adams, Brenda Chow, Gabby Silberman, Rod D'Silva, John Clevenger, C.J. Hwang, Vladimir Parfenov, Yong Yu, Boba Mannova, Kiyoshi Ishihata, Katsuhiko Kakehi, Debbie Kilbride, Roy Andersson, Tom Verhoeff, Vladimir Parfenov, Roman Elizarov, Tim deBoer, Chris Rudin, the Traxlers, Fredrik Neimela, Greg Lee, Jan Madey, Nik Tapus, Ali Orooji, Orlando Madrigal, Sallie Henry, Raewyn Boersen, Ricardo Dahab among a few of the great champions of the contest.

Maybe I will tell you why the contest should be called Melinda's Programming Contest. I haven't yet touched the hem of the garment of acknowledgement or even skimmed the surface of the great debt I owe to the ICPC family.

I hope you enjoy the book. Give Miguel Revilla and the University of Valladolid a real pat on the back. He is the first Fellow of the Competitive Learning Institute and has done the lion's share of work pulling this book together.

In whatever small way I have contributed to the harmony of the ICPC community, I can never express my good fortune to be married to the **Mom of the ICPC**, Marsha Henderson Poucher or the joy I have in my daughters Elaine, Karen, and Melinda, my grandchild Kristen, and my sons-in-laws Dale Chang and Ken Patterson. Family makes a difference.

William B. Poucher
Baylor University, Texas

March 2009

ABOUT THE CONTEST

The ACM International Collegiate Programming Contest (ICPC) traces its roots to a competition held at Texas A&M in 1970 hosted by the Alpha Chapter of the UPE Computer Science Honor Society. The idea quickly gained popularity within the United States and Canada as an innovative initiative to challenge the top students in the emerging field of computer science.

The contest evolved into a multi-tier competition with the first Finals held at the ACM Computer Science Conference in 1977. Operating under the auspices of ACM and headquartered at Baylor University since 1989, the contest has expanded into a global network of universities hosting regional competitions that advance teams to the ACM-ICPC World Finals.

Since IBM became sponsor in 1997, the contest has increased by a factor of eight. Participation has grown to involve several tens of thousands of the finest students and faculty in computing disciplines at 1,838 universities from 88 countries on six continents.

The contest fosters creativity, teamwork, and innovation in building new software programs, and enables students to test their ability to perform under pressure. Quite simply, it is the oldest, largest, and most prestigious programming contest in the world.

The annual event is comprised of several levels of competition:

- *Local Contests* – Universities choose teams or hold local contests to select one or more teams to represent them at the next level of competition. Selection takes place from a field of over 300,000 students in computing disciplines worldwide.

- *Regional Contests* (September to December 2008) – This year, participation increased from 6,700 to 7,109 teams representing 1,838 universities from 88 countries on six continents competing at 259 sites.

- *World Finals* (April 18-22, 2009, Stockholm) – One hundred (100) world finalist teams will compete for awards, prizes and bragging rights in Stockholm hosted by KTH - Royal Institute of Technology. These teams represent the best of the great universities on six continents - the cream of the crop.

Battle of the Brains

The contest pits teams of three university students against eight or more complex, real-world problems, with a grueling five-hour deadline. Huddled around a single computer, competitors race against the clock in a battle of logic, strategy and mental endurance.

Teammates collaborate to rank the difficulty of the problems, deduce the requirements, design test beds, and build software systems that solve the problems under the intense scrutiny of expert judges. For a well-versed computer science student, some of the problems require precision only. Others require a knowledge and understanding of advanced algorithms. Still others are simply too hard to solve – except, of course, for the world's brightest problem-solvers.

Judging is relentlessly strict. The students are given a problem statement - not a requirements document. They are given an example of test data, but they do not have access to the judges' test data and acceptance criteria. Each incorrect solution submitted is assessed a time penalty. You don't want to waste your customer's time when you are dealing with the supreme court of computing. The team that solves the most problems in the fewest attempts in the least cumulative time is declared the winner.

To learn more about the ICPC, please visit http://acmicpc.org or http://icpc.baylor.edu/. Visit IBM's podcast series at http://battleofthebrains.podbean.com/ for insights from past contestants and current IBM executives.

Contest Growth

ACM, IBM, and Baylor University are thrilled that the contest continues to attract the best and brightest students from around the world, with tens of thousands of participants on 7,109 teams representing 1,838 universities in 88 countries. Since the beginning of IBM's sponsorship in 1997, when 840 teams competed, participation has increased by more than a factor of eight. For more information on previous contests, and last year's final standings and problem sets, please see http://icpc.baylor.edu / or http://www.ibm.com/university/acmcontest/.

CONTENTS

WORLD FINALS 1991

SAN ANTONIO, TEXAS

World Champion

STANFORD UNIVERSITY

Michael Patrick Frank
Sean Quinlan
David Magerman
Carl Witty

Director of Judging

Dick Rinewalt   *Texas Christian University*

Chief Judge

Jo Perry   *North Carolina State University*

Judges

Tom Nute	*Texas Christian University*
Lavon Page	*North Carolina State University*
Bob Roggio	*University of North Florida*
Brian Rudolph	*Michigan Technical University*
Patrick Ryan	*TechnoSolutions, Inc.*
Stanley Wileman, Jr.	*University of Nebraska at Omaha*

UVa Online Judge problem numbers

208	A	Firetruck
209	B	Triangular Vertices
210	C	Concurrency Simulator
211	D	The Domino Effect
212	E	Use of Hospital Facilities
213	F	Message Decoding
214	G	Code Generation

A   Firetruck

The Center City fire department collaborates with the transportation department to maintain maps of the city which reflects the current status of the city streets. On any given day, several streets are closed for repairs or construction. Firefighters need to be able to select routes from the firestations to fires that do not use closed streets.

Central City is divided into non-overlapping fire districts, each containing a single firestation. When a fire is reported, a central dispatcher alerts the firestation of the district where the fire is located and gives a list of possible routes from the firestation to the fire. You must write a program that the central dispatcher can use to generate routes from the district firestations to the fires.

Input

The city has a separate map for each fire district. Streetcorners of each map are identified by positive integers less than 21, with the firestation always on corner #1. The input file contains several test cases representing different fires in different districts.

- The first line of a test case consists of a single integer which is the number of the streetcorner closest to the fire.

- The next several lines consist of pairs of positive integers separated by blanks which are the adjacent streetcorners of open streets. (For example, if the pair 4 7 is on a line in the file, then the street between streetcorners 4 and 7 is open. There are no other streetcorners between 4 and 7 on that section of the street.)

- The final line of each test case consists of a pair of 0's.

Output

For each test case, your output must identify the case by number (CASE #1, CASE #2, etc). It must list each route on a separate line, with the streetcorners written in the order in which they appear on the route. And it must give the total number routes from firestation to the fire. Include only routes which do not pass through any streetcorner more than once. (For obvious reasons, the fire department doesn't want its trucks driving around in circles.)

Output from separate cases must appear on separate lines.

The following sample input and corresponding correct output represents two test cases.

Sample Input

```
6
1 2
1 3
3 4
3 5
4 6
5 6
2 3
2 4
0 0
4
2 3
3 4
5 1
1 6
7 8
8 9
2 5
5 7
3 1
1 8
4 6
6 9
0 0
```

Sample Output

```
CASE 1:
1 2 3 4 6
1 2 3 5 6
1 2 4 3 5 6
1 2 4 6
1 3 2 4 6
1 3 4 6
1 3 5 6
There are 7 routes from the firestation to streetcorner 6.
CASE 2:
1 3 2 5 7 8 9 6 4
1 3 4
1 5 2 3 4
1 5 7 8 9 6 4
1 6 4
1 6 9 8 7 5 2 3 4
1 8 7 5 2 3 4
1 8 9 6 4
There are 8 routes from the firestation to streetcorner 4.
```

B   Triangular Vertices

Consider the points on an infinite grid of equilateral triangles as shown below:

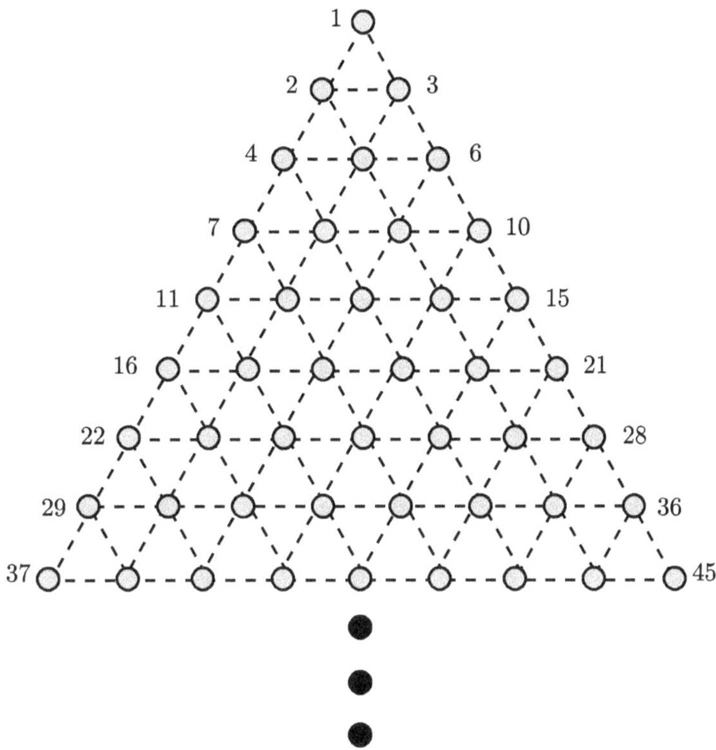

Note that if we number the points from left to right and top to bottom, then groups of these points form the vertices of certain geometric shapes. For example, the sets of points {1,2,3} and {7,9,18} are the vertices of triangles, the sets {11,13,26,24} and {2,7,9,18} are the vertices of parallelograms, and the sets {4,5,9,13,12,7} and {8,10,17,21,32,34} are the vertices of hexagons.

Write a program which will repeatedly accept a set of points on this triangular grid, analyze it, and determine whether the points are the vertices of one of the following "acceptable" figures: triangle, parallelogram, or hexagon. In order for a figure to be acceptable, it must meet the following two conditions:

    1)   Each side of the figure must coincide with an edge in the grid.

and   2)   All sides of the figure must be of the same length.

Input

The input will consist of an unknown number of point sets. Each point set will appear on a separate line in the file. There are at most six points in a set and the points are limited to the range $1 \ldots 32767$.

Output

For each point set in the input file, your program should deduce from the number of points in the set which geometric figure the set potentially represents; e.g., six points can only represent a hexagon, etc. The output must be a series of lines listing each point set followed by the results of your analysis.

Sample Input

```
1 2 3
11 13 29 31
26 11 13 24
4 5 9 13 12 7
1 2 3 4 5
47
11 13 23 25
```

Sample Output

```
1 2 3 are the vertices of a triangle
11 13 29 31 are not the vertices of an acceptable figure
26 11 13 24 are the vertices of a parallelogram
4 5 9 13 12 7 are the vertices of a hexagon
1 2 3 4 5 are not the vertices of an acceptable figure
47 are not the vertices of an acceptable figure
11 13 23 25 are not the vertices of an acceptable figure
```

C Concurrency Simulator

Programs executed concurrently on a uniprocessor system appear to be executed at the same time, but in reality the single CPU alternates between the programs, executing some number of instructions from each program before switching to the next. You are to simulate the concurrent execution of up to ten programs on such a system and determine the output that they will produce.

The program that is currently being executed is said to be running, while all programs awaiting execution are said to be ready. A program consists of a sequence of no more than 25 statements, one per line, followed by an end statement. The statements available are listed below.

Statement Type	Syntax
Assignment	*variable* = *constant*
Output	**print** *variable*
Begin Mutual Exclusion	**lock**
End Mutual Exclusion	**unlock**
Stop Execution	**end**

A *variable* is any single lowercase alphabetic character and a *constant* is an unsigned decimal number less than 100. There are only 26 variables in the computer system, and they are shared among the programs. Thus assignments to a variable in one program affect the value that might be printed by a different program. All variables are initially set to zero.

Each statement requires an integral number of time units to execute. The running program is permitted to continue executing instructions for a period of time called its quantum. When a program's time *quantum* expires, another ready program will be selected to run. Any instruction currently being executed when the time quantum expires will be allowed to complete.

Programs are queued first-in-first-out for execution in a *ready queue*. The initial order of the ready queue corresponds to the original order of the programs in the input file. This order can change, however, as a result of the execution of **lock** and **unlock** statements.

The **lock** and **unlock** statements are used whenever a program wishes to claim mutually exclusive access to the variables it is manipulating. These statements always occur in pairs, bracketing one or more other statements. A **lock** will always precede an **unlock**, and these statements will never be nested. Once a program successfully executes a **lock** statement, no other program may successfully execute a **lock** statement until the locking program runs and executes the corresponding **unlock** statement. Should a running program attempt to execute a **lock** while one is already in effect, this program will be placed at the end of the *blocked queue*. Programs blocked in this fashion lose any of their current time quantum remaining. When an **unlock** is executed, any program at the head of the blocked queue is moved to the head of the ready queue. The first statement this program will execute when it runs will be the **lock** statement that previously failed. Note that it is up to the programs involved to enforce the mutual exclusion protocol through correct usage of **lock** and **unlock** statements. (A renegade program with no **lock**/**unlock** pair could alter any variables it wished, despite the proper use of **lock**/**unlock** by the other programs.)

Input

The first line of the input file consists of seven integers separated by spaces. These integers specify (in order): the number of programs which follow, the unit execution times for each of the five statements (in the order given above), and the number of time units comprising the time quantum. The remainder of the input consists of the programs, which are correctly formed from statements according to the rules described above.

All program statements begin in the first column of a line. Blanks appearing in a statement should be ignored. Associated with each program is an identification number based upon its location in the input data (the first program has ID = 1, the second has ID = 2, etc.).

Output

Your output will contain of the output generated by the print statements as they occur during the simulation. When a print statement is executed, your program should display the program ID, a colon, a space, and the value of the selected variable. Output from separate print statements should appear on separate lines.

A sample input and correct output are shown below.

Sample Input	Sample Output

```
3 1 1 1 1 1 1
a = 4
print a
lock
b = 9
print b
unlock
print b
end
a = 3
print a
lock
b = 8
print b
unlock
print b
end
b = 5
a = 17
print a
print b
lock
b = 21
print b
unlock
print b
end
```

```
1: 3
2: 3
3: 17
3: 9
1: 9
1: 9
2: 8
2: 8
3: 21
3: 21
```

D   The Domino Effect

A standard set of Double Six dominoes contains 28 pieces (called bones) each displaying two numbers from 0 (blank) to 6 using dice-like pips. The 28 bones, which are unique, consist of the following combinations of pips:

```
Bone #    Pips      Bone #    Pips      Bone #    Pips      Bone #    Pips
   1     0 | 0         8     1 | 1        15     2 | 3        22     3 | 6
   2     0 | 1         9     1 | 2        16     2 | 4        23     4 | 4
   3     0 | 2        10     1 | 3        17     2 | 5        24     4 | 5
   4     0 | 3        11     1 | 4        18     2 | 6        25     4 | 6
   5     0 | 4        12     1 | 5        19     3 | 3        26     5 | 5
   6     0 | 5        13     1 | 6        20     3 | 4        27     5 | 6
   7     0 | 6        14     2 | 2        21     3 | 5        28     6 | 6
```

All the Double Six dominoes in a set can he laid out to display a 7 x 8 grid of pips. Each layout corresponds at least one "map" of the dominoes. A map consists of an identical 7 x 8 grid with the appropriate bone numbers substituted for the pip numbers appearing on that bone. An example of a 7 x 8 grid display of pips and a corresponding map of bone numbers is shown below.

```
        7 x 8 grid of pips                    map of bone numbers
    6   6   2   6   5   2   4   1         28 28 14   7 17 17 11 11
    1   3   2   0   1   0   3   4         10 10 14   7  2  2 21 23
    1   3   2   4   6   6   5   4          8  4 16 25 25 13 21 23
    1   0   4   3   2   1   1   2          8  4 16 15 15 13  9  9
    5   1   3   6   0   4   5   5         12 12 22 22  5  5 26 26
    5   5   4   0   2   6   0   3         27 24 24  3  3 18  1 19
    6   0   5   3   4   2   0   3         27  6  6 20 20 18  1 19
```

Write a program that will analyze the pattern of pips in any 7×8 layout of a standard set of dominoes and produce a map showing the position of all dominoes in the set. If more than one arrangement of dominoes yield the same pattern, your program should generate a map of each possible layout.

Input

The input file will contain several of problem sets. Each set consists of seven lines of eight integers from 0 through 6, representing an observed pattern of pips. Each set is corresponds to a legitimate configuration of bones (there will be at least one map possible for each problem set). There is no intervening data separating the problem sets.

Output

Correct output consists of a problem set label (beginning with Set #1) followed by an echo printing of the problem set itself. This is followed by a map label for the set and the map(s) which correspond to the problem set. (Multiple maps can be output in any order.) After all maps for a problem set have been printed, a summary line stating the number of possible maps appears.

At least one line is skipped between the output from different problem sets as well as before the text lines. One line separates also the different maps within the same problem set.

Sample Input

```
5 4 3 6 5 3 4 6
0 6 0 1 2 3 1 1
3 2 6 5 0 4 2 0
5 3 6 2 3 2 0 6
4 0 4 1 0 0 4 1
5 2 2 4 4 1 6 5
5 5 3 6 1 2 3 1
4 2 5 2 6 3 5 4
5 0 4 3 1 4 1 1
1 2 3 0 2 2 2 2
1 4 0 1 3 5 6 5
4 0 6 0 3 6 6 5
4 0 1 6 4 0 3 0
6 5 3 6 2 1 5 3
```

Sample Output

```
Layout #1:
    5    4    3    6    5    3    4    6
    0    6    0    1    2    3    1    1
    3    2    6    5    0    4    2    0
    5    3    6    2    3    2    0    6
    4    0    4    1    0    0    4    1
    5    2    2    4    4    1    6    5
    5    5    3    6    1    2    3    1

Maps resulting from layout #1 are:
    6   20   20   27   27   19   25   25
    6   18    2    2    3   19    8    8
   21   18   28   17    3   16   16    7
   21    4   28   17   15   15    5    7
   24    4   11   11    1    1    5   12
   24   14   14   23   23   13   13   12
   26   26   22   22    9    9   10   10

There are 1 solution(s) for layout #1.

Layout #2:
    4    2    5    2    6    3    5    4
    5    0    4    3    1    4    1    1
    1    2    3    0    2    2    2    2
    1    4    0    1    3    5    6    5
    4    0    6    0    3    6    6    5
    4    0    1    6    4    0    3    0
    6    5    3    6    2    1    5    3

Maps resulting from layout #2 are:
   16   16   24   18   18   20   12   11
    6    6   24   10   10   20   12   11
    8   15   15    3    3   17   14   14
    8    5    5    2   19   17   28   26
   23    1   13    2   19    7   28   26
   23    1   13   25   25    7    4    4
   27   27   22   22    9    9   21   21

   16   16   24   18   18   20   12   11
    6    6   24   10   10   20   12   11
    8   15   15    3    3   17   14   14
    8    5    5    2   19   17   28   26
   23    1   13    2   19    7   28   26
   23    1   13   25   25    7   21    4
   27   27   22   22    9    9   21    4

There are 2 solution(s) for layout #2.
```

E Use of Hospital Facilities

County General Hospital is trying to chart its course through the troubled waters of the economy and shifting population demographics. To support the planning requirements of the hospital, you have been asked to develop a simulation program that will allow the hospital to evaluate alternative configurations of operating rooms, recovery rooms and operations guidelines. Your program will monitor the usage of operating rooms and recovery room beds during the course of one day.

County General Hospital has several operating rooms and recovery room beds. Each surgery patient is assigned to an available operating room and following surgery the patient is assigned to one of the recovery room beds. The amount of time necessary to transport a patient from an operating room to a recovery room is fixed and independent of the patient. Similarly, both the amount of time to prepare an operating room for the next patient and the amount of time to prepare a recovery room bed for a new patient are fixed.

All patients are officially scheduled for surgery at the same time, but the order in which they actually go into the operating rooms depends on the order of the patient roster. A patient entering surgery goes into the lowest numbered operating room available. For example, if rooms 2 and 4 become available simultaneously, the next patient on the roster not yet in surgery goes into room 2 and the next after that goes into room 4 at the same time. After surgery, a patient is taken to the available recovery room bed with the lowest number. If two patients emerge from surgery at the same time, the patient with the lower number will be the first assigned to a recovery room bed. (If in addition the two patients entered surgery at the same time, the one first on the roster is first assigned a bed.)

Input

The input file contains data for a single simulation run. All numeric data in the input file are integers, and successive integers on the same line are separated by blanks. The first line of the file is the set of hospital configuration parameters to be used for this run. The parameters are, in order:

> Number of operating rooms (maximum of 10)
> Number of recovery room beds (maximum of 30)
> Starting hour for 1st surgery of day (based on a 24-hour clock)
> Minutes to transport patient from operating room to recovery room
> Minutes to prepare operating room for next patient
> Minutes to prepare recovery room bed for next patient
> Number of surgery patients for the day (maximum of 100)

This initial configuration data will be followed by pairs of lines of patient data as follows:

> Line 1:   Last name of patient (maximum of 8 characters)
> Line 2:   Minutes required for surgery   Minutes required in the recovery room

Patient records in the input file are ordered according to the patient roster, which determines the order in which patients are scheduled for surgery. The number of recovery room beds specified in any configuration will be sufficient to handle patients arriving from surgery (No queuing of patients for recovery room beds will be required). Computed times will not extend past 24:00.

Output

Correct output shows which room and bed are used by each patient, and the time period they use them along with a summary of the utilization of hospital facilities for that day. The output file consists of a set of two tables describing the results of the simulation run.

The first table is in columnar form with appropriate column labels to show the number of each patient (in the order the patient roster), the patient's last name, the operating room number, the time surgery beings and ends, the recovery bed number and the time the patient enters and leaves the recovery room bed. The second table will also be in columnar form with appropriate column labels summarizing the utilization of operating rooms and recovery room beds. This summary indicates the facility type (room or bed), the facility number, the number of minutes used and percentage of available time utilized. Available time is defined as the time in minutes from the starting time for first surgery of day to the ending time of the last patient in a recovery room bed.

Sample input

```
5 12 07 5 15 10 16
Jones
28 140
Smith
120 200
Thompson
23 75
Albright
19 82
Poucher
133 209
Comer
74 101
Perry
93 188
Page
111 223
Roggio
69 122
Brigham
42 79
Nute
22 71
Young
38 140
Bush
26 121
Cates
120 248
Johnson
86 181
White
92 140
```

Sample output

```
Patient          Operating Room           Recovery Room
#  Name       Room#  Begin   End     Bed#  Begin     End
--------------------------------------------------------
1  Jones        1    7:00   7:28      3    7:33    9:53
2  Smith        2    7:00   9:00      1    9:05   12:25
3  Thompson     3    7:00   7:23      2    7:28    8:43
4  Albright     4    7:00   7:19      1    7:24    8:46
5  Poucher      5    7:00   9:13      5    9:18   12:47
6  Comer        4    7:34   8:48      4    8:53   10:34
7  Perry        3    7:38   9:11      2    9:16   12:24
8  Page         1    7:43   9:34      6    9:39   13:22
9  Roggio       4    9:03  10:12      9   10:17   12:19
10 Brigham      2    9:15   9:57      8   10:02   11:21
11 Nute         3    9:26   9:48      7    9:53   11:04
12 Young        5    9:28  10:06      3   10:11   12:31
13 Bush         1    9:49  10:15     10   10:20   12:21
14 Cates        3   10:03  12:03      8   12:08   16:16
15 Johnson      2   10:12  11:38      4   11:43   14:44
16 White        5   10:21  11:53      7   11:58   14:18


Facility Utilization
Type  # Minutes   % Used
------------------------
Room  1     165    29.68
Room  2     248    44.60
Room  3     258    46.40
Room  4     162    29.14
Room  5     263    47.30
Bed   1     282    50.72
Bed   2     263    47.30
Bed   3     280    50.36
Bed   4     282    50.72
Bed   5     209    37.59
Bed   6     223    40.11
Bed   7     211    37.95
Bed   8     327    58.81
Bed   9     122    21.94
Bed  10     121    21.76
Bed  11       0     0.00
Bed  12       0     0.00
```

F Message Decoding

Some message encoding schemes require that an encoded message be sent in two parts. The first part, called the header, contains the characters of the message. The second part contains a pattern that represents the message. You must write a program that can decode messages under such a scheme.

The heart of the encoding scheme for your program is a sequence of "key" strings of 0's and 1's as follows:

$$0, 00, 01, 10, 000, 001, 010, 011, 100, 101, 110, 0000, 0001, \ldots, 1011, 1110, 00000, \ldots$$

The first key in the sequence is of length 1, the next 3 are of length 2, the next 7 of length 3, the next 15 of length 4, etc. If two adjacent keys have the same length, the second can be obtained from the first by adding 1 (base 2). Notice that there are no keys in the sequence that consist only of 1's.

The keys are mapped to the characters in the header in order. That is, the first key (0) is mapped to the first character in the header, the second key (00) to the second character in the header, the kth key is mapped to the kth character in the header. For example, suppose the header is:

AB#TANCnrtXc

Then 0 is mapped to A, 00 to B, 01 to #, 10 to T, 000 to A, ..., 110 to X, and 0000 to c.

The encoded message contains only 0's and 1's and possibly carriage returns, which are to be ignored. The message is divided into segments. The first 3 digits of a segment give the binary representation of the length of the keys in the segment. For example, if the first 3 digits are 010, then the remainder of the segment consists of keys of length 2 (00, 01, or 10). The end of the segment is a string of 1's which is the same length as the length of the keys in the segment. So a segment of keys of length 2 is terminated by 11. The entire encoded message is terminated by 000 (which would signify a segment in which the keys have length 0). The message is decoded by translating the keys in the segments one-at-a-time into the header characters to which they have been mapped.

Input

The input file contains several data sets. Each data set consists of a header, which is on a single line by itself, and a message, which may extend over several lines. The length of the header is limited only by the fact that key strings have a maximum length of 7 (111 in binary). If there are multiple copies of a character in a header, then several keys will map to that character. The encoded message contains only 0's and 1's, and it is a legitimate encoding according to the described scheme. That is, the message segments begin with the 3-digit length sequence and end with the appropriate sequence of 1's. The keys in any given segment are all of the same length, and they all correspond to characters in the header. The message is terminated by 000.

Carriage returns may appear anywhere within the message part. They are *not* to be considered as part of the message.

Output

For each data set, your program must write its decoded message on a separate line. There should not be blank lines between messages.

```
TNM AEIOU
0010101100011
1010001001110110011
11000
$#**\
01000001011011000111001000101000
```

Sample output

```
TAN ME
##*\$
```

G   Code Generation

Your employer needs a backend for a translator for a very SIC machine (Simplified Instructional Computer, apologies to Leland Beck). Input to the translator will be arithmetic expressions in postfix form and the output will be assembly language code.

The target machine has a single register and the following instructions, where the operand is either an identifier or a storage location.

L	load the operand into the register
A	add the operand to the contents of the register
S	subtract the operand from the contents of the register
M	multiply the contents of the register by the operand
D	divide the contents of the register by the operand
N	negate the contents of the register
ST	store the contents of the register in the operand location

An arithmetic operation replaces the contents of the register with the expression result. Temporary storage locations are allocated by the assembler for an operand of the form "$n" where **n** is a single digit.

Input

The input file consists of several legitimate postfix expressions, each on a separate line. Expression operands are single letters and operators are the normal arithmetic operators (+, -, *, /) and unary negation (@).

Output

Output must be assembly language code that meets the following requirements:

1. One instruction per line with the instruction mnemonic separated from the operand (if any) by one blank.

2. One blank line must separate the assembly code for successive expressions.

3. The original order of the operands must be preserved in the assembly code.

4. Assembly code must be generated for each operator as soon as it is encountered.

5. As few temporaries as possible should be used (given the above restrictions).

6. For each operator in the expression, the minimum number of instructions must be generated (given the above restrictions).

Sample input

```
AB+CD+EF++GH+++
AB+CD+-
```

Sample output

```
L A
A B
ST $1
L C
A D
ST $2
L E
A F
A $2
ST $2
L G
A H
A $2
A $1

L A
A B
ST $1
L C
A D
N
A $1
```

WORLD FINALS 1992

KANSAS CITY, MISSOURI

World Champion

UNIVERSITY OF MELBOURNE

Andrew Conway
Craig Dillon
Stephen Simmons

Director of Judging

Dick Rinewalt	*Texas Christian University*

Chief Judge

Jo Perry	*North Carolina State University*

Judges

Dave Brennan	*Microsoft*
David Elizandro	*Tennessee Tech University*
Tom Nute	*Texas Christian University*
Lavon Page	*North Carolina State University*
Patrick Ryan	*TechnoSolutions, Inc.*
Kevin Schott	*Shawnee State University*
Laurie White	*Mercer University*
Stanley Wileman, Jr.	*University of Nebraska at Omaha*

UVa Online Judge problem numbers

215	A	Spreadsheet Calculator
216	B	Getting in Line
217	C	Radio Direction Finder
218	D	Moth Eradication
219	E	Department of Redundancy Department
220	F	Othello
221	G	Urban Elevations

A Spreadsheet Calculator

A spreadsheet is a rectangular array of cells. Cells contain data or expressions that can be evaluated to obtain data. A "simple" spreadsheet is one in which data are integers and expressions are mixed sums and differences of integers and cell references. For any expression, if each cell that is referenced contains an integer, then the expression can be replaced by the integer to which the expression evaluates. You are to write a program which evaluates simple spreadsheets.

Input

Input consists of a sequence of simple spreadsheets. Each spreadsheet begins with a line specifying the number of rows and the number of columns. No spreadsheet contains more than 20 rows or 10 columns. Rows are labeled by capital letters A through T. Columns are labeled by decimal digits 0 through 9. Therefore, the cell in the first row and first column is referenced as A0; the cell in the twentieth row and fifth column is referenced as T4.

Following the specification of the number of rows and columns is one line of data for each cell, presented in row-major order. (That is, all cells for the first row come first, followed by all cells for the second row, etc.)

Each cell initially contains a signed integer value or an expression involving unsigned integer constants, cell references, and the operators + (addition) and - (subtraction).

If a cell initially contains a signed integer, the corresponding input line will begin with an optional minus sign followed by one or more decimal digits.

If a cell initially contains an expression, its input line will contain one or more cell references or unsigned integer constants separated from each other by + and - signs. Such a line must begin with a cell reference. No expression contains more than 75 characters. No line of input contains leading blanks. No expression contains any embedded blanks. However, any line may contain trailing blanks.

The end of the sequence of spreadsheets is marked by a line specifying 0 rows and 0 columns.

Output

For each spreadsheet in the input, you are to determine the value of each expression and display the resulting spreadsheet as a rectangular array of numbers with the rows and columns appropriately labeled. In each display, all numbers for a column must appear right-justified and aligned with the column label.

Operators are evaluated left to right in each expression; values in cells are always less than 10,000 in absolute value. Since expressions may reference cells that themselves contain expressions, the order in which cells are evaluated is dependent on the expressions themselves.

If one or more cells in a spreadsheet contain expressions with circular references, then the output for that spreadsheet should contain only a list of the unevaluated cells in row-major order, one per line, with each line containing the cell label, a colon, a blank, and the cell's original expression.

A blank line should appear following the output for each spreadsheet.

Sample Input

```
2 2
A1+B1
5
3
B0-A1
3 2
A0
5
C1
7
A1+B1
B0+A1
0 0
```

Sample Output

```
        0      1
A       3      5
B       3     -2

A0: A0
B0: C1
C1: B0+A1
```

B   Getting in Line

Computer networking requires that the computers in the network be linked.

This problem considers a "linear" network in which the computers are chained together so that each is connected to exactly two others except for the two computers on the ends of the chain which are connected to only one other computer. A picture is shown below. Here the computers are the black dots and their locations in the network are identified by planar coordinates (relative to a coordinate system not shown in the picture).

Distances between linked computers in the network are shown in feet.

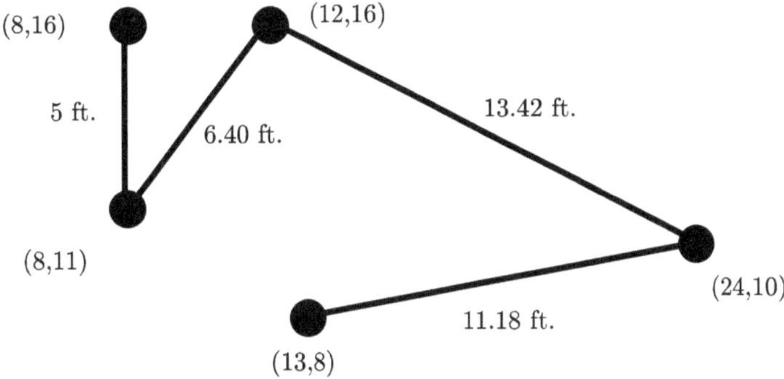

For various reasons it is desirable to minimize the length of cable used.

Your problem is to determine how the computers should be connected into such a chain to minimize the total amount of cable needed. In the installation being constructed, the cabling will run beneath the floor, so the amount of cable used to join 2 adjacent computers on the network will be equal to the distance between the computers plus 16 additional feet of cable to connect from the floor to the computers and provide some slack for ease of installation.

The picture below shows the optimal way of connecting the computers shown above, and the total length of cable required for this configuration is $(4+16)+ (5+16) + (5.83+16) + (11.18+16) = 90.01$ feet.

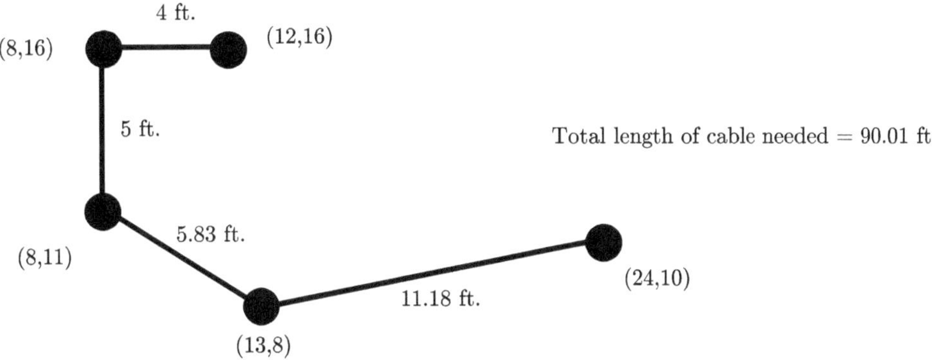

Input

The input file will consist of a series of data sets. Each data set will begin with a line consisting of a single number indicating the number of computers in a network. Each network has at least 2 and at most 8 computers. A value of 0 for the number of computers indicates the end of input.

After the initial line in a data set specifying the number of computers in a network, each additional line in the data set will give the coordinates of a computer in the network. These coordinates will be integers in the range 0 to 150. No two computers are at identical locations and each computer will be listed once.

Output

The output for each network should include a line which tells the number of the network (as determined by its position in the input data), and one line for each length of cable to be cut to connect each adjacent pair of computers in the network. The final line should be a sentence indicating the total amount of cable used.

In listing the lengths of cable to be cut, traverse the network from one end to the other. (It makes no difference at which end you start.) Use a format similar to the one shown in the sample output, with a line of asterisks separating output for different networks and with distances in feet printed to 2 decimal places.

Sample Input

```
6
5 19
55 28
38 101
28 62
111 84
43 116
5
11 27
84 99
142 81
88 30
95 38
3
132 73
49 86
72 111
0
```

Sample Output

```
**************************************************************
Network #1
Cable requirement to connect (5,19) to (55,28) is 66.80 feet.
Cable requirement to connect (55,28) to (28,62) is 59.42 feet.
Cable requirement to connect (28,62) to (38,101) is 56.26 feet.
Cable requirement to connect (38,101) to (43,116) is 31.81 feet.
Cable requirement to connect (43,116) to (111,84) is 91.15 feet.
Number of feet of cable required is 305.45.
**************************************************************
Network #2
Cable requirement to connect (11,27) to (88,30) is 93.06 feet.
Cable requirement to connect (88,30) to (95,38) is 26.63 feet.
Cable requirement to connect (95,38) to (84,99) is 77.98 feet.
Cable requirement to connect (84,99) to (142,81) is 76.73 feet.
Number of feet of cable required is 274.40.
**************************************************************
Network #3
Cable requirement to connect (132,73) to (72,111) is 87.02 feet.
Cable requirement to connect (72,111) to (49,86) is 49.97 feet.
Number of feet of cable required is 136.99.
```

C   Radio Direction Finder

A boat with a directional antenna can determine its present position with the help of readings
from local beacons. Each beacon is located at a known position and emits a unique signal. When
a boat detects a signal, it rotates its antenna until the signal is at maximal strength. This gives
a relative bearing to the position of the beacon. Given a previous beacon reading (the time, the
relative bearing, and the position of the beacon), a new beacon reading is usually sufficient to
determine the boat's present position. You are to write a program to determine, when possible,
boat positions from pairs of beacon readings.

For this problem, the positions of beacons and boats are relative to a rectangular coordinate
system. The positive x-axis points east; the positive y-axis points north. The course is the direction
of travel of the boat and is measured in degrees clockwise from north. That is, north is 0°, east is
90°, south is 180°, and west is 270°. The relative bearing of a beacon is given in degrees clockwise
relative to the course of the boat. A boat's antenna cannot indicate on which side the beacon is
located. A relative bearing of 90° means that the beacon is toward 90° or 270°.

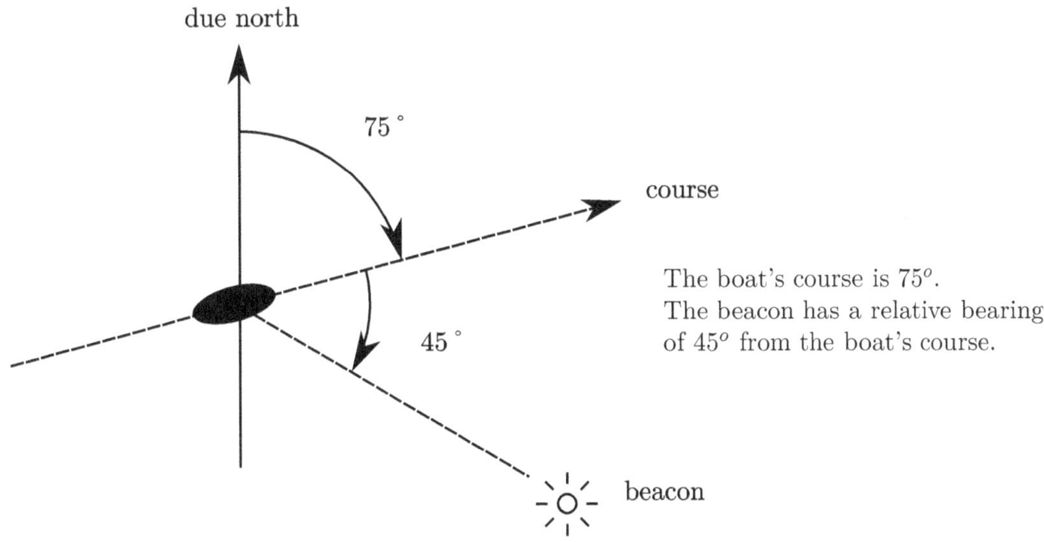

Input

The first line of input is an integer specifying the number of beacons (at most 30). Following that
is a line for each beacon. Each of those lines begins with the beacon's name (a string of 20 or
fewer alphabetic characters), the x-coordinate of its position, and the y-coordinate of its position.
These fields are single-space separated.

Coming after the lines of beacon information is an integer specifying a number of boat scenarios
to follow. A boat scenario consists of three lines, one for velocity and two for beacon readings.

Data on input line	Meaning of data
course speed	the boat's course, the speed at which it is traveling
time#1 name#1 angle#1	time of first beacon reading, name of first beacon, relative bearing of first beacon
time#2 name#2 angle#2	time of second reading, name of second beacon, relative bearing of second beacon

All times are given in minutes since midnight measured over a single 24-hour period. The speed is the distance (in units matching those on the rectangular coordinate system) over time. The second line of a scenario gives the first beacon reading as the time of the reading (an integer), the name of the beacon, and the angle of the reading as measured from the boat's course. These 3 fields have single space separators. The third line gives the second beacon reading. The time for that reading will always be at least as large as the time for the first reading.

Output

For each scenario, your program should print the scenario number (Scenario 1, Scenario 2, etc.) and a message indicating the position (rounded to 2 decimal places) of the boat as of the time of the *second* beacon reading. If it is impossible to determine the position of the boat, the message should say "Position cannot be determined." Sample input and corresponding correct output are shown below.

Sample Input

```
4
First 2.0 4.0
Second 6.0 2.0
Third 6.0 7.0
Fourth 10.0 5.0
2
0.0 1.0
1 First 270.0
2 Fourth 90.0
116.5651 2.2361
4 Third 126.8699
5 First 319.3987
```

Sample Output

```
Scenario 1: Position cannot be determined
Scenario 2: Position is (6.00, 5.00)
```

D Moth Eradication

Entomologists in the Northeast have set out traps to determine the influx of Jolliet moths into the area. They plan to study eradication programs that have some potential to control the spread of the moth population.

The study calls for organizing the traps in which moths have been caught into compact regions, which will then be used to test each eradication program. A region is defined as the polygon with the minimum length perimeter that can enclose all traps within that region. For example, the traps (represented by dots) of a particular region and its associated polygon are illustrated below.

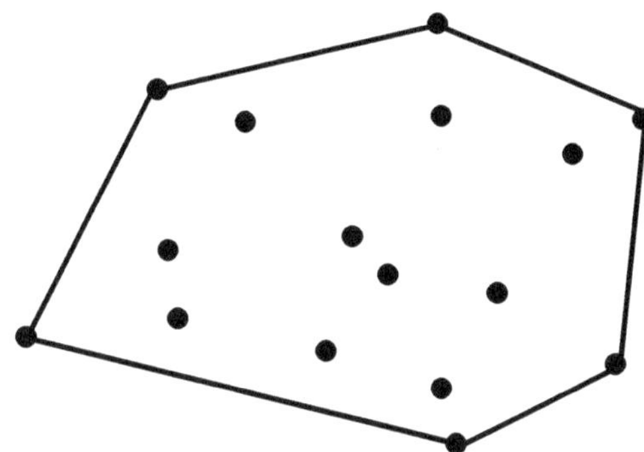

You must write a program that can take as input the locations of traps in a region and output the locations of traps that lie on the perimeter of the region as well as the length of the perimeter.

Input

The input file will contain records of data for several regions. The first line of each record contains the number (an integer) of traps for that region. Subsequent lines of the record contain 2 real numbers that are the x- and y-coordinates of the trap locations. Data within a single record will not be duplicated. End of input is indicated by a region with 0 traps.

Output

Output for a single region is displayed on at least 3 lines:

First line: The number of the region. (The first record corresponds to `Region #1`, the second to `Region #2`, etc.)

Next line(s):   A listing of all the points that appear on the perimeter of the region. The points must be identified in the standard form "(x-coordinate,y-coordinate)" rounded to a single decimal place. The starting point for this listing is irrelevant, but the listing must be oriented *clockwise* and *begin and end with the same point*. For collinear points, any order which describes the minimum length perimeter is acceptable.

Last line: The length of the perimeter of the region rounded to 2 decimal places.

One blank line must separate output from consecutive input records.

Sample Input

```
3
1 2
4 10
5 12.3
6
0 0
1 1
3.1 1.3
3 4.5
6 2.1
2 -3.2
7
1 0.5
5 0
4 1.5
3 -0.2
2.5 -1.5
0 0
2 2
0
```

Sample Output

```
Region #1:
(1.0,2.0)-(4.0,10.0)-(5.0,12.3)-(1.0,2.0)
Perimeter length = 22.10

Region #2:
(0.0,0.0)-(3.0,4.5)-(6.0,2.1)-(2.0,-3.2)-(0.0,0.0)
Perimeter length = 19.66

Region #3:
(0.0,0.0)-(2.0,2.0)-(4.0,1.5)-(5.0,0.0)-(2.5,-1.5)-(0.0,0.0)
Perimeter length = 12.52
```

E Department of Redundancy Department

When designing tables for a relational database, a functional dependency (FD) is used to express the relationship between the different fields. A functional dependency is concerned with the relationship of values of one set of fields to those of another set of fields.

The notation X->Y is used to denote that when supplied values to the field(s) in set X, the assigned value for each field in set Y can be determined. For example, if a database table is to contain fields for the *social security number* (S), *name* (N), *address* (A), and *phone* (P) and each person has been assigned a unique value for S, the S field functionally determines the N, A and P fields. This is written as S->NAP.

Develop a program that will identify each redundant FD in each input group of FDs. An FD is redundant if it can be derived using other FDs in the group.

For example, if the group contains the FDs A->B, B->C, and A->C, then the third FD is redundant since the field set C can be derived using the first two. (The A fields determine values for the B fields, which in turn determine values for the fields in C.) In the group A->B, B->C, C->A, A->C, C->B, and B->A, all the FDs are redundant.

Input

The input file contains an arbitrary number of groups of FDs. Each group is preceded by a line containing an integer no larger than 100 specifying the number of FDs in that group. A group with zero FDs indicates the end of the input.

Each FD in the group appears on a separate line containing two non-empty lists of field names separated by the characters - and >. The lists of field names contain only uppercase alphabetic characters. Functional dependency lines contain no blanks or tabs. There are no trivially redundant FDs (for example, A->A).

For identification purposes, groups are numbered sequentially, starting with 1; the FDs are also numbered sequentially, starting with 1 in each group.

Output

For each group, in order, your program must identify the group, each redundant FD in the group, and a sequence of the other FDs in the group which were used to determine the indicated FD is redundant. If more than one sequence of FDs can be used to show another FD is redundant, any such sequence is acceptable, even if it is not the shortest proof sequence. Each FD in an acceptable proof sequence must, however, be necessary. For example, in the set number 3 of the sample below, the sequence of FDs '2 4' can be used to show that the FD 5 is redundante, and then the solution 'FD 5 is redundant using FDs: 2 4' is also acceptable

If a group of FDs contains no redundancy, display No redundant FDs.

Sample Input

```
3
A->BD
BD->C
A->C
6
P->RST
VRT->SQP
PS->T
Q->TR
QS->P
SR->V
5
A->B
A->C
B->D
C->D
A->D
3
A->B
B->C
A->D
0
```

Sample Output

```
Set number 1
    FD 3 is redundant using FDs: 1 2

Set number 2
    FD 3 is redundant using FDs: 1
    FD 5 is redundant using FDs: 4 6 2

Set number 3
    FD 5 is redundant using FDs: 1 3

Set number 4
    No redundant FDs.
```

F   Othello

Othello is a game played by two people on an 8 x 8 board, using disks that are white on one side and black on the other. One player places disks with the white side up and the other player places disks with the black side up. The players alternate placing one disk on an unoccupied space on the board. In placing a disk, the player **must** bracket at least one of the other color disks. Disks are bracketed if they are in a straight line horizontally, vertically, or diagonally, with a disk of the current player's color at each end of the line. When a move is made, **all** the disks that were bracketed are changed to the color of the player making the move. (It is possible that disks will be bracketed across more than one line in a single move.)

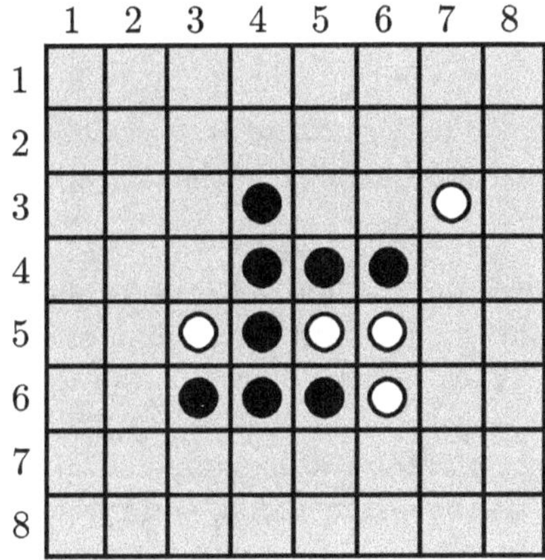

Legal Moves for White
(2,3),(3,3),(3,5),(3,6)
(6,2),(7,3),(7,4),(7,5)

Board Configuration after
White Moves to (7,3)

Write a program to read a series of Othello games.

Input

The first line of the input is the number of games to be processed. Each game consists of a board configuration followed by a list of commands. The board configuration consists of 9 lines. The first 8 specify the current state of the board. Each of these 8 lines contains 8 characters, and each of these characters will be one of the following:

'-' indicating an unoccupied square
'B' indicating a square occupied by a black disk
'W' indicating a square occupied by a white disk

The ninth line is either a 'B' or a 'W' to indicate which is the current player. You may assume that the data is legally formatted.

Then a set of commands follows. The commands are to list all possible moves for the current player, make a move, or quit the current game. There is one command per line with no blanks in the input.

Output

The commands and the corresponding outputs are formatted as follows:

List all possible moves for the current player. The command is an 'L' in the first column of the line. The program should go through the board and print all legal moves for the current player in the format (x, y) where x represents the row of the legal move and y represents its column. These moves should be printed in row major order which means:

1) all legal moves in row number i will be printed before any legal move in row number j if j is greater than i

and 2) if there is more than one legal move in row number i, the moves will be printed in ascending order based on column number.

All legal moves should be put on one line. If there is no legal move because it is impossible for the current player to bracket any pieces, the program should print the message "`No legal move.`"

Make a move. The command is an 'M' in the first column of the line, followed by 2 digits in the second and third column of the line. The digits are the row and the column of the space to place the piece of the current player's color, *unless the current player has no legal move.* If the current player has no legal move, the current player is first changed to the other player and the move will be the move of the new current player. You may assume that the move is then legal. You should record the changes to the board, including adding the new piece and changing the color of all bracketed pieces. At the end of the move, print the number of pieces of each color on the board in the format "`Black - ` xx `White - ` yy" where xx is the number of black pieces on the board and yy is the number of white pieces on the board. After a move, the current player will be changed to the player that did not move.

Quit the current game. The command will be a 'Q' in the first column of the line. At this point, print the final board configuration using the same format as was used in the input. This terminates input for the current game.

You may assume that the commands will be syntactically correct. Put one blank line between output from separate games and no blank lines anywhere else in the output.

Sample Input

```
2
--------
--------
--------
---WB---
---BW---
--------
--------
--------
W
L
M35
```

```
L
Q
WWWWB---
WWWB----
WWB-----
WB------
--------
--------
--------
--------
B
L
M25
L
Q
```

Sample Output

```
(3,5) (4,6) (5,3) (6,4)
Black -  1 White -  4
(3,4) (3,6) (5,6)
--------
--------
----W---
---WW---
---BW---
--------
--------
--------

No legal move.
Black -  3 White - 12
(3,5)
WWWWB---
WWWWW---
WWB-----
WB------
--------
--------
--------
--------
```

G   Urban Elevations

An elevation of a collection of buildings is an orthogonal projection of the buildings onto a vertical plane. An external elevation of a city would show the skyline and the faces of the "visible" buildings of the city as viewed from outside the city from a certain direction. A southern elevation shows no sides; it shows the perfectly rectangular faces of buildings or parts of faces of buildings not obstructed on the south by taller buildings. For this problem, you must write a program that determines which buildings of a city are visible in a southern elevation.

For simplicity, assume all the buildings for the elevation are perfect rectangular solids, each with two sides that run directly east-west and two running directly north-south. Your program will find the buildings that appear in a southern elevation based on knowing the positions and heights of each city building. That data can be illustrated by a map of the city as in the diagram on the left below. The southern elevation for that city is illustrated in the diagram on the right.

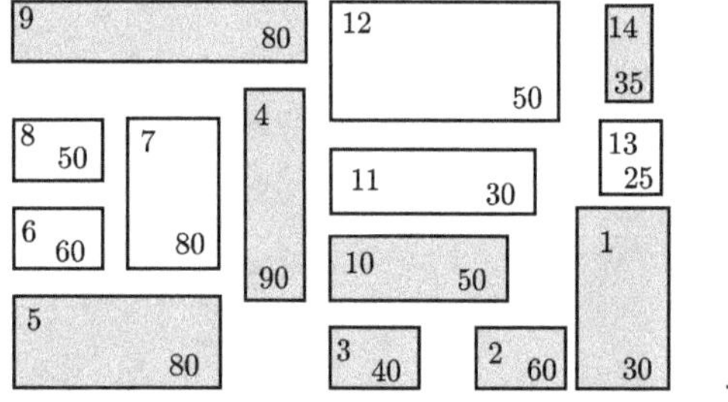

City map. Boldface numbers (in the upper left of each building) identify the buildings. Plain numbers (lower right) are the buildings heights.

Southern Elevation. Only the shaded buildings on the left are visible.

Input

Input for your program consists of the numeric description of maps of several cities. The first line of each map contains the number of buildings in the city (a non-negative integer less than 101). Each subsequent line of a map contains data for a single building – 5 real numbers separated by spaces in the following order:

> x-coordinate of the southwest corner
> y-coordinate of the southwest corner
> width of the building (length of the south side)
> depth of the building (length of the west side)
> height of the building

Each map is oriented on a rectangular coordinate system so that the positive x-axis points east and the positive y-axis points north. Assume that all input for each map corresponds to a legitimate map (the number of buildings is the same as the number of subsequent lines of input for the map; no two buildings in a single map overlap). Input is terminated by the number 0 representing a map with no buildings.

Output

Buildings are numbered according to where their data lines appear in the map's input data – building #1 corresponding to the first line of building data, building #2 data to the next line, and building #*n* to the *n*th line of building data for that map. (Buildings on subsequent maps also begin their numbering with 1.)

For each map, output begins with line identifying the map (`map #1`, `map #2`, etc.) On the next line the numbers of the visible buildings as they appear in the southern elevation, ordered south-to-north, west-to-east. This means that if building *n* and building *m* are visible buildings and if the southwest corner of building *n* is west of the southwest corner of building *m*, then number *n* is printed before number *m*. If building *n* and building *m* have the same *x*-coordinate for their southwest corners and if building *n* is south of building *m*, then the number *n* is printed before the number *m*.

For this program, a building is considered visible whenever the part of its southern face that appears in the elevation has strictly positive area. One blank line must separate output from consecutive input records.

Sample Input

```
14
160 0 30 60 30
125 0 32 28 60
95 0 27 28 40
70 35 19 55 90
0 0 60 35 80
0 40 29 20 60
35 40 25 45 80
0 67 25 20 50
0 92 90 20 80
95 38 55 12 50
95 60 60 13 30
95 80 45 25 50
165 65 15 15 25
165 85 10 15 35
0
```

Sample Output

```
For map #1, the visible buildings are numbered as follows:
5 9 4 3 10 2 1 14
```

WORLD FINALS 1993

INDIANAPOLIS, INDIANA

World Champion

HARVARD UNIVERSITY

Derrick Bass
Tony Hsieh
Craig Silverstein

Director of Judging
Dick Rinewalt   *Texas Christian University*

Chief Judge
Jo Perry   *North Carolina State University*

Judges

Dave Brennan	*Microsoft*
David Elizandro	*Tennessee Tech University*
Robin O'Leary	*Swansea*
Lavon Page	*North Carolina State University*
Patrick Ryan	*TechnoSolutions, Inc.*
Laurie White	*Mercer University*
Stanley Wileman, Jr.	*University of Nebraska at Omaha*

UVa Online Judge problem numbers

222	A	Budget Travel
223	B	Classifying Lots in a Subdivision
224	C	Kissin' Cousings
225	D	Golygons
226	E	MIDI Preprocessing
227	F	Puzzle
228	G	Resource Allocation
229	H	Scanner

A Budget Travel

An American travel agency is sometimes asked to estimate the minimum cost of traveling from one city to another by automobile. The travel agency maintains lists of many of the gasoline stations along the popular routes. The list contains the location and the current price per gallon of gasoline for each station on the list.

In order to simplify the process of estimating this cost, the agency uses the following rules of thumb about the behavior of automobile drivers.

- A driver never stops at a gasoline station when the gasoline tank contains more than half of its capacity unless the car cannot get to the following station (if there is one) or the destination with the amount of gasoline in the tank.

- A driver always fills the gasoline tank completely at every gasoline station stop.

- When stopped at a gasoline station, a driver will spend \$2.00 on snacks and goodies for the trip.

- A driver needs no more gasoline than necessary to reach a gasoline station or the city limits of the destination. There is no need for a "safety margin."

- A driver always begins with a full tank of gasoline.

- The amount paid at each stop is rounded to the nearest cent (where 100 cents make a dollar).

You must write a program that estimates the minimum amount of money that a driver will pay for gasoline and snacks to make the trip.

Input

Program input will consist of several data sets corresponding to different trips. Each data set consists of several lines of information. The first 2 lines give information about the origin and destination. The remaining lines of the data set represent the gasoline stations along the route, with one line per gasoline station. The following shows the exact format and meaning of the input data for a single data set.

Line 1: One real number – the distance from the origin to the destination

Line 2: Three real numbers followed by an integer

- The first real number is the gallon capacity of the automobile's fuel tank.
- The second is the miles per gallon that the automobile can travel.
- The third is the cost in dollars of filling the automobiles tank in the origination city.
- The integer (less than 51) is the number of gasoline stations along the route.

Each remaining line: Two real numbers

- The first is the distance in miles from the origination city to the gasoline station.
- The second is the price (in cents) per gallon of gasoline sold at that station.

All data for a single data set are positive. Gasoline stations along a route are arranged in nondescending order of distance from the origin. No gasoline station along the route is further from the origin than the distance from the origin to the destination. There are always enough stations appropriately placed along the each route for any car to be able to get from the origin to the destination.

The end of data is indicated by a line containing a single negative number.

Output

For each input data set, your program must print the data set number and a message indicating the minimum total cost of the gasoline and snacks rounded to the nearest cent. That total cost must include the initial cost of filling the tank at the origin. Sample input data for 2 separate data sets and the corresponding correct output follows.

Sample Input

```
475.6
11.9 27.4 14.98 6
102.0 99.9
220.0 132.9
256.3 147.9
275.0 102.9
277.6 112.9
381.8 100.9
516.3
15.7 22.1 20.87 3
125.4 125.9
297.9 112.9
345.2 99.9
-1
```

Sample Output

```
Data Set #1
  minimum cost = $27.31
Data Set #2
  minimum cost = $38.09
```

B   Classifying Lots in a Subdivision

A subdivision consists of plots of land with each plot having a polygonal boundary. A surveyor has surveyed the plots, and has given the location of all boundary lines. That is the only information available, however, and more information is desired about the plots in the subdivision. Specifically, planners wish to classify the lots by the number of boundary line segments (B=3,4,5,...) on the perimeter of the lots.

Write a program that will take as input the surveyor's data and produce as output the desired information about the nature of the lots in the subdivision.

Input

The input file consists of several data sets. Each data set begins with a line containing the number of line segments ($4 \leq N \leq 200$) in the survey. The following N lines each contain four integers representing the Cartesian (x, y) coordinate pairs for the N points of a boundary line segment. The input file is terminated with a 0.

Output

For each data set, provide output listing the number of lots in each classification of boundary line segment counts (B=3,4,5,...). Do not include in your output those cases in which the classification has no members. The output for each data set will begin with a line containing an appropriately labeled data set number. Output for successive data sets will be separated by a blank line.

Figures 1 and 2 show two hypothetical subdivisions. In Figure 1 there are 12 boundary line segments, and in Figure 2 there are 27. The sample input file below contains the data for these two test cases. The plot in the upper left hand corner of Figure 2 has one line running from (16,16) to (17,18) and another from (17,18) to (19,22). Thus this lot has a perimeter comprised of 5 boundary line segments, though geometrically the lot is a 4-sided region. Similarly the perimeter of the plot in the upper left hand corner of Figure 1 is comprised of 6 boundary line segments, though the lot is pentagonal in shape.

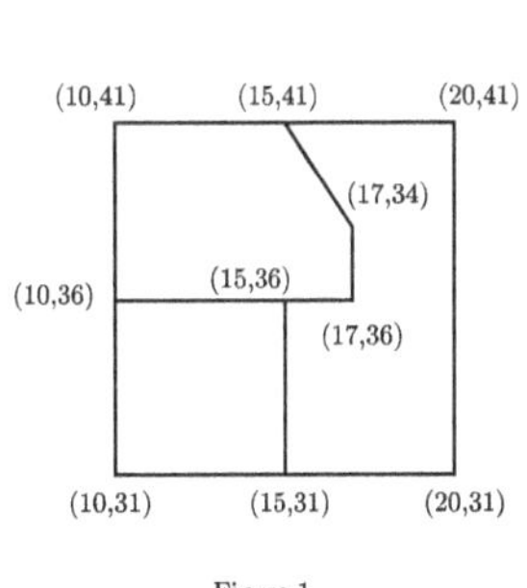

Figure 1

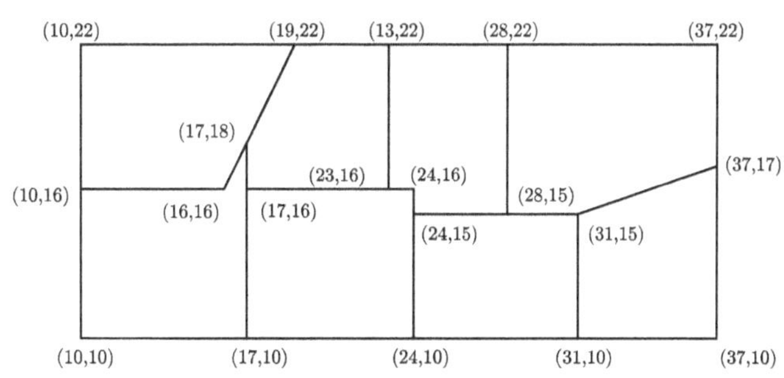

Figure 2

Sample Input

```
12
10 41 15 41
15 41 20 41
10 36 15 36
15 36 17 36
10 31 15 31
15 31 20 31
10 41 10 36
10 36 10 31
15 41 17 34
17 34 17 36
15 36 15 31
20 41 20 31
27
10 22 19 22
19 22 23 22
23 22 28 22
28 22 37 22
10 16 16 16
17 16 23 16
23 16 24 16
24 15 28 15
28 15 31 15
10 10 17 10
17 10 24 10
24 10 31 10
31 10 37 10
10 22 10 16
10 16 10 10
17 18 17 16
17 16 17 10
24 16 24 15
24 15 24 10
23 22 23 16
28 22 28 15
31 15 31 10
37 22 37 17
37 17 37 10
16 16 17 18
17 18 19 22
31 15 37 17
0
```

Sample Output

```
Case 1
Number of lots with perimeter consisting of 4 surveyor's lines = 1
Number of lots with perimeter consisting of 6 surveyor's lines = 1
Number of lots with perimeter consisting of 7 surveyor's lines = 1
Total number of lots = 3

Case 2
Number of lots with perimeter consisting of 4 surveyor's lines = 1
Number of lots with perimeter consisting of 5 surveyor's lines = 4
Number of lots with perimeter consisting of 6 surveyor's lines = 3
Total number of lots = 8
```

Assumptions:

1. *Each data set corresponds to a rectangular subdivision (as in Figures 1 and 2). The boundaries of the rectangular subdivision are parallel to the x and y axes.*

2. *All coordinates in the input file are positive integers in the range 1 to 10,000.*

3. *Boundary line segments in the input file do not extend past corners of lots. For example, in Figure 1 the surveyor must survey from the point (10,41) to (15,41) and from (15,41) to (20,41) rather than surveying the entire line (10,41) to (20,41).*

4. *At least one boundary line segment in each lot lies on the subdivisions bounding rectangle.*

C   Kissin' Cousins

The Oxford English Dictionary defines cousin as follows:

> **cous'in** (kŭzn), n. (Also *first cousin*) child of one's uncle or aunt; *my second (third...) cousin*, my parents first (second...) cousins child; *my first cousin once (twice...) removed*, my first cousin's child (grandchild...), also my parent's (grandparent's...) first cousin.

Put more precisely, any two persons whose closest common ancestor is $(m + 1)$ generations away from one person and $(m + 1) + n$ generations away from the other are mth cousins $n$ce removed. Normally, $m \geq 1$ and $n \geq 0$, but being used to computers counting from 0, in this problem we require $m \geq 0$ and $n \geq 0$. This extends the normal definition so that siblings are zeroth cousins. We write such a relationship as `cousin-`m`-`n.

If one of the persons is an ancestor of the other, p generations away where $p \geq 1$, they have a relationship `descendant-`p. You may assume that a person is not an ancestor of himself/herself.

A relationship `cousin-`m_1`-`n_1 is *closer* than a relationship `cousin-`m_2`-`n_2 if $m_1 < m_2$ or ($m_1 = m_2$ and $n_1 < n_2$). A relationship `descendant-`p_1 is *closer* than a relationship `descendant-`p_2 if $p_1 < p_2$. A `descendant-`p relationship is always closer than a `cousin-`m`-`n relationship.

Write a program that accepts definitions of simple relationships between individuals and displays the closest `cousin` or `descendant` relationship, if any, which exists between arbitrary pairs of individuals.

Input

Each line in the input begins with one of the characters **#**, **R**, **F** or **E**.

'#' lines are comments. Ignore them.

'R' lines direct your program to record a relationship between two different individuals. The first 5 characters following the 'R' constitute the name of the first person; the next 5 characters constitute the name of the second. Case is significant. Following the names, possibly separated from them by blanks, is a non-negative integer, k, defining the relationship. If k is 0, then the named individuals are siblings. If k is 1, then the first named person is a child of the second. If k is 2, then the first named person is a grandchild of the second, and so forth. Ignore anything on the line following the integer.

'F' lines are queries; your program is to find the closest relationship, if any, which exists between the two different persons whose 5 character names follow the 'F'. Ignore anything on the line following the second name. A query should be answered only with regard to 'R' lines which precede the query in the input.

'E' There will be one 'E' line to mark the end of the input data. Ignore anything on or after the 'E' line.

Output

For each 'F' line, your program is to report the closest relationship that exists between the two persons named *aaaaa* and *bbbbb* in one of the following formats:

aaaaa and *bbbbb* are descendant-*p*.
aaaaa and *bbbbb* are cousin-*m*-*n*.

with m, n and p replaced by integers calculated as defined above. If no relationship exists between the pair, your program is to output the following:

aaaaa and *bbbbb* are not related.

Sample Input

```
# A Comment!
RFred Joe  1 Fred is Joe's son
RFran Fred 2
RJake Fred 1
RBill Joe  1
RBill Sue  1
RJean Sue  1
RJean Don  1
RPhil Jean 3
RStan Jean 1
RJohn Jean 1
RMary Don  1
RSusanMary 4
RPeg  Mary 2
FFred Joe
FJean Jake
FPhil Bill
FPhil Susan
FJake Bill
FDon  Sue
FStan John
FPeg  John
FJean Susan
FFran Peg
FJohn Avram
RAvramStan  99
FJohn Avram
FAvramPhil
E
```

Diagram of the Sample Input

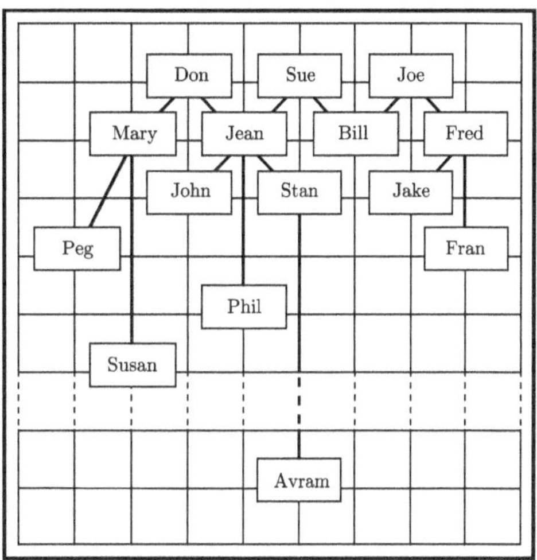

Sample Output

```
Fred  and Joe   are descendant-1.
Jean  and Jake  are not related.
Phil  and Bill  are cousin-0-3.
Phil  and Susan are cousin-3-1.
Jake  and Bill  are cousin-0-1.
Don   and Sue   are not related.
Stan  and John  are cousin-0-0.
Peg   and John  are cousin-1-1.
Jean  and Susan are cousin-0-4.
Fran  and Peg   are not related.
John  and Avram are not related.
John  and Avram are cousin-0-99.
Avram and Phil  are cousin-2-97.
```

D   Golygons

Imagine a country whose cities have all their streets laid out in a regular grid. Now suppose that a tourist with an obsession for geometry is planning expeditions to several such cities.

Starting each expedition from the central cross-roads of a city, the intersection labelled (0,0), our mathematical visitor wants to set off north, south, east or west, travel one block, and view the sights at the intersection (0,1) after going north, (0,-1) after going south, (1,0) after going east or (-1,0) after going west. Feeling ever more enthused by the regularity of the city, our mathematician would like to walk a longer segment before stopping next, going two blocks.

What's more, our visitor doesn't want to carry on in the same direction as before, nor wishes to double back, so will make a 90° turn either left or right. The next segment should be three blocks, again followed by a right-angle turn, then four, five, and so on with ever-increasing lengths until finally, at the end of the day, our weary traveller returns to the starting point, (0,0).

The possibly self-intersecting figure described by these geometrical travels is called a golygon.

Unfortunately, our traveller will making these visits in the height of summer when road works will disrupt the stark regularity of the cities' grids. At some intersections there will be impassable obstructions. Luckily, however, the country's limited budget means there will never be more than 50 road works blocking the streets of any particular city. In an attempt to gain accountability to its citizens, the city publishes the plans of road works in advance. Our mathematician has obtained a copy of these plans and will ensure that no golygonal trips get mired in molten tar.

Write a program that constructs all possible golygons for a city.

Input

Since our tourist wants to visit several cities, the input file will begin with a line containing an integer specifying the number of cities to be visited.

For each city there will follow a line containing a positive integer not greater than 20 indicating the length of the longest edge of the golygon. That will be the length of the last edge which returns the traveler to (0,0). Following this on a new line will be an integer from 0 to 50 inclusive which indicates how many intersections are blocked. Then there will be this many pairs of integers, one pair per line, each pair indicating the x and y coordinates of one blockage.

Output

For each city in the input, construct all possible golygons. Each golygon must be represented by a sequence of characters from the set {n,s,e,w} on a line of its own. Following the list of golygons should be a line indicating how many solutions were found. This line should be formatted as shown in the example output. A blank line should appear following the output for each city.

Sample Input

```
2
8
2
-2 0
6 -2
8
2
2 1
-2 0
```

Sample Output

```
wsenenws
Found 1 golygon(s).

Found 0 golygon(s).
```

Diagram of the 1st City

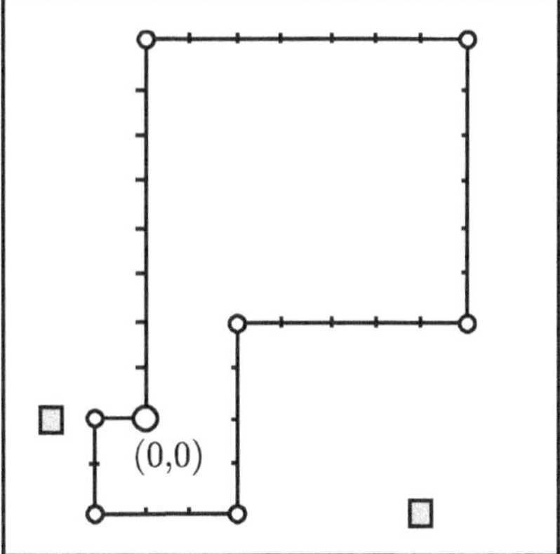

E   MIDI Preprocessing

MIDI (Musical Instrument Digital Interface) is a standard for communication involving computers and synthesized music instruments. Part of the standard defines commands, which when transmitted to a synthesizer, begin and end the sounding of a particular note. In this problem we will consider processing simple MIDI "programs." In the following example, three simultaneous notes (a chord, with note numbers 60, 70 and 80) are played for 10 time units immediately followed by a single note (number 62) for 2 time units.

```
0 ON 60
0 ON 70
0 ON 80
10 OFF 60
10 OFF 80
10 OFF 70
10 ON 62
12 OFF 62
```

Much existing music cannot be directly translated to this program form. Sometimes a note is already "on" when the written music indicates that it is to be sounded again. For example:

```
0 ON 60
10 ON 60
12 OFF 60
20 OFF 60
```

A synthesizer will interpret this program to sound note 60 for 12 time units, not 20 as indicated. We will not hear the separate sounding of the note at time 10, since turning on a note that is already sounding will be ignored. By analogy, consider turning a light on and off. If it's on, turning it on again is ineffective. Likewise, the first time that a light is turned off, it is off!

When a note already on is to be sounded again, the program can be "fixed" by inserting an OFF command for that note 1 time unit before the second ON command. Since there are already at least two OFF commands in such circumstances, only the last of these should be retained; the other should be eliminated from the program. The "fixed" program will cause the synthesizer to behave as if the same note had been played twice in rapid succession.

Another problem exists in programs that turn a note on and off at the same time. Depending on the ordering of the events in the program, either the note will be prematurely ended (if the OFF command appears after the ON), or the second sounding of the note will not be heard. For example:

```
0 ON 60          0 ON 60
10 ON 60         10 OFF 60
10 OFF 60        10 ON 60
20 OFF 60        20 OFF 60
```

In the example on the left, the note will be turned off at time 10. The example on the right doesn't leave the note off long enough to allow a human listener to detect the "punctuation" in the sound. In both cases the correction is the same: move the OFF command so it is executed by the synthesizer 1 time unit before the corresponding ON command.

If an OFF command inserted 1 time unit before an ON as a result of the "fix" occurs at exactly the same time as the preceding ON, the second ON and the OFF that occurs at the same time should be eliminated.

Write a program that will accept an arbitrary number of MIDI programs and "fix" them as described above.

Input

Each program contains an arbitrary number of lines. Each line contains, in order, the time that the command is sent to the synthesizer (a non-negative integer), a command (either ON or OFF), and a note (an integer in the range 1 to 127). These items are separated by one or more blanks. Each program except the last is terminated with a line containing only the integer -1. The last program is terminated by a line containing only the integer -2.

Output

The output is to be a "fixed" MIDI program in the same format as the input.

Assumptions:

1. *The ON and OFF commands will always be in upper case letters.*
2. *The times associated with programs are in non-decreasing order.*
3. *All notes are initially OFF.*
4. *If different notes are to be turned on or off simultaneously, the order in which the corresponding commands appear is unimportant.*
5. *Each ON command will have a matching OFF command following it in the program.*
6. *For ONE time and ONE tone, there is a maximum of 1 command ON and one command OFF.*

<table>
<tr><td>

Sample Input

```
0 ON 60
10 ON 60
12 OFF 60
20 OFF 60
-1
0 ON 60
5 ON 70
10 ON 60
10 OFF 60
15 OFF 70
15 ON 70
20 OFF 60
20 OFF 70
-1
0 ON 60
1 OFF 60
1 ON 60
10 OFF 60
-2
```

</td><td>

Sample Output

```
0 ON 60
9 OFF 60
10 ON 60
20 OFF 60
-1
0 ON 60
5 ON 70
9 OFF 60
10 ON 60
14 OFF 70
15 ON 70
20 OFF 60
20 OFF 70
-1
0 ON 60
10 OFF 60
-2
```

</td></tr>
</table>

F   Puzzle

A children's puzzle that was popular 30 years ago consisted of a 5×5 frame which contained 24 small squares of equal size. A unique letter of the alphabet was printed on each small square. Since there were only 24 squares within the frame, the frame also contained an empty position which was the same size as a small square. A square could be moved into that empty position if it were immediately to the right, to the left, above, or below the empty position. The object of the puzzle was to slide squares into the empty position so that the frame displayed the letters in alphabetical order.

The illustration below represents a puzzle in its original configuration and in its configuration after the following sequence of 6 moves:

1)   The square above the empty position moves.
2)   The square to the right of the empty position moves.
3)   The square to the right of the empty position moves.
4)   The square below the empty position moves.
5)   The square below the empty position moves.
6)   The square to the left of the empty position moves.

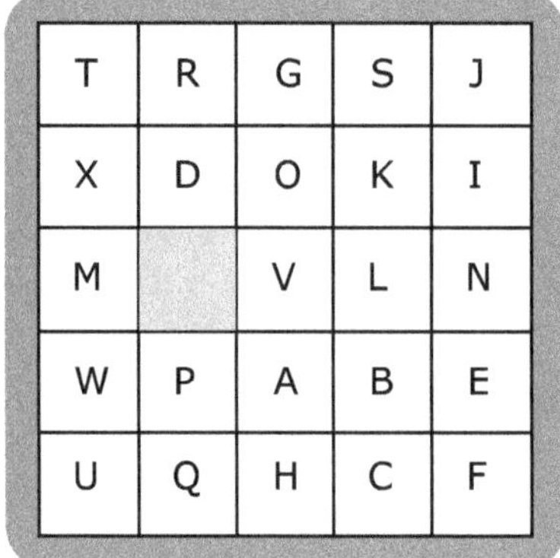

Original puzzle configuration

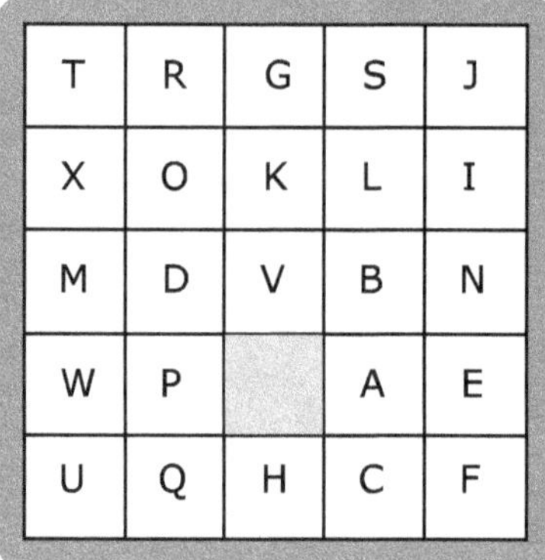

Puzzle configuration after the
sequence of described moves

Write a program to display resulting frames given their initial configurations and sequences of moves.

Input

Input for your program consists of several puzzles. Each is described by its initial configuration and the sequence of moves on the puzzle. The first 5 lines of each puzzle description are the starting configuration. Subsequent lines give the sequence of moves.

The first line of the frame display corresponds to the top line of squares in the puzzle. The other lines follow in order. The empty position in a frame is indicated by a blank. Each display line contains exactly 5 characters, beginning with the character on the leftmost square (or a blank if the leftmost square is actually the empty frame position). The display lines will correspond to a legitimate puzzle.

The sequence of moves is represented by a sequence of As, Bs, Rs, and Ls to denote which square moves into the empty position. A denotes that the square above the empty position moves; B denotes that the square below the empty position moves; L denotes that the square to the left of the empty position moves; R denotes that the square to the right of the empty position moves. It is possible that there is an illegal move, even when it is represented by one of the 4 move characters. If an illegal move occurs, the puzzle is considered to have no final configuration. This sequence of moves may be spread over several lines, but it always ends in the digit 0. The end of data is denoted by the character Z.

Output

Output for each puzzle begins with an appropriately labeled number (`Puzzle #1`, `Puzzle #2`, etc.). If the puzzle has no final configuration, then a message to that effect should follow. Otherwise that final configuration should be displayed.

Format each line for a final configuration so that there is a single blank character between two adjacent letters. Treat the empty square the same as a letter. For example, if the blank is an interior position, then it will appear as a sequence of 3 blanks – one to separate it from the square to the left, one for the empty position itself, and one to separate it from the square to the right.

Separate output from different puzzle records by one blank line.

Note: The first record of the sample input corresponds to the puzzle illustrated above.

Sample Input

```
TRGSJ
XDOKI
M VLN
WPABE
UQHCF
ARRBBL0
ABCDE
FGHIJ
KLMNO
PQRS
TUVWX
AAA
LLLL0
ABCDE
FGHIJ
KLMNO
PQRS
TUVWX
AAAAABBRRRLL0
Z
```

Sample Output

```
Puzzle #1:
T R G S J
X O K L I
M D V B N
W P   A E
U Q H C F

Puzzle #2:
  A B C D
F G H I E
K L M N J
P Q R S O
T U V W X

Puzzle #3:
This puzzle has no final configuration.
```

G   Resource Allocation

A software development firm is willing to hire new programmers and to spend more money for hardware and software systems in order to increase productivity in its programming divisions. For lack of a better idea, management has defined increased productivity for a division as "incremental lines of code" that the division produces. The company needs a resource allocation model to determine how the money and new programmers should be divided among the divisions in order to maximize the total productivity increase.

Each programming division is limited in how effectively it can utilize any new resources. For example, one particular division will be able to use 0, 3, 5, or 6 new programmers effectively. (The personnel organization within that division prevents it from being able to use 1, 2, 4, 7 or more new programmers.) This gives 4 options for allocating new programmers to that division. There are only 3 different options for allocation of additional money to that division. Therefore, there are 12 possible allocation scenarios in this example. For each scenario, the company has estimated the incremental lines of code that would be produced by that division.

You must write a program that recommends a precise allocation of resources among the divisions. For each division, your program must determine how many new programmers and how much money should be allocated. Allocation of new programmers and money must be made to maximize the total productivity increase – the sum of incremental lines of code over all divisions. The total number of programmers allocated cannot exceed the total number of programmers that the company is willing to hire. The total amount of money cannot exceed the total amount budgeted for the entire company. In the case where there are multiple optimal solutions, your program may recommend any one of them.

Input

Input for your program consists of several allocation problems. All input data are non-negative integers. The first 3 lines of input for each problem consists of:

d number of programming divisions
         $(0 < d \leq 20$ except when d is the end-of-file sentinel$)$
p total number of new programmers
b total amount of money budgeted for new computing resources

Following those 3 lines are input records for each programming division. The first record is for division #1, the second for division #2, etc. Each division record is organized as follows:

n	number of new programmer options $(0 \leq n \leq 10)$
$x_1 x_2 \ldots x_n$	list of new programmer options
	(numbers are separated by blanks)
k	number of new budget options $(0 \leq k \leq 10)$
$b_1 b_2 \ldots b_k$	cost of each new budget option (separated by blanks)
$n \times k$ table of integers	the (i, j) table entry is the incremental lines of code produced
	for allocation of x_i new programmers and b_j additional budget

It is possible to allocate 0 new programmers to any division and \$0 for new hardware and software – resulting in no increase in productivity for that division. This "null" allocation will be explicitly shown.

Each allocation problem begins on a new line. The end of input is signified by an allocation "problem" with 0 divisions. No input lines follow that line.

Output

Output for each problem begins with a line identifying the problem that is solved (`problem #1`, `problem #2`, etc.). This is followed by a blank line then 3 lines that tell the total amount of money to be spent, the total number of new programmer to be hired, and the total anticipated new productivity for an optimal resource allocation.

Output for each division comes next. The first line identifies the division by number. The remaining 3 lines indicate the division's budget, the number of new programmers for the division, and the expected incremental lines of code to be produced. One blank line appears between output for successive divisions. Two blank lines appear between output for successive problems. The exact formatting of the output is not critical, but all output must be easy to read and well-identified.

Note: A sample input file which contains one complete allocation problem is shown below. In this problem, there are 3 programming divisions. The company is willing to hire up to 10 new programmers and spend up to $90,000 on new computing resources. For division #1, the expenditure of $50,000 on new computing resources and allocation of 6 new programmers would result in the production of 40,000 incremental lines of code.

Sample Input

```
3
10
90000
4
0 2 5 6
4
0 20000 50000 70000
      0    10000    20000    50000
  60000    20000    10000    40000
  20000    10000    30000    40000
  30000    10000    40000    30000
5
0 1 3 4 8
3
0 40000 80000
      0    50000    30000
  50000    40000    60000
  20000    30000    50000
  80000    90000    50000
  30000    40000    70000
3
0  4  6
5
0   50000   30000   40000   50000
      0   30000   50000   60000   30000
  10000   20000   30000   40000   50000
  20000   30000   40000   50000   60000
0
```

Sample Output

```
Optimal resource allocation problem #1

Total budget: $80000
Total new programmers: 6
Total productivity increase: 210000

Division #1 resource allocation:
Budget:  $0
Programmers: 2
Incremental lines of code: 60000

Division #2 resource allocation:
Budget:  $40000
Programmers: 4
Incremental lines of code: 90000

Division #3 resource allocation:
Budget:  $40000
Programmers: 0
Incremental lines of code: 60000
```

H   Scanner

A body scanner works by scanning a succession of horizontal slices through the body; the slices
are imaged one at a time. The image slices can be reassembled to form a three dimensional model
of the object. Write a program to construct a two dimensional image slice using data captured
during the scan.

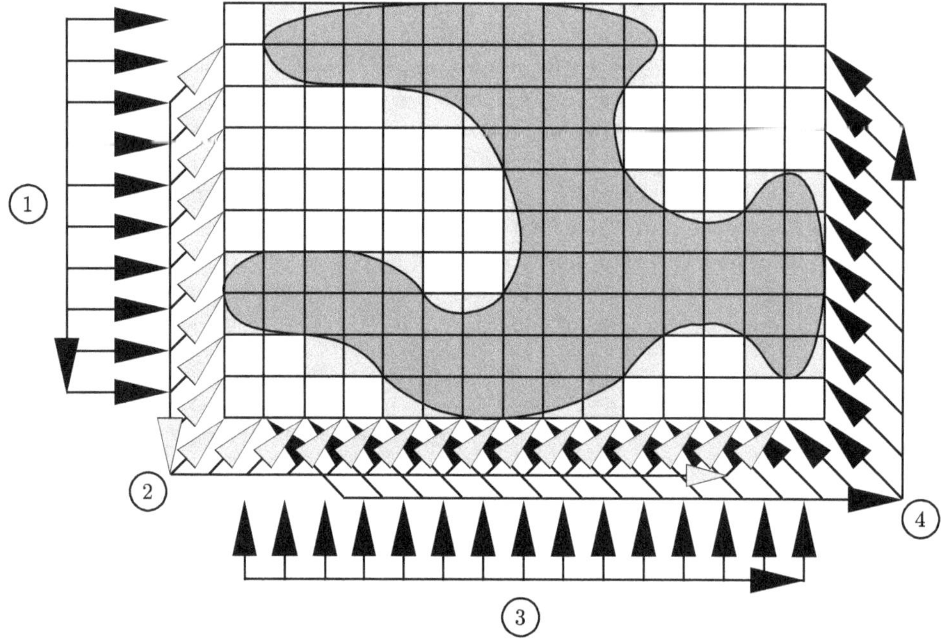

The scanner consists of four arrays of sensors arranged around a 10×15 matrix. Array 1
consists of 10 sensors pointing to the right, array 2 has 24 sensors pointing diagonally to the top
right, array 3 has 15 sensors pointing to the top and array 4 has 24 sensors pointing to the top
left. Each sensor records the thickness of that portion of the object directly in front of that sensor.

Readings from the arrays of sensors are recorded in counterclockwise order. Within an array
of sensors, data are also recorded counterclockwise. A complete scan consists of 73 readings.

Input

The input file begins with a line with an integer indicating the number of image slices to follow.
For each image slice, there are separate lines with 10, 24, 15, and 24 integers representing sensor
data from sensor arrays 1 through 4 respectively. The order of the readings is indicated in the
diagram.

Output

For each slice, your program should print 10 lines of 15 cells. To indicate that the cell represents
a part of the object, print a hash character (#) for the cell; to indicate that the cell is not a part
of the object, print a period (.). Between successive output image slices, print a blank line.

It is possible for the result of a scan to be ambiguous, in that case you will have to output a
blank picture as shown in the sample output.

Sample Input (First one describing object above)

```
2
10 10 6 4 6 8 13 15 11 6
0 1 2 2 2 2 4 5 5 6 7 6 5 6 6 6 5 5 6 6 3 2 2 1 0
2 4 5 5 7 6 7 10 10 10 7 3 3 5 5
0 0 1 3 4 4 4 4 3 4 5 7 8 8 9 9 6 4 4 2 0 0 0 0
10 10 6 4 6 8 13 15 11 6
0 1 2 2 2 2 4 5 5 6 7 6 5 6 6 6 5 5 6 6 3 2 2 1 0
2 4 5 5 7 6 7 10 10 10 7 3 3 5 5
0 0 1 3 4 4 4 4 3 2 5 7 8 8 9 9 6 4 4 2 0 0 0 0
```

Sample Output

```
.#########....
.##########....
....######.....
......####.....
.......####..##
.......########
#####..########
###############
..#########..##
....######.....

.............
.............
.............
.............
.............
.............
.............
.............
.............
.............
```

WORLD FINALS 1994

PHOENIX, ARIZONA

World Champion

UNIVERSITY OF WATERLOO

Seiji Ando
Ian Goldberg
Ka-Ping Yee

Director of Judging
Dick Rinewalt — *Texas Christian University*

Chief Judge
Jo Perry — *North Carolina State University*

Judges
David Elizandro — *Tennessee Tech University*
Robin O'Leary — *Swansea*
Lavon Page — *North Carolina State University*
Patrick Ryan — *TechnoSolutions, Inc.*
Laurie White — *Mercer University*
Stanley Wileman, Jr. — *University of Nebraska at Omaha*

UVa Online Judge problem numbers
230   A   Borrowers
231   B   Testing the CATCHER
232   C   Crossword Answers
233   D   Package Pricing
234   E   Switching Channels
235   F   Typesetting
236   G   VTAS - Vessel Traffic Advisory Service
237   H   Monitoring Wheelchair Patients

A   Borrowers

> I mean your *borrowers of books* – those mutilators of collections, spoilers of the symmetry of shelves, and creators of odd volumes.
>
> – (Charles Lamb, *Essays of Elia* (1823) 'The Two Races of Men')

Like Mr. Lamb, librarians have their problems with borrowers too. People don't put books back where they should. Instead, returned books are kept at the main desk until a librarian is free to replace them in the right places on the shelves. Even for librarians, putting the right book in the right place can be very time-consuming. But since many libraries are now computerized, you can write a program to help.

When a borrower takes out or returns a book, the computer keeps a record of the title. Periodically, the librarians will ask your program for a list of books that have been returned so the books can be returned to their correct places on the shelves. Before they are returned to the shelves, the returned books are sorted by author and then title using the ASCII collating sequence. Your program should output the list of returned books in the same order as they should appear on the shelves. For each book, your program should tell the librarian which book (including those previously shelved) is already on the shelf before which the returned book should go.

Input

First, the stock of the library will be listed, one book per line, in no particular order. Initially, they are all on the shelves. No two books have the same title. The format of each line will be:

        "*title*" **by** *author*

The end of the stock listing will be marked by a line containing only the word:

        END

Following the stock list will be a series of records of books borrowed and returned, and requests from librarians for assistance in restocking the shelves. Each record will appear on a single line, in one of the following formats:

        BORROW "*title*"
        RETURN "*title*"
        SHELVE

The list will be terminated by a line containing only the word:

        END

Output

Each time the SHELVE command appears, your program should output a series of instructions for the librarian, one per line, in the format:

        Put "*title*$_1$" **after** "*title*$_2$"

or, for the special case of the book being the first in the collection:

        Put "*title*" **first**

After the set of instructions for each SHELVE, output a line containing only the word:

        END

Assumptions & Limitations:

1. A title is at most 80 characters long.
2. An author is at most 80 characters long.
3. A title will not contain the double quote (") character.

Sample Input

```
"The Canterbury Tales" by Chaucer, G.
"Algorithms" by Sedgewick, R.
"The C Programming Language" by Kernighan, B. and Ritchie, D.
END
BORROW "Algorithms"
BORROW "The C Programming Language"
RETURN "Algorithms"
RETURN "The C Programming Language"
SHELVE
END
```

Sample Output

```
Put "The C Programming Language" after "The Canterbury Tales"
Put "Algorithms" after "The C Programming Language"
END
```

B   Testing the CATCHER

A military contractor for the Department of Defense has just completed a series of preliminary tests for a new defensive missile called the CATCHER which is capable of intercepting multiple incoming offensive missiles. The CATCHER is supposed to be a remarkable defensive missile. It can move forward, laterally, and downward at very fast speeds, and it can intercept an offensive missile without being damaged. But it does have one major flaw. Although it can be fired to reach any initial elevation, it has no power to move higher than the last missile that it has intercepted.

The tests which the contractor completed were computer simulations of battlefield and hostile attack conditions. Since they were only preliminary, the simulations tested only the CATCHER's vertical movement capability. In each simulation, the CATCHER was fired at a sequence of offensive missiles which were incoming at fixed time intervals. The only information available to the CATCHER for each incoming missile was its height at the point it could be intercepted and where it appeared in the sequence of missiles. Each incoming missile for a test run is represented in the sequence only once.

The result of each test is reported as the sequence of incoming missiles and the total number of those missiles that are intercepted by the CATCHER in that test.

The General Accounting Office wants to be sure that the simulation test results submitted by the military contractor are attainable, given the constraints of the CATCHER. You must write a program that takes input data representing the pattern of incoming missiles for several different tests and outputs the maximum numbers of missiles that the CATCHER can intercept for those tests. For any incoming missile in a test, the CATCHER is able to intercept it if and only if it satisfies one of these two conditions:

1. The incoming missile is the first missile to be intercepted in this test.

-or-

2. The missile was fired after the last missile that was intercepted and it is not higher than the last missile which was intercepted.

Input

The input data for any test consists of a sequence of one or more non-negative integers, all of which are less than or equal to 32,767, representing the heights of the incoming missiles (the test pattern). The last number in each sequence is -1, which signifies the end of data for that particular test and is not considered to represent a missile height. The end of data for the entire input is the number -1 as the first value in a test; it is not considered to be a separate test.

Output

Output for each test consists of a test number (`Test #1`, `Test #2`, etc.) and the maximum number of incoming missiles that the CATCHER could possibly intercept for the test. That maximum number appears after an identifying message. There must be at least one blank line between output for successive data sets.

Note: The number of missiles for any given test is not limited. If your solution is based on an inefficient algorithm, it **may not** execute in the allotted time.

Sample Input

```
389
207
155
300
299
170
158
65
-1
23
34
21
-1
-1
```

Sample Output

```
Test #1:
  maximum possible interceptions: 6

Test #2:
  maximum possible interceptions: 2
```

C Crossword Answers

A crossword puzzle consists of a rectangular grid of black and white squares and two lists of definitions (or descriptions). One list of definitions is for "words" to be written left to right across white squares in the rows and the other list is for words to be written down white squares in the columns. (A word is a sequence of alphabetic characters.) To solve a crossword puzzle, one writes the words corresponding to the definitions on the white squares of the grid.

The definitions correspond to the rectangular grid by means of sequential integers on "eligible" white squares. White squares with black squares immediately to the left or above them are "eligible." White squares with no squares either immediately to the left or above are also "eligible." No other squares are numbered. All of the squares on the first row are numbered.

The numbering starts with 1 and continues consecutively across white squares of the first row, then across the eligible white squares of the second row, then across the eligible white squares of the third row and so on across all of the rest of the rows of the puzzle. The picture below illustrates a rectangular crossword puzzle grid with appropriate numbering.

1	2	3	██	4	5	6
██	7		██	8		
9			10	██	11	
12		██	13	14		
██	15	16	██	17		██
18			██	19		20

An "across" word for a definition is written on a sequence of white squares in a row starting on a numbered square that does not follow another white square in the same row. The sequence of white squares for that word goes across the row of the numbered square, ending immediately before the next black square in the row or in the rightmost square of the row.

A "down" word for a definition is written on a sequence of white squares in a column starting on a numbered square that does not follow another white square in the same column. The sequence of white squares for that word goes down the column of the numbered square, ending immediately before the next black square in the column or in the bottom square of the column. Every white square in a correctly solved puzzle contains a letter.

You must write a program that takes several solved crossword puzzles as input and outputs the lists of across and down words which constitute the solutions.

Input

Each puzzle solution in the input starts with a line containing two integers r and c ($1 \leq r \leq 10$ and $1 \leq c \leq 10$), where r (the first number) is the number of rows in the puzzle and c (the second number) is the number of columns in the puzzle. The r rows of input which follow each contain c characters (excluding the end-of-line) which describe the solution. Each of those c characters is an alphabetic character which is part of a word or the character '*', which indicates a black square.

The end of input is indicated by a line consisting of the single number '0'.

Output

Output for each puzzle consists of an identifier for the puzzle (`puzzle #1:`, `puzzle #2:`, etc.) and the list of across words followed by the list of down words. Words in each list must be output one-per-line in increasing order of the number of their corresponding definitions.

The heading for the list of across words is "`Across`". The heading for the list of down words is "`Down`". In the case where the lists are empty (all squares in the grid are black), the `Across` and `Down` headings should still appear.

Separate output for successive input puzzles by a blank line.

<table>
<tr><td>

Sample Input

```
2 2
AT
*O
6 7
AIM*DEN
*ME*ONE
UPON*TO
SO*ERIN
*SA*OR*
IES*DEA
0
```

</td><td>

Sample Output

```
puzzle #1:
Across
  1.AT
  3.O
Down
  1.A
  2.TO

puzzle #2:
Across
  1.AIM
  4.DEN
  7.ME
  8.ONE
  9.UPON
 11.TO
 12.SO
 13.ERIN
 15.SA
 17.OR
 18.IES
 19.DEA
Down
  1.A
  2.IMPOSE
  3.MEO
  4.DO
  5.ENTIRE
  6.NEON
  9.US
 10.NE
 14.ROD
 16.AS
 18.I
 20.A
```

</td></tr>
</table>

D   Package Pricing

The Green Earth Trading Company sells 4 different sizes of energy-efficient fluorescent light bulbs for use in home lighting fixtures. The light bulbs are expensive, but last much longer than ordinary incandescent light bulbs and require much less energy. To encourage customers to buy and use the energy- efficient light bulbs, the company catalogue lists special packages which contain a variety of sizes and numbers of the light bulbs. The price of a package is always substantially less than the total price of the individual bulbs in the package. Customers typically want to buy several different sizes and numbers of bulbs. You are to write a program to determine the least expensive collection of packages that satisfy any customer's request.

Input

The input file is divided into two parts. The first one describes the packages which are listed in the catalogue. The second part describes individual customer requests. The 4 sizes of light bulbs are identified in the input file by the characters "a", "b", "c", and "d".

The first part of the input file begins with an integer n $(1 \leq n \leq 50)$ indicating the number of packages described in the catalogue. Each of the n lines that follows is a single package description. A package description begins with a catalogue number (a positive integer) followed by a price (a real number), and then the sizes and corresponding numbers of the light bulbs in the package. Between 1 and 4 different sizes of light bulbs will be listed in each description. The listing format for these size-number pairs is a blank, a character ("a", "b", "c", or "d") representing a size, another blank, and then an integer representing the number of light bulbs of that size in the package. These size-number pairs will not appear in any particular order, and there will be no duplicate sizes listed in any package. The following line describes a package with catalogue number 210 and price \$76.95 which contains 3 size "a" bulbs, 1 size "c" bulb, and 4 size "d" bulbs.

```
210 76.95 a 3 c 1 d 4
```

The second part of the input file begins with a line containing a single positive integer m representing the number of customer requests. Each of the remaining m lines is a customer request. A listing of sizes and corresponding numbers of light bulbs constitutes a request. Each list contains only the size-number pairs, formatted the same way that the size-number pairs are formatted in the catalogue descriptions. Unlike the catalogue descriptions, however, a customer request may contain duplicate sizes. The following line represents a customer request for 1 size "a" bulb, 2 size "b" bulbs, 2 size "c" bulbs, and 5 size "d" bulbs.

```
a 1 d 5 b 1 c 2 b 1
```

Output

For each request, print the customer number (1 through m, 1 for the first customer request, 2 for the second, ..., m for the mth customer), a colon, the total price of the packages which constitute the least expensive way to fill the request, and then the combination of packages that the customer should order to fill that request.

Prices should be shown with exactly two significant digits to the right of the decimal. The combination of packages must be written in ascending order of catalogue numbers. If more than one of the same type package is to be ordered, then the number ordered should follow the catalogue number in parentheses. You may assume that each customer request can be filled. In some cases, the least expensive way to fill a customer request may contain more light bulbs of some sizes than necessary to fill the actual request. This is acceptable. What matters is that the customers receive *at least* what they request.

Sample Input

```
5
10 25.00 b 2
502 17.95 a 1
3 13.00 c 1
55 27.50 b 1 d 2 c 1
6 52.87 a 2 b 1 d 1 c 3
6
d 1
b 3
b 3 c 2
b 1 a 1 c 1 d 1 a 1
b 1 b 2 c 3 c 1 a 1 d 1
b 3 c 2 d 1 c 1 d 2 a 1
```

Sample Output

```
1:    27.50 55
2:    50.00 10(2)
3:    65.50 3 10 55
4:    52.87 6
5:    90.87 3 6 10
6:   100.45 55(3) 502
```

E Switching Channels

CPN (The Couch Potato Network) owns several cable channels. They would like to arrange the timing of programmes so viewers can switch channels without missing the end of one programme or the beginning of another. To do this they have identified certain times, called "alignment points," where ideally one programme should end and another should begin. Some of these alignment points are more important than others. For example, the time when the nightly news begins is an important alignment point. Since many viewers watch the news, they would be less likely to watch a CPN programme whose ending time causes them to miss the beginning of the news, or which starts before the news finishes. Your task is to write a solution which determines the best order in which programmes can be shown on one channel.

A "miss" time is the absolute value of the difference between the time of an alignment point and the nearest time of the beginning or end of a programme. The "total miss time" at a particular level of importance is the sum of all the miss times for alignment points at that level of importance. One programme order is better than another if it has a lower total miss time at some level of importance and the same total miss time at all higher levels of importance (if any).

Input

Your solution must accept multiple input data sets. Each set will begin with an integer, p ($0 \leq p \leq 8$), specifying the number of programmes to be ordered. When a data set beginning with 0 is encountered, your solution should terminate. Following p on the same line will be p integers specifying the lengths of the programmes in minutes. There is no significance to the order in which these are given.

The next line of input specifies the alignment points. The total number of such points, a ($0 \leq a \leq 8$), appears first followed by a pairs of integers. The first integer in each pair, i ($1 \leq i \leq 5$), gives the importance of the alignment point. Alignment points marked 1 are most important; those marked 2 are of secondary importance, etc. The second integer in each pair, t, specifies the time when the alignment point occurs. No two alignment points in the same data set will have the same value of t.

Output

Your solution must output three lines for each data set. The first line identifies the data set being processed and should be in the form:

`Data set `n

where n is the number of the data set (1 for the first data set, 2 for the second, etc.). On the following line, your solution should output the lengths of the programmes in the order in which they should be shown to achieve the best synchronization with the alignment points. On the third line, output the total number of minutes by which the alignment points were missed (the sum of all total miss times).

There may be more than one best programme order for an input data set. Any one of these best orders is acceptable.

Sample Input

```
4   30 45 45 15
3   1 60   2 90   3 15
6   10 15 13 18 25 33
4   1 30   2 15   2 45   1 60
0
```

Sample Output

```
Data set 1
  Order: 15 45 30 45
  Error: 0
Data set 2
  Order: 15 13 33 25 18 10
  Error: 19
```

F Typesetting

Proportional fonts are so called because characters require varying amounts of space on the printed line. The size in which text is "set," usually measured in points, also affects the space required for each character. In this problem you are given a number of paragraphs of text to set. Each paragraph may include special "words" to select the font and point size.

Input

The input starts with the font width table. These data give the widths of 10- point characters in six different fonts. The first line contains the number of characters in the table, N $(0 \le N \le 100)$. Each of the next N lines contain a character in column 1 and then 6 integers representing the width of that character in each of the 6 different fonts. Widths are given in an arbitrary measurement called "units." The width of each 10-point character will be greater than zero units, and less than 256 units. Character widths scale linearly with point size. Thus if a 10-point "A" is 12 units wide, a 20-point "A" is 24 units wide.

The remainder of the input consists of paragraphs to be typeset. Each paragraph begins with a line containing two integers, L and W. L is the number of input lines of text for the paragraph (these immediately follow the first line), and W is the width allowed for each typeset line, in units. The initial font at the beginning of each paragraph is always font 1, and the initial point size in which characters are to be set is 10. Fonts are numbered 1 through 6, corresponding to columns 1 through 6 in the font width table. An empty paragraph (one for which L is 0) will mark the end of the input data. No output is to be produced for this empty paragraph.

The words in each paragraph are sequences of no more than 8 non-blank characters separated by spaces (that is, blanks – no tab characters will appear in the input). Spaces at the ends of input lines are irrelevant, and spaces between words are significant only to the extent that they separate words. Each character in each word will appear in the width table. Case is significant for all characters in the input data.

The special tokens "*f1", "*f2", "*f3", "*f4", "*f5", and "*f6" are used to select a particular font to be used in setting the text that follows it. The token "*sN", where N is an integer in the range 1 to 99 indicates that N point characters are to be used in setting the following text. These tokens will always be separated from words and other tokens by at least one blank. Note that style and size changes made in one paragraph do not carry over to the next paragraph, and that many such changes may appear in a single paragraph.

For each paragraph, try to set as many words per line as possible, ensuring that each word is followed by at least the width of a blank (which will always appear in the font width table) with the same point size and style as the characters in the preceding word, except for the last word on the line. The last word in a typeset line must not have any following space.

When scaling fonts, round the scaled character widths to the nearest integer, rounding upward in cases where the rounded value is half way between two consecutive integers. Thus, if a particular 10 point character occupies 9 units of space, a 15 point character would occupy 14 units of space, as would a 16 point character. A 14 point character, however, would occupy only 13 units of space.

Output

For each paragraph, first display the paragraph number (1, 2, ...). Then, for each typeset line in the paragraph, display the line number, the first and last words on that line, and the total number of units of white space that follow the last character printed on the line. (This is just the number of units of space available on the line not occupied by characters or spaces between characters.)

If a single word exceeds the width of a line, set it on a line by itself. In the output for that line, show only that single word, and a negative amount of white space equal to the excess width of the word.

Sample Input

```
4
A 10 20 30 12 22 32
B 1 2 3 4 5 6
C 9 10 8 3 5 2
  2 4 6 3 5 7
2 80
*f2  AAA BBB CCC
  ABC *s15 CBA AABC CACA
3 100
AAA
AAA BBB CCC
ABC CBA AABC CACA
0 0
```

Sample Output

```
Paragraph 1
Line 1: AAA ... BBB (10 whitespace)
Line 2: CCC ... ABC (14 whitespace)
Line 3: CBA ... CBA (32 whitespace)
Line 4: AABC ... AABC (2 whitespace)
Line 5: CACA (-10 whitespace)
Paragraph 2
Line 1: AAA ... CCC (4 whitespace)
Line 2: ABC ... AABC (26 whitespace)
Line 3: CACA ... CACA (62 whitespace)
```

G VTAS - Vessel Traffic Advisory Service

In order to promote safety and efficient use of port facilities, the Association of Coastal Merchants (ACM) has developed a concept for a Vessel Traffic Advisory Service (VTAS) that will provide traffic advisories for vessels transiting participating ports.

The concept is built on a computer program that maintains information about the traffic patterns and reported movements of vessels within the port over multiple days. For each port, the traffic lanes are defined between waypoints. The traffic lanes have been designated as directional to provide traffic separation and flow controls. Each port is represented by a square matrix containing the distances (in nautical miles) along each valid traffic lane. The distances are defined from each row waypoint to each column waypoint. A distance of 0 indicates that no valid traffic lane exists between the two waypoints.

Vessel traffic enters the port at a waypoint and transits the traffic lanes. A vessel may begin its transit at any of the waypoints and must follow a valid connected route via the valid traffic lanes. A vessel may end its transit at any valid waypoint.

The service provided by the VTAS to transiting vessels includes:

- Projection of arrival times at waypoints

- Notification of invalid routes

- Projected encounters with other vessels on each leg of the transit. An "encounter" occurs when two vessels are between common waypoints (either traffic lane) at a common time

- Warning of close passing with another vessel in the vicinity of a waypoint (within 3 minutes of projected waypoint arrival)

Reported times will be rounded to the nearest whole minute. Time is maintained based on a 24 hour clock (i.e. 9 am is 0900, 9 PM is 2100, midnight is 0000). Speed is measured in knots which is equal to 1 nautical mile per hour.

Input

The input file for the computer program include a Port Specification to provide the description of the traffic patterns within the port and a Traffic List which contains the sequence of vessels entering the port and their intended tracks. The end of the input is indicated by a Vessel Name beginning with an "*"

Port Specification : Number of Waypoints in Port (an integer N)
Waypoint ID List (N single-character designators)
Waypoint Connection Matrix (N rows of N real values specifying
the distances between waypoints in nautical miles)
Traffic List: Vessel Name (alphabetic characters)
Time at first waypoint (on 24-hour clock)
and Planned Transit Speed (in knots)
Planned Route (ordered list of waypoints)

Output

The output shall provide for each vessel as it enters the port a listing indicating the arrival of the vessel and its planned speed followed by a table containing the waypoints in its route and projected arrival at each waypoint. Following this table will be appropriate messages indicating:

- Notification of Invalid Routes

- Projected Encounters on each leg

- Warning of close passing at waypoints

All times are to be printed as four-digit integers with leading zeros when necessary.

Assumptions & Limitations:

1. *Vessel names are at most 20 characters long.*

2. *There are at most 20 waypoints in a port and at most 20 waypoints in any route.*

3. *There will be at most 20 vessels in port at any time.*

4. *A vessel will complete its transit in at most 12 hours.*

5. *No more than 24 hours will elapse between vessel entries.*

Sample Input

```
6
ABCDEF
0 3 0 0 0 0
3 0 0 2 0 0
0 3 0 0 0 0
0 0 0 0 3 0
0 0 2 0 0 4
0 0 0 0 4 0
Tug
2330 12
ABDEF
WhiteSailboat
2345 6
ECBDE
TugWBarge
2355 5
DECBA
PowerCruiser
   0 15
FECBA
LiberianFreighter
   7 18
ABDXF
ChineseJunk
  45 8
ACEF
*****
```

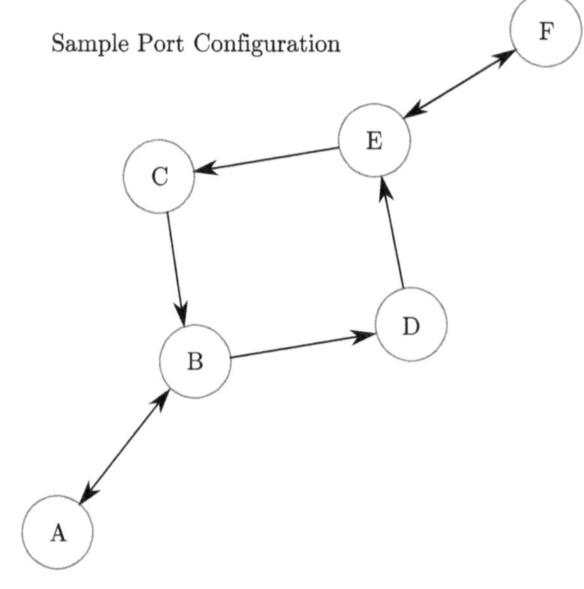

Sample Output

```
Tug entering system at 2330 with a planned speed of 12.0 knots
        Waypoint:    A    B    D    E    F
        Arrival:    2330 2345 2355 0010 0030

WhiteSailboat entering system at 2345 with a planned speed of 6.0 knots
        Waypoint:    E    C    B    D    E
        Arrival:    2345 0005 0035 0055 0125

TugWBarge entering system at 2355 with a planned speed of 5.0 knots
        Waypoint:    D    E    C    B    A
        Arrival:    2355 0031 0055 0131 0207
Projected encounter with Tug on leg between Waypoints D & E
** Warning ** Close passing with Tug at Waypoint D

PowerCruiser entering system at 0000 with a planned speed of 15.0 knots
        Waypoint:    F    E    C    B    A
        Arrival:    0000 0016 0024 0036 0048
Projected encounter with Tug on leg between Waypoints F & E
Projected encounter with WhiteSailboat on leg between Waypoints C & B
** Warning ** Close passing with WhiteSailboat at Waypoint B

LiberianFreighter entering system at 0007 with a planned speed of 18.0 knots
**> Invalid Route Plan for Vessel: LiberianFreighter

ChineseJunk entering system at 0045 with a planned speed of 8.0 knots
**> Invalid Route Plan for Vessel: ChineseJunk
```

H Monitoring Wheelchair Patients

A researcher at a rehabilitation facility is studying the use that a patient makes of a motorized wheelchair in a restricted area at the facility. The chair's motor is connected to the axle by a chain drive. Therefore both wheels turn at the same speed and the chair can travel only in a straight line. The patient can stop the chair, rotate the wheels, and thereby change the direction only while the wheelchair is stopped. To help monitor its usage, the chair is equipped with a compass, a clock, and a speedometer. A recording device records each time interval that the chair is in motion, the average speed during the time interval, and the compass bearing during the time interval. The compass is a standard compass in which 0° is north, 90° is east, and so forth.

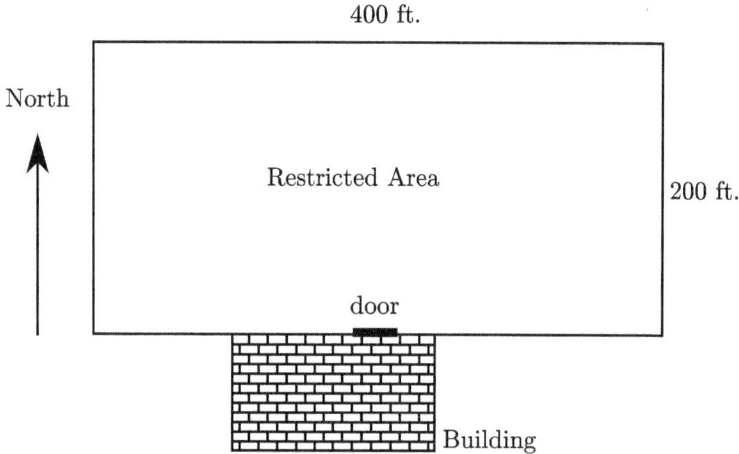

   A map of the restricted area is shown. The restricted area is a 200 ft by 400 ft rectangular area of the lawn. Patients enter the restricted area from the door of a building located on the southern edge of the restricted area. The door is at the center of the 400 ft southern boundary, as shown in the figure.

   The recording device turns itself on when the patient enters the restricted area through the door and monitors the patient's movements for up to 1 hour. Time is measured in seconds from 0 to 3,600, with time 0 being the time the patient initially enters the restricted area through the door. The device records 4 numbers to describe the motion of the wheelchair during any interval when the motor is in operation. The first two numbers give the time the motion begins and ends; the third number gives the speed during the time interval; and the fourth number gives the compass bearing during the time interval. (During each time interval the wheelchair maintains constant speed and bearing.) For example, the recorded line

        10.6   15.9   2.8   274

would indicate that between times $t_1 = 10.6$ and $t_2 = 15.9$ seconds the wheelchair was traveling at speed of 2.8 ft/sec with compass bearing (direction) 274°. Times are recorded to 0.1 sec, speeds are recorded to 0.1 ft/sec, and bearings are recorded to a whole number of degrees.

   Your job is to analyze the data from the wheelchair's recording device. Specifically, you must determine the following:

1) Did the patient ever leave the restricted area? If so, determine the first time that the patient left the restricted area and determine at what point on the perimeter of the restricted area the wheelchair crossed out of the restricted area. If the patient did not leave the restricted area, what was the distance from the door to the farthest point the patient reached within the area?

2) What was the total distance that the patient traveled?

For the purpose of answering these questions, use coordinates with the location (0,0) corresponding to the southwest corner of the restricted area and the location (400,200) corresponding to the northeast corner. Since the recorder switches on when the patient passes through the door, the position of the patient at time $t = 0.0$ is always (200,0). Patients will be traveling north when they enter the restricted area.

Input

The input data consists of several data sets. The first line of each data set has an integer which is the number of lines recorded by the device. Each subsequent line in the data set consists of the four numbers recorded by the device during a particular time interval. The end of data is indicated by a data set whose first line consists of the number 0.

In the first data set of the sample input, the patient entered through the door (at time 0.0) and for the first 5 seconds was traveling due north at 3 ft/sec. From time $t = 7$ to $t = 9$ he traveled at a speed of 2 ft/sec with a compass bearing of $30°$. He then stopped, changed his bearing to $60°$, and then traveled at 4 ft/sec from time $t = 10$ to time $t = 100$. Ten seconds later (at time $t = 110$) he headed due north at 2 ft/sec until $t = 200$.

Output

The output for each data set begins with an identification of that case. The output indicates whether the patient departed from the restricted area and if so the time and point of departure on the perimeter. If not, the maximum distance the patient reached from the door is provided. For each case, the total distance that the patient traveled is provided. Format your output so that the same labeling information is included as shown in the sample output, with a line of asterisks separating the cases.

Assumptions and requirements:

1. *Within each data set, time intervals will be listed in chronological order, with the first time interval always having time 0.0 as the time of entry into the restricted area. All times will be given with one decimal place accuracy and will be in the range 0.0 to 3600.0 inclusive. For each time interval specified, the duration of the time interval will be positive, i.e. the second time specified will be greater than the first.*

2. *Speeds will be in the range 0.1 to 9.9 ft/sec.*

3. *Compass bearings will be given as a whole number of degrees and will be in the range 0 to 359 inclusive. The initial compass bearing for the first line of data in each data set will be 0.*

4. *Within each line of data, numbers will be separated by at least one blank space.*

5. *All numerical results will be displayed with one decimal place of accuracy as shown in the sample output.*

6. *If the patient goes out of the restricted area, his location may include negative coordinates. However, you don't have to worry about the wheelchair crashing through the walls of the building.*

Sample Input

```
4
0.0 5.0 3.0 0
7.0 9.0 2.0 30
10.0 100.0 4.0 60
110.0 200.0 2.0 0
3
0.0 20.0 2.0 0
500.0 600.0 1.0 270
3000.0 3100.0 1.0 0
7
0.0 5.3 2.1 0
19.8 35.6 2.7 346
42.0 78.4 2.3 15
1181.4 1192.1 1.7 117
2107.0 2193.6 2.1 295
2196.3 2201.2 2.0 298
2704.3 2709.2 1.5 208
0
```

Sample Output

```
Case Number 1
Left restricted area at point (400.0,132.8) and time 67.2 sec.
Total distance traveled was 559.0 feet
***************************************
Case Number 2
No departure from restricted area
Maximum distance patient traveled from door was 172.0 feet
Total distance traveled was 240.0 feet
***************************************
Case Number 3
Left restricted area at point (67.0,200.0) and time 2191.4 sec.
Total distance traveled was 354.7 feet
***************************************
```

WORLD FINALS 1995

NASHVILLE, TENNESSEE

World Champion

ALBERT-LUDWIGS-UNIVERSITAT FREIBURG

Matthias Ruhl
Christian Wetzel
Phillip Zembrod

Director of Judging
Dick Rinewalt   *Texas Christian University*

Chief Judge
Jo Perry   *North Carolina State University*

Judges

Owen Astrachan	*Duke University*
David Elizandro	*Tennessee Tech University*
Robin O'Leary	*Swansea*
Lavon Page	*North Carolina State University*
Robert Roos	*Allegheny College*
Patrick Ryan	*TechnoSolutions, Inc.*
Laurie White	*Mercer University*
Stanley Wileman, Jr.	*University of Nebraska at Omaha*

UVa Online Judge problem numbers

238	A	Jill's Bike
239	B	*Tempus et mobilius.* Time and motion
240	C	Variable Radix Huffman Encoding
241	D	Sail Race
242	E	Stamps and Envelope Size
243	F	Theseus and the Minotaur
244	G	Train Time
245	H	Uncompress

A   Jill's Bike

Jill Bates hates climbing hills. Jill rides a bicycle everywhere she goes, but she always wants to go the easiest and shortest way possible. The good news is that she lives in Greenhills, which has all its roads laid out in a strictly rectangular grid – east-west roads are *streets*; north-south roads are *avenues* and the distance between any two adjacent grid points is the same. The bad news is that Greenhills is very hilly and has many one-way roads.

In choosing a route between where she starts and where she ends, Jill has three rules:

1. Avoid any climb of more than 10 meters between adjacent grid points.

2. Never go the wrong way on a one-way road.

3. Always travel the shortest possible route.

Your program should help Jill find an acceptable route.

Input

The input file contains data in the following form:

- The first line contains two integers, separated by one or more spaces. The first integer n represents the number of streets, and the second integer m represents the number of avenues, $1 \leq n \leq 20$, $1 \leq m \leq 20$.

- The next n lines contain the altitudes of grid points. Each line represents a street and contains a sequence of m integers separated by one or more spaces. These integers represent the altitude in meters of the grid points along that street. Even if a particular street and avenue have no intersection, the altitude is still given for that grid point.

- One or more lines follow that define the one-way roads. Each road is represented by two pairs of integers, separated by one or more spaces, in the form:

  > *street*   *avenue*   *street*   *avenue*

  The first street and avenue define the starting point of the road and the second pair define the ending point. Since Greenhills is a strict grid, if the two points are not adjacent in the grid, the road passes through all the intervening grid points. For example,

  ```
  5 7 5 10
  ```

  represents roads 5-7 to 5-8, 5-8 to 5-9, and 5-9 to 5-10. Road definitions are terminated by a line containing four zeroes in the above format.

- Finally, one or more lines will follow that contain pairs of grid points between which Jill wants to find an optimal path, in the form:

  > *street*   *avenue*   *street*   *avenue*

  As before, the integer pairs are separated by one or more spaces. The end of the input set is defined by a line containing four zeroes, formatted as before.

You may assume that all street and avenue numbers are within the bounds defined by the first line of input, and that all road definitions are strictly north-south or east-west.

Output

For each path query in the input file, output a sequence of grid points, from the starting grid point to the ending grid point, which meets Jill's three rules. Output grid points as '*street-avenue*' separated by the word 'to'. If there is more than one path that meets Jill's criteria, any such path will be acceptable. If no route satisfies all the criteria, or if the starting and ending grid points are the same, output an appropriate message to that effect. Output a blank line between each output set.

Sample Input

```
3 4
10 15 20 25
19 30 35 30
10 19 26 20
1 1 1 4
2 1 2 4
3 4 3 3
3 3 1 3
1 4 3 4
2 4 2 1
1 1 2 1
0 0 0 0
1 1 2 2
2 3 2 3
2 2 1 1
0 0 0 0
```

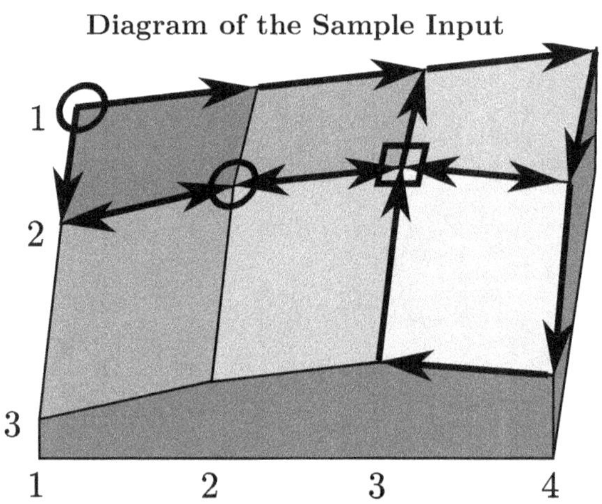

Sample Output

```
1-1 to 1-2 to 1-3 to 1-4 to 2-4 to 2-3 to 2-2

To get from 2-3 to 2-3, stay put!

There is no acceptable route from 2-2 to 1-1.
```

B *Tempus et mobilius.* Time and motion

...and movement has long been used to measure time. For example, the ball clock is a simple device which keeps track of the passing minutes by moving ball- bearings. Each minute, a rotating arm removes a ball bearing from the queue at the bottom, raises it to the top of the clock and deposits it on a track leading to indicators displaying minutes, five-minutes and hours. These indicators display the time between 1:00 and 12:59, but without 'a.m.' or 'p.m.' indicators. Thus 2 balls in the minute indicator, 6 balls in the five- minute indicator and 5 balls in the hour indicator displays the time 5:32.

Unfortunately, most commercially available ball clocks do not incorporate a date indication, although this would be simple to do with the addition of further carry and indicator tracks. However, all is not lost! As the balls migrate through the mechanism of the clock, they change their relative ordering in a predictable way. Careful study of these orderings will therefore yield the time elapsed since the clock had some specific ordering. The length of time which can be measured is limited because the orderings of the balls eventually begin to repeat. Your program must compute the time before repetition, which varies according to the total number of balls present.

Operation of the Ball Clock

Every minute, the least recently used ball is removed from the queue of balls at the bottom of the clock, elevated, then deposited on the minute indicator track, which is able to hold four balls. When a fifth ball rolls on to the minute indicator track, its weight causes the track to tilt. The four balls already on the track run back down to join the queue of balls waiting at the bottom in reverse order of their original addition to the minutes track. The fifth ball, which caused the tilt, rolls on down to the five-minute indicator track. This track holds eleven balls. The twelfth ball carried over from the minutes causes the five-minute track to tilt, returning the eleven balls to the queue, again in reverse order of their addition. The twelfth ball rolls down to the hour indicator.

The hour indicator also holds eleven balls, but has one extra fixed ball which is always present so that counting the balls in the hour indicator will yield an hour in the range one to twelve. The twelfth ball carried over from the five-minute indicator causes the hour indicator to tilt, returning the eleven free balls to the queue, in reverse order, before the twelfth ball itself also returns to the queue.

Input

The input defines a succession of ball clocks. Each clock operates as described above. The clocks differ only in the number of balls present in the queue at one o'clock when all the clocks start. This number is given for each clock, one per line and does not include the fixed ball on the hours indicator. Valid numbers are in the range 27 to 127. A zero signifies the end of input.

Output

For each clock described in the input, your program should report the number of balls given in the input and the number of days (24-hour periods) which elapse before the clock returns to its initial ordering.

Sample Input

```
30
45
0
```

Sample Output

```
30 balls cycle after 15 days.
45 balls cycle after 378 days.
```

C Variable Radix Huffman Encoding

Huffman encoding is a method of developing an optimal encoding of the symbols in a *source alphabet* using symbols from a *target alphabet* when the frequencies of each of the symbols in the source alphabet are known. Optimal means the average length of an encoded message will be minimized. In this problem you are to determine an encoding of the first N uppercase letters (the source alphabet, S_1 through S_N, with frequencies f_1 through f_N) into the first R decimal digits (the target alphabet, T_1 through T_R).

Consider determining the encoding when $R = 2$. Encoding proceeds in several passes. In each pass the two source symbols with the lowest frequencies, say S_1 and S_2, are grouped to form a new "combination letter" whose frequency is the sum of f_1 and f_2. If there is a tie for the lowest or second lowest frequency, the letter occurring earlier in the alphabet is selected. After some number of passes only two letters remain to be combined. The letters combined in each pass are assigned one of the symbols from the target alphabet.

The letter with the lower frequency is assigned the code 0, and the other letter is assigned the code 1. (If each letter in a combined group has the same frequency, then 0 is assigned to the one earliest in the alphabet. For the purpose of comparisons, the value of a "combination letter" is the value of the earliest letter in the combination.) The final code sequence for a source symbol is formed by concatenating the target alphabet symbols assigned as each combination letter using the source symbol is formed.

The target symbols are concatenated in the reverse order that they are assigned so that the first symbol in the final code sequence is the last target symbol assigned to a combination letter.

The two illustrations below demonstrate the process for $R = 2$.

Symbol	Frequency
A	5
B	7
C	8
D	15

Pass 1: A and B grouped
Pass 2: {A,B} and C grouped
Pass 3: {A,B,C} and D grouped
Resulting codes: A=110, B=111, C=10, D=0
Avg. length=(3*5+3*7+2*8+1*15)/35=1.91

Symbol	Frequency
A	7
B	7
C	7
D	7

Pass 1: A and B grouped
Pass 2: C and D grouped
Pass 3: {A,B} and {C,D} grouped
Resulting codes: A=00, B=01, C=10, D=11
Avg. length=(2*7+2*7+2*7+2*7)/28=2.00

When R is larger than 2, R symbols are grouped in each pass. Since each pass effectively replaces R letters or combination letters by 1 combination letter, and the last pass must combine

R letters or combination letters, the source alphabet must contain $k*(R-1)+R$ letters, for some integer k.

Since N may not be this large, an appropriate number of fictitious letters with zero frequencies must be included. These fictitious letters are not to be included in the output. In making comparisons, the fictitious letters are later than any of the letters in the alphabet.

Now the basic process of determining the Huffman encoding is the same as for the $R=2$ case. In each pass, the R letters with the lowest frequencies are grouped, forming a new combination letter with a frequency equal to the sum of the letters included in the group. The letters that were grouped are assigned the target alphabet symbols 0 through $R-1$. 0 is assigned to the letter in the combination with the lowest frequency, 1 to the next lowest frequency, and so forth. If several of the letters in the group have the same frequency, the one earliest in the alphabet is assigned the smaller target symbol, and so forth.

The illustration below demonstrates the process for $R=3$.

Symbol	Frequency
A	5
B	7
C	8
D	15

Pass 1: ? (fictitious symbol), A and B are grouped
Pass 2: {?,A,B}, C and D are grouped
Resulting codes: A=11, B=12, C=0, D=2
Avg. length=(2*5+2*7+1*8+1*15)/35=1.34

Input

The input will contain one or more data sets, one per line. Each data set consists of an integer value for R (between 2 and 10), an integer value for N (between 2 and 26), and the integer frequencies f_1 through f_N, each of which is between 1 and 999.

The end of data for the entire input is the number 0 for R; it is not considered to be a separate data set.

Output

For each data set, display its number (numbering is sequential starting with 1) and the average target symbol length (rounded to two decimal places) on one line. Then display the N letters of the source alphabet and the corresponding Huffman codes, one letter and code per line. The examples below illustrate the required output format.

Sample Input

```
2 5 5 10 20 25 40
2 5 4 2 2 1 1
3 7 20 5 8 5 12 6 9
4 6 10 23 18 25 9 12
0
```

Sample Output

```
Set 1; average length 2.10
    A: 1100
    B: 1101
    C: 111
    D: 10
    E: 0

Set 2; average length 2.20
    A: 11
    B: 00
    C: 01
    D: 100
    E: 101

Set 3; average length 1.69
    A: 1
    B: 00
    C: 20
    D: 01
    E: 22
    F: 02
    G: 21

Set 4; average length 1.32
    A: 32
    B: 1
    C: 0
    D: 2
    E: 31
    F: 33
```

D Sail Race

The Atlantic Coastal Mariners (ACM) sailing club is building a race planning tool to estimate durations of sailboat races with various race courses, wind directions, and types of sailboats. You must write a program to help with that task.

A race course is defined by marks with up to 10 marks per race course. A sailboat must sail to all marks in the specified order. The marks are identified as x- and y-coordinates on a hypothetical grid with a single unit equal to one nautical mile (nm). The positive y-axis is oriented due north and the positive x-axis is oriented due east. The race course is in open waters without any navigational limitations.

For purposes of this planning tool, the only driving force controlling a sailboat is the wind. The wind determines the sailboat's speed of advance and limits its direction of travel. The wind is constant for the duration of each race and is specified in terms of the direction from which the wind is blowing and its speed in nautical miles per hour (kts). Wind direction is specified as a compass bearing in degrees measured clockwise from 000.0^o as north.

Sailboats cannot steer any closer to the wind than a given "point angle" off the wind direction. In order to make progress closer to the wind direction, the sailboat must tack back and forth across the wind, steering no closer to the wind than its point angle. Each time the sailboat tacks or passes a mark it incurs a tack penalty. For this simulation, each sailboat will travel each leg of a race (the portion of a race between successive marks) with the minimum number of tacks and the minimum possible distance. Courses and directions are specified as compass bearings in degrees measured clockwise from 000.0^o as north.

The speed of a sailboat is determined by the sailboat design, wind speed, and direction steered relative to the wind. In the figure, the wind direction is 45° and the point angle is 40°. This means then that this sailboat cannot steer between 5° and 85° because it cannot point that closely into the wind.

For this problem, the ratio of sailboat speed to wind speed is one of three ratios, selected as shown in the table below according to the angle off the wind :

Angle off wind	Applicable ratio
$\geq$ point angle and $<$ reach angle	point speed ratio
$\geq$ reach angle and $<$ downwind angle	reach speed ratio
$\geq$ downwind angle	downwind speed ratio

For instance, if the boat is steering at an angle off the wind which is between the reach angle and downwind angle then

$$\text{boat speed} = \text{reach speed ratio} \times \text{wind speed}$$

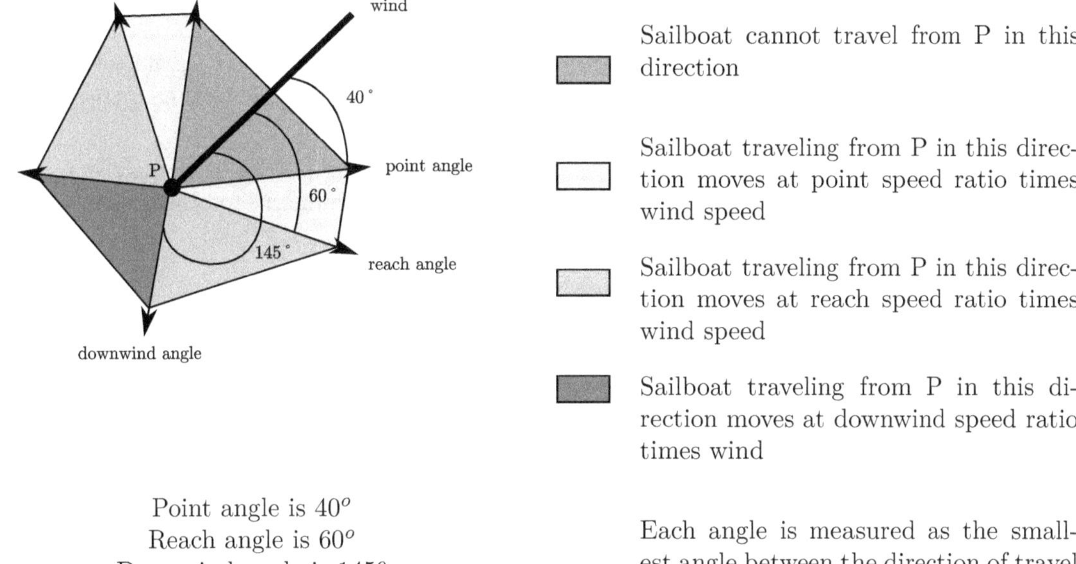

Point angle is 40°
Reach angle is 60°
Downwind angle is 145°

Input

Your solution must accept multiple input data sets. Each data set represents a different race course to be evaluated for a single sailboat. The data set begins with a line with 4 numbers: wind direction (real), wind speed (real), tack penalty (real), and number of marks n (integer). The next line contains six real numbers: point angle, point speed ratio, reach angle, reach speed ratio, downwind angle, downwind speed ratio.

The subsequent n lines of the data set represent the n race marks in the order in which they must be reached. Each line begins with a 2-character mark id followed by the x-coordinate then y-coordinate of the mark.

The end of input is denoted by a line of four 0's.

Output

The output for your program consists of various data calculated for each input data set. Values should be presented with the following precisions and units.

Courses, tacks, directions	0.1 degree	Distance	0.01 nm
Speed	0.1 kts	Time	0.01 hours

Output for each race begins with a header containing the number of the data set (1 for the first, 2 for the second, etc.) and the number of legs. The next line is the total length of the race course, measured as the sum of distances between successive marks.

For each leg of the course, the leg number, beginning and ending mark id's, course from the beginning to end marks of the leg, and the leg distance is presented. This is followed by a listing of the tacks necessary to complete the leg. The tacks for each race are numbered sequentially, with tack numbers beginning with 1 for each race. For each tack, the tack number, the projected sailboat speed, the course steered, and the length of that tack are presented.

The summary output for each data set includes the total number of tacks, the total distance traveled for the race, the estimated race duration, and the total tack penalty time incurred by the sailboat after leaving the first mark.

The exact format of the output is not specified, but all output should be organized so that it is in the specified order, appropriately labeled and follows given numeric specifications.

Sample Input

```
45 10 .1 6
45 0.5 90 0.75 135 0.67
M1 15 10
M2 25 20
M3 22 30
M4 5 25
M5 10 15
M6 10 10
0 0 0 0
```

Sample Output

```
==========================
Race 1 has 5 legs
The race layout is  58.48 nm long
------------------------------

Leg 1 from Mark M1 to M2 == > Direction:  45.0  Distance:  14.14 nm
Tack 1 ==> Speed:  5.0   Direction:  90.0  Distance: 10.00 nm
Tack 2 ==> Speed:  5.0   Direction:   0.0  Distance: 10.00 nm

Leg 2 from Mark M2 to M3 == > Direction: 343.3  Distance:  10.44 nm
Tack 3 ==> Speed:  5.0   Direction: 343.3  Distance: 10.44 nm

Leg 3 from Mark M3 to M4 == > Direction: 253.6  Distance:  17.72 nm
Tack 4 ==> Speed:  6.7   Direction: 253.6  Distance: 17.72 nm

Leg 4 from Mark M4 to M5 == > Direction: 153.4  Distance:  11.18 nm
Tack 5 ==> Speed:  7.5   Direction: 153.4  Distance: 11.18 nm

Leg 5 from Mark M5 to M6 == > Direction: 180.0  Distance:   5.00 nm
Tack 6 ==> Speed:  6.7   Direction: 180.0  Distance:  5.00 nm


------------------------------------
Race 1 was 64.34 nm long with 6 tack legs
Estimated Race Duration is 11.47 hours with 0.50 hours of Tack Penalty
==========================
```

E Stamps and Envelope Size

Philatelists have collected stamps since long before postal workers were disgruntled. An excess of stamps may be bad news to a country's postal service, but good news to those that collect the excess stamps. The postal service works to minimize the number of stamps needed to provide seamless postage coverage. To this end you have been asked to write a program to assist the postal service.

Envelope size restricts the number of stamps that can be used on one envelope. For example, if 1 cent and 3 cent stamps are available and an envelope can accommodate 5 stamps, all postage from 1 to 13 cents can be "covered":

Postage	Number of $1\rlap{/}c$ Stamps	Number of $3\rlap{/}c$ Stamps
1	1	0
2	2	0
3	0	1
4	1	1
5	2	1
6	0	2
7	1	2
8	2	2
9	0	3
10	1	3
11	2	3
12	0	4
13	1	4

Although five 3 cent stamps yields an envelope with 15 cents postage, it is not possible to cover an envelope with 14 cents of stamps using at most five 1 and 3 cent stamps. Since the postal service wants maximal coverage without gaps, the maximal coverage is 13 cents.

Input

The first line of each data set contains the integer S, representing the maximum of stamps that an envelope can accommodate. The second line contains the integer N, representing the number of sets of stamp denominations in the data set. Each of the next N lines contains a set of stamp denominations. The first integer on each line is the number of denominations in the set, followed by a list of stamp denominations, in order from smallest to largest, with each denomination separated from the others by one or more spaces. There will be at most S denominations on each of the N lines. The maximum value of S is 10, the largest stamp denomination is 100, the maximum value of N is 10.

The input is terminated by a data set beginning with zero (S is zero).

Output

Output one line for each data set giving the maximal no-gap coverage followed by the stamp denominations that yield that coverage in the following format:

`max coverage =` $<value>$ `:` $<denominations>$

If more than one set of denominations in a set yields the same maximal no-gap coverage, the set with the fewest number of denominations should be printed (this saves on stamp printing costs). If two sets with the same number of denominations yield the same maximal no-gap coverage, then the set with the lower maximum stamp denomination should be printed. For example, if five stamps fit on an envelope, then stamp sets of 1, 4, 12, 21 and 1, 5, 12, 28 both yield maximal no-gap coverage of 71 cents. The first set would be printed because both sets have the same number of denominations but the first set's largest denomination (21) is lower than that of the second set (28). If multiple sets in a sequence yield the same maximal no-gap coverage, have the same number of denominations, and have equal largest denominations, then any one of the sets is acceptable.

Sample Input

```
5
2
4 1 4 12 21
4 1 5 12 28
10
2
5 1 7 16 31 88
5 1 15 52 67 99
6
2
3 1 5 8
4 1 5 7 8
0
```

Sample Output

```
max coverage =  71 :  1  4 12 21
max coverage = 409 :  1  7 16 31 88
max coverage =  48 :  1  5  7  8
```

F Theseus and the Minotaur

Those of you with a classical education may remember the legend of Theseus and the Minotaur. This is an unlikely tale involving a bull-headed monster, lovelorn damsels, balls of silk and an underground maze full of twisty little passages all alike. In line with the educational nature of this contest, we will now reveal the true story.

The maze was a series of caverns connected by passages. Theseus managed to smuggle into the labyrinth with him a supply of candles and a small tube of phosphorescent paint with which he could mark his way, or, more specifically, the exits he used. He knew that he would be lowered into a passage between two caverns, and that if he could find and kill the Minotaur he would be set free. His intended strategy was to move cautiously along a passage until he came to a cavern and then turn right (he was left-handed and wished to keep his sword away from the wall) and feel his way around the edge of the cavern until he came to an exit. If this was unmarked, he would mark it and enter it; if it was marked he would ignore it and continue around the cavern. If he heard the Minotaur in a cavern with him, he would light a candle and kill the Minotaur, since the Minotaur would be blinded by the light. If, however, he met the Minotaur in a passage he would be in trouble, since the size of the passage would restrict his movements and he would be unable to either light a candle or fight adequately. When he entered a cavern that had been previously entered by the Minotaur he would light a candle and leave it there and then turn right (as usual) but take the Minotaur's exit.

In the meantime, the Minotaur was also searching for Theseus. He was bigger and slower-moving but he knew the caverns well and hence, unlikely as it may seem, every time he emerged from a passage into a cavern, so did Theseus, albeit usually in a different one. The Minotaur turned left when he entered a cavern and traveled clockwise around it until he came to an unmarked (by him) exit, at which point he would mark it and take it. If he sensed that the cavern he was about to enter had a candle burning in it, he would turn and flee back up the passage he had just used, arriving back at the previous cavern to complete his 'turn.'

Consider the following labyrinth as an example

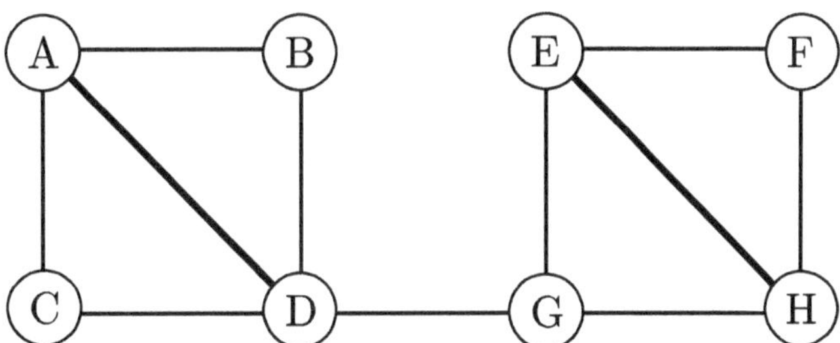

Assume that Theseus starts off between A and C going toward C, and that the Minotaur starts off between F and H going toward H. After entering C, Theseus will move to D, whereas the Minotaur, after entering H will move to G. Theseus will then move towards G while the Minotaur will head for D and Theseus will be killed in the corridor between D and G. If, however, Theseus starts off as before and the Minotaur starts off between D and G then, while Theseus moves from C to D to G, the Minotaur moves from G to E to F. When Theseus enters G he detects that the Minotaur has been there before him and heads for E, and not for H, reaching it as the Minotaur reaches H. The Minotaur is thwarted in his attempt to get to G and turns back, arriving in H just as Theseus, still 'following' the Minotaur arrives in F. The Minotaur tries E and is again thwarted and arrives back at H just as Theseus arrives in hot pursuit. Thus the Minotaur is slain in H.

Write a program that will simulate Theseus' pursuit of the Minotaur.

Input

Input will consist of a series of labyrinths. Each labyrinth will contain a series of cavern descriptors, one per line. Each line will contain a cavern identifier (a single upper case character) followed by a colon (:) and a list of caverns reachable from it (in counterclockwise order). No cavern will be connected to itself. The cavern descriptors will not be ordered in any way. The description of a labyrinth will be terminated by a line starting with a @ character, followed by two pairs of cavern identifiers. The first pair indicates the passage in which Theseus starts, and the second in which the Minotaur starts. The travel in a starting passage is toward the cavern whose identifier is the second character in the pair. The file will be terminated by a line consisting of a single #.

A final encounter is possible for each input data set.

Output

Output will consist of one line for each labyrinth. Each line will specify who gets killed and where. Note that if the final encounter takes place in a passage it should be specified from Theseus' point of view. Follow the format shown in the example below exactly, which describes the situations referred to above.

Sample Input

```
A:BCD
D:BACG
F:HE
G:HED
B:AD
E:FGH
H:FEG
C:AD
@ACFH
A:BCD
D:BACG
F:HE
G:HED
B:AD
E:FGH
H:FEG
C:AD
@ACDG
#
```

Sample Output

```
Theseus is killed between D and G
The Minotaur is slain in H
```

G   Train Time

City transportation planners are developing a light rail transit system to carry commuters between the suburbs and the downtown area. Part of their task includes scheduling trains on different routes between the outermost stations and the metro center hub.

Part of the planning process consists of a simple simulation of train travel. A simulation consists of a series of scenarios in which two trains, one starting at the metro center and one starting at the outermost station of the same route, travel toward each other along the route. The transportation planners want to find out where and when the two trains meet. You are to write a program to determine those results.

This model of train travel is necessarily simplified. All scenarios are based on the following assumptions.

1. All trains spend a fixed amount of time at each station.

2. All trains accelerate and decelerate at the same constant rate. All trains have the same maximum possible velocity.

3. When a train leaves a station, it accelerates (at a constant rate) until it reaches its maximum velocity. It remains at that maximum velocity until it begins to decelerate (at the same constant rate) as it approaches the next station. Trains leave stations with an initial velocity of zero (0.0) and they arrive at stations with terminal velocity zero. Adjacent stations on each route are far enough apart to allow a train to accelerate to its maximum velocity before beginning to decelerate.

4. Both trains in each scenario make their initial departure at the same time.

5. There are at most 30 stations along any route.

Input

All input values are real numbers. Data for each scenario are in the following format.

$d_1\ d_2\ \ldots\ d_n$ 0.0   For a single route, the list of distances (in miles – there are 5,280 feet in a mile) from each station to the metro center hub, separated by one or more spaces. Stations are listed in ascending order, starting with the station closest to the metro center hub (station 1) and continuing to the outermost station. All distances are greater than zero. The list is terminated by the sentinel value 0.0.

v The maximum train velocity, in feet/minute.

s The constant train acceleration rate in feet/minute^2.

m The number of minutes a train stays in a station.

The series of runs is terminated by a data set which begins with the number -1.0.

Output

For each scenario, output consists of the following labeled data.

1. The number of the scenario (numbered consecutively, starting with **Scenario #1**).

2. The time when the two trains meet in terms of minutes from starting time. All times must be displayed to one decimal place. Also, if the trains meet in a station, output the station number where they meet.

3. The distance in miles between the metro center hub and the place where the two trains meet. Distances must be displayed to three decimal places.

Sample Input

```
15.0 0.0
5280.0
10560.0
5.0
3.5 7.0 0.0
5280.0
10560.0
2.0
3.4 7.0 0.0
5280.0
10560.0
2.0
-1.0
```

Sample Output

```
Scenario #1:
   Meeting time: 7.8 minutes
   Meeting distance: 7.500 miles from metro center hub

Scenario #2:
   Meeting time: 4.0 minutes
   Meeting distance: 3.500 miles from metro center hub, in station 1

Scenario #3:
   Meeting time: 4.1 minutes
   Meeting distance: 3.400 miles from metro center hub, in station 1
```

H Uncompress

A simple scheme for creating a compressed version of a text file can be used for files which contain no digit characters. The compression scheme requires making a list of the words in the uncompressed file. When a non-alphabetic character is encountered in the uncompressed file, it is copied directly into the compressed file. When a word is encountered in the uncompressed file, it is copied directly into the compressed file only if this is the first occurrence of the word. In that case, the word is put at the front of the list. If it is not the first occurrence, the word is not copied to the compressed file. Instead, its position in the list is copied into the compressed file and the word is moved to the front of the list. The numbering of list positions begins at 1.

Write a program that takes a compressed file as input and generates a reproduction of the original uncompressed file as output. You can assume that no word contains more than 50 characters and that the original uncompressed file contains no digit characters.

For the purposes of this problem, a word is defined to be a maximal sequence of upper- and lower-case letters. Words are case-sensitive – the word `abc` is not the same as the word `Abc`. For example,

`x-ray`	contains 2 words:	`x` and `ray`
`Mary's`	contains 2 words:	`Mary` and `s`
`It's a winner`	contains 4 words:	`It` and `s` and `a` and `winner`

There is no upper limit on the number of different words in the input file. The end of the input file is signified by the number 0 on a line by itself. The terminating 0 merely indicates the end of the input and should not be part of the output produced by your program.

Sample Input

```
Dear Sally,

    Please, please do it--1 would 4
Mary very, 1 much.  And 4 6
8 everything in 5's power to make
14 pay off for you.

    -- Thank 2 18 18--
0
```

Sample Output

```
Dear Sally,

    Please, please do it--it would please
Mary very, very much.  And Mary would
do everything in Mary's power to make
it pay off for you.

    -- Thank you very much--
```

WORLD FINALS 1996

PHILADELPHIA, PENNSYLVANIA

World Champion

UNIVERSITY OF CALIFORNIA AT BERKELEY

Scott McPeak
Ben Rudiak-Gould
Amit Sahai

Director of Judging
Dick Rinewalt   *Texas Christian University*

Chief Judge
Jo Perry   *North Carolina State University*

Judges
Owen Astrachan   *Duke University*
David Elizandro   *Tennessee Tech University*
Mark Measures   *Baylor University*
Robin O'Leary   *Swansea*
Robert Roos   *Allegheny College*
Patrick Ryan   *TechnoSolutions, Inc.*
Laurie White   *Mercer University*
Stanley Wileman, Jr.   *University of Nebraska at Omaha*

UVa Online Judge problem numbers
246   A   10-20-30
247   B   Calling Circles
248   C   Cutting Corners
249   D   Bang the Drum Slowly
250   E   Pattern Matching Prelims
251   F   Nondeterministic Trellis Automata
252   G   Trucking

A   10-20-30

A simple solitaire card game called 10-20-30 uses a standard deck of 52 playing cards in which suit is irrelevant. The value of a face card (king, queen, jack) is 10. The value of an ace is one. The value of each of the other cards is the face value of the card (2, 3, 4, etc.). Cards are dealt from the top of the deck. You begin by dealing out seven cards, left to right forming seven piles. After playing a card on the rightmost pile, the next pile upon which you play a card is the leftmost pile.

For each card placed on a pile, check that pile to see if one of the following three card combinations totals 10, 20, or 30.

1.   the first two and last one,
2.   the first one and the last two, or
3.   the last three cards.

If so, pick up the three cards and place them on the bottom of the deck. For this problem, always check the pile in the order just described. Collect the cards in the order they appear on the pile and put them at the bottom of the deck. Picking up three cards may expose three more cards that can be picked up. If so, pick them up. Continue until no more sets of three can be picked up from the pile.

For example, suppose a pile contains 5 9 7 3 where the 5 is at the first card of the pile, and then a 6 is played. The first two cards plus the last card $(5 + 9 + 6)$ sum to 20. The new contents of the pile after picking up those three cards becomes 7 3. Also, the bottommost card in the deck is now the 6, the card above it is the 9, and the one above the 9 is the 5.

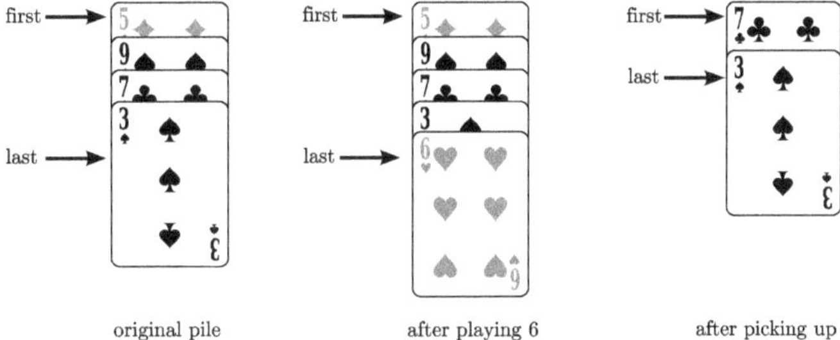

original pile   after playing 6   after picking up

If a queen were played instead of the six, $5 + 9 + 10 = 24$, and $5 + 3 + 10 = 18$, but $7 + 3 + 10 = 20$, so the last three cards would be picked up, leaving the pile as 5 9.

original pile   after playing queen   after picking up

If a pile contains only three cards when the three sum to 10, 20, or 30, then the pile "disappears" when the cards are picked up. That is, subsequent play skips over the position that the now-empty pile occupied. You win if all the piles disappear. You lose if you are unable to deal a card. It is also possible to have a draw if neither of the previous two conditions ever occurs.

Write a program that will play games of 10-20-30 given initial card decks as input.

Input

Each input set consists of a sequence of 52 integers separated by spaces and/or ends of line. The integers represent card values of the initial deck for that game. The first integer is the top card of the deck. Input is terminated by a single zero (0) following the last deck.

Output

For each input set, print whether the result of the game is a win, loss, or a draw, and print the number of times a card is dealt before the game results can be determined. (A draw occurs as soon as the state of the game is repeated.) Use the format shown in the "Sample Output" section.

Sample Input

```
2 6 5 10 10 4 10 10 10 4 5 10 4 5 10 9 7 6 1 7 6 9 5 3 10 10 4 10 9 2 1
10 1 10 10 10 3 10 9 8 10 8 7 1 2 8 6 7 3 3 8 2
4 3 2 10 8 10 6 8 9 5 8 10 5 3 5 4 6 9 9 1 7 6 3 5 10 10 8 10 9 10 10 7
2 6 10 10 4 10 1 3 10 1 1 10 2 2 10 4 10 7 7 10
10 5 4 3 5 7 10 8 2 3 9 10 8 4 5 1 7 6 7 2 6 9 10 2 3 10 3 4 4 9 10 1 1
10   5 10 10 1 8 10 7 8 10 6 10 10 10 9 6 2 10 10
0
```

Sample Output

```
Win : 66
Loss: 82
Draw: 73
```

B Calling Circles

If you've seen television commercials for long-distance phone companies lately, you've noticed that many companies have been spending a lot of money trying to convince people that they provide the best service at the lowest cost. One company has "calling circles." You provide a list of people that you call most frequently. If you call someone in your calling circle (who is also a customer of the same company), you get bigger discounts than if you call outside your circle. Another company points out that you only get the big discounts for people in your calling circle, and if you change who you call most frequently, it's up to you to add them to your calling circle.

LibertyBell Phone Co. is a new company that thinks they have the calling plan that can put other companies out of business. LibertyBell has calling circles, but they figure out your calling circle for you. This is how it works. LibertyBell keeps track of all phone calls. In addition to yourself, your calling circle consists of all people whom you call and who call you, either directly or indirectly.

For example, if Ben calls Alexander, Alexander calls Dolly, and Dolly calls Ben, they are all within the same circle. If Dolly also calls Benedict and Benedict calls Dolly, then Benedict is in the same calling circle as Dolly, Ben, and Alexander. Finally, if Alexander calls Aaron but Aaron doesn't call Alexander, Ben, Dolly, or Benedict, then Aaron is not in the circle.

You've been hired by LibertyBell to write the program to determine calling circles given a log of phone calls between people.

Input

The input file will contain one or more data sets. Each data set begins with a line containing two integers, n and m. The first integer, n, represents the number of different people who are in the data set. The maximum value for n is 25. The remainder of the data set consists of m lines, each representing a phone call. Each call is represented by two names, separated by a single space. Names are first names only (unique within a data set), are case sensitive, and consist of only alphabetic characters; no name is longer than 25 letters.

For example, if Ben called Dolly, it would be represented in the data file as

```
Ben Dolly
```

Input is terminated by values of zero (0) for n and m.

Output

For each input set, print a header line with the data set number, followed by a line for each calling circle in that data set. Each calling circle line contains the names of all the people in any order within the circle, separated by comma-space (a comma followed by a space). Output sets are separated by blank lines.

Sample Input

```
5 6
Ben Alexander
Alexander Dolly
Dolly Ben
Dolly Benedict
Benedict Dolly
Alexander Aaron
14 34
John Aaron
Aaron Benedict
Betsy John
Betsy Ringo
Ringo Dolly
Benedict Paul
John Betsy
John Aaron
Benedict George
Dolly Ringo
Paul Martha
George Ben
Alexander George
Betsy Ringo
Alexander Stephen
Martha Stephen
Benedict Alexander
Stephen Paul
Betsy Ringo
Quincy Martha
Ben Patrick
Betsy Ringo
Patrick Stephen
Paul Alexander
Patrick Ben
Stephen Quincy
Ringo Betsy
Betsy Benedict
Betsy Benedict
Betsy Benedict
Betsy Benedict
Betsy Benedict
Betsy Benedict
Quincy Martha
0 0
```

Sample Output

```
Calling circles for data set 1:
Ben, Alexander, Dolly, Benedict
Aaron

Calling circles for data set 2:
John, Betsy, Ringo, Dolly
Aaron
Benedict
Paul, George, Martha, Ben, Alexander, Stephen, Quincy, Patrick
```

C Cutting Corners

Bicycle messengers who deliver documents and small items to businesses have long been part of the guerrilla transportation services in several major U.S. cities. The cyclists of Boston are a rare breed of riders. They are notorious for their speed, their disrespect for one-way streets and traffic signals, and their brazen disregard for cars, taxis, buses, and pedestrians.

Bicycle messenger services are very competitive. Billy's Bicycle Messenger Service is no exception. To boost its competitive edge and to determine its actual expenses, BBMS is developing a new scheme for pricing deliveries that depends on the shortest route messengers can travel. You are to write a program to help BBMS determine the distances for these routes.

The following assumptions help simplify your task:

- Messengers can ride their bicycles anywhere at ground level except inside buildings.

- Ground floors of irregularly shaped buildings are modeled by the union of the interiors of rectangles. By agreement any intersecting rectangles share interior space and are part of the same building.

- The defining rectangles for two separate buildings never touch, although they can be quite close. (Bicycle messengers- skinny to a fault-can travel between any two buildings. They can cut the sharpest corners and run their skinny tires right down the perimeters of the buildings.)

- The starting and stopping points are never inside buildings.

- There is always some route from the starting point to the stopping point.

Your program must be able to process several scenarios. Each scenario defines the buildings and the starting and stopping points for a delivery route. The picture below shows a bird's-eye view of a typical scenario.

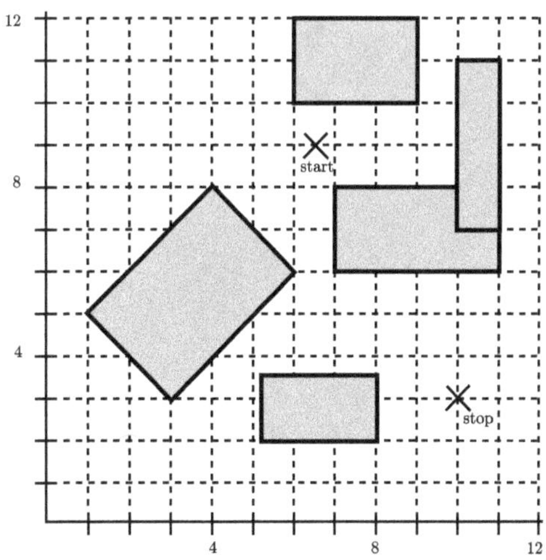

Input

The input file represents several scenarios. Input for each scenario consists of lines as follows:

First line: n
    The number of rectangles describing the buildings in the scenario. $0 \leq n \leq 20$
Second line: $x_1\ y_1\ x_2\ y_2$
    The x- and y-coordinates of the starting and stopping points of the route.
Remaining n lines: $x_1\ y_1\ x_2\ y_2\ x_3\ y_3$
    The x- and y-coordinates of three vertices of a rectangle.

    The x and y-coordinates of all input data are real numbers between 0 and 1000 inclusive. Successive coordinates on a line are separated by one or more blanks. The integer -1 follows the data of the last scenario.

Output

Output should number each scenario (`Scenario #1`, `Scenario #2`, etc.) and give the distance of the shortest route from starting to stopping point as illustrated in the Sample Output below. The distance should be written with two digits to the right of the decimal point. Output for successive scenarios should be separated by blank lines.

Sample Input

```
5
6.5     9       10  3
1       5       3   3       6   6
5.25    2       8   2       8   3.5
6       10      6   12      9   12
7       6       11  6       11  8
10      7       11  7       11  11
-1
```

Sample Output

```
Scenario #1
   route distance: 7.28
```

D Bang the Drum Slowly

Many years ago the "primary memory" of most computer systems was a magnetic drum. Read-/write heads were placed so they could access data from the magnetic outer surface as the drum rotated along its horizontal axis. The following illustration gives the basic idea:

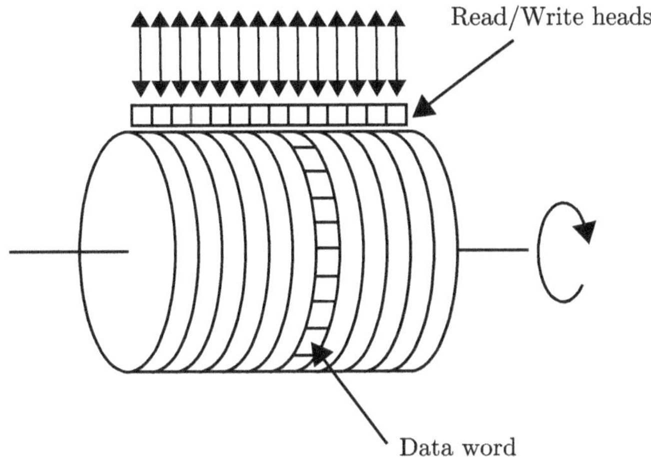

As the drum rotated, the data word under the read/write head(s) could be accessed. The drum continued to rotate after an instruction was fetched. After the execution of an instruction, the word ready to be accessed by the read/write head(s) was typically many words away. To minimize the delay that would occur if instructions to be executed sequentially were placed in consecutive words on the drum, designers of these machines frequently included the next instruction's drum address as a field in the instruction (that is, each instruction included an explicit "next instruction" address). Then "optimizing" assemblers could fill in the next instruction field with the address of the first available word ready to be read by the drum as soon as the current instruction was completed.

In this problem we want to determine the average execution times of simple programs without loops. We will consider only a single read/write head on a single track. Assume that the words on that track have sequential addresses numbered 1 through n. All instructions require the same length of time to execute, specifically the same time as it takes the drum to rotate past t words. t does not include the time to read the instruction from the drum, nor does it include the additional rotational delay that might be required if the next instruction isn't at the "optimum" address. However, these factors must be included in calculating the average execution time.

There are three types of instructions: terminal, conditional and unconditional. Terminal instructions don't have a "next instruction" address, since they terminate the execution of a program. Conditional instructions have two "next instruction" addresses, and unconditional instructions have only one "next instruction" address.

The execution time of a program run is the time taken from beginning to read the first instruction until the terminal instruction has executed. To calculate the average execution time of a program, every possible run time is weighted (multiplied) by the probability of the run. We assume equal probability of taking each path of a branch in a conditional instruction. The sum of all weighted run times is the average execution time of the program.

Assumptions:

- *At the beginning of each test case the drum is positioned so that the instruction at location 1 is about to be read. Each program begins execution with the word in location 1.*

- *The time to read an instruction is one time unit.*

- *There will always be at least one terminal instruction, but there may be several.*

Input

The input consists of a number of test cases. The input for each test case begins with a line containing integer values for n $(1 < n < 50)$ and t $(0 < t < n)$. This line is followed by a sequence of lines each of which contains integers representing an instruction address and zero, one, or two branch addresses. Specifically, for each instruction there is a location (between 1 and n), the number of "next instruction" addresses (0 for a terminal instruction, 1 for an unconditional instruction, and 2 for a conditional instruction), and that many branch addresses. The last instruction is followed by '0' on a line by itself. The input set is terminated by values of 0 for both n and t.

Output

For each test case, print the case number (they are numbered sequentially starting with 1) and the average execution time for the program. Execution times must be accurate to and displayed with four fractional digits.

Sample Input

```
10 5
1 0
0
10 5
1 1 6
6 0
0
10 5
1 1 7
7 0
0
10 5
1 2 7 8
7 0
8 0
0
10 6
8 0
7 1 3
3 0
1 2 7 8
0
0 0
```

Sample Output

```
Case 1. Execution time = 6.0000
Case 2. Execution time = 21.0000
Case 3. Execution time = 12.0000
Case 4. Execution time = 12.5000
Case 5. Execution time = 26.5000
```

E   Pattern Matching Prelims

Some algorithms for optical character recognition compare a scanned image with templates of "perfect" characters. Part of the difficulty with such comparisons is deciding where to start the comparison. This is because the characters in the scanned image are subject to noise and distortion, resulting in changes in size, position, and orientation.

A procedure that is sometimes used to deal with changes in position matches the "center of gravity" of the scanned character and the templates against which it is compared. In this problem you are to determine the "centers of gravity" of scanned images of characters.

For our purposes, a scanned image will be a rectangular array of real numbers, each of which represents the gray-scale value of a point in a scanned image. Each gray-scale value will be between 0 (representing a totally white region) and 1 (representing a totally black region). The array will have no more than 25 rows and 25 columns.

The center of gravity is a particular element of an array. Suppose a center of gravity is in the ith row and jth column. Then the difference between the sum of the elements of the two array portions above and below the ith row is minimal. Likewise, the difference of the sums of the elements in the two array portions to the left and to the right of the jth column is minimal.

Consider the array shown below, which might have resulted from scanning a lower case "o." The center of gravity for this array is uniquely in row 3, column 3. The difference of the sum of the elements in each array portion formed by ignoring the third row is 0.1 (the sums are 5.55 and 5.65). The difference of the sum of each array portion formed by ignoring the third column is 0.0 (the sums are both 5.60).

0.7	0.75	0.7	0.75	0.8
0.55	0.3	0.2	0.1	0.7
0.8	0.1	0.0	0.0	0.8
0.7	0.0	0.0	0.0	0.8
0.8	0.9	0.8	0.75	0.9

Input

The input will consist of a sequence of scanned character images. Input for each image will begin with two integers specifying the number of rows and columns in the scanned data. This will be immediately followed by the scanned gray-scale data given in row-major order. A pair of zeroes will follow the data for the last input image.

Output

For each input character image, display its number (they are sequentially numbered starting with 1) and the row and column corresponding to the center of gravity. If there is more than one center of gravity, the one with the largest row and column should be displayed. The sample that follows illustrates a reasonable output format.

Sample Input

```
5 5
0.1 0.2 0.1 0.2 0.1
0.1 0.2 0.3 0.1 0.1
0.2 0.3 0.1 0.1 0.3
0.4 0.1 0.1 0.1 0.2
0.2 0.2 0.3 0.3 0.1

5 10
0.1 0.1 0.1 0.1 0.1 0.1 0.1 0.1 0.1 0.1
0.2 0.2 0.2 0.2 0.2 0.2 0.2 0.2 0.2 0.2
0.3 0.3 0.3 0.3 0.3 0.3 0.3 0.3 0.3 0.3
0.4 0.4 0.4 0.4 0.4 0.4 0.4 0.4 0.4 0.4
0.5 0.5 0.5 0.5 0.5 0.5 0.5 0.5 0.5 0.6

0 0
```

Sample Output

```
Case 1: center at (3, 3)
Case 2: center at (4, 6)
```

F   Nondeterministic Trellis Automata

A nondeterministic trellis automaton (NTA) is a kind of parallel machine composed of identical finite-state processors arranged in an infinite triangular trellis. The top, or apex, of the triangle is a single processor. The next row has two processors and each successive row of an NTA has one more processor than the row above it. Each processor in an NTA is connected to two children in the row below it. Computation in an NTA occurs bottom up; the state of each processor in a row is based on the state of the processor's children and a transition table. The input to an NTA is the initial configuration of one row of processors. The input is specified by a string that gives the initial state of each processor in a row so that an n-character string specifies the initial configuration for a row of n processors. Computation proceeds up the NTA to the apex by nondeterministically calculating the state of each processor in a row based on the transition table and the state of the processor's children in the row below.

Some states are identified as accepting states. Some transitions are computed nondeterministically. An input is *accepted* if some computation puts the apex processor into an accepting state. An input is *rejected* if no computation puts the apex processor into an accepting state. For example, the table below shows transitions for a 3-state NTA. States are labeled by characters "a", "b", and "c"; the only accepting state is "c".

State transition table:

states={a,b,c}
accepting={c}

	right child a	right child b	right child c
left child a	a	a	c
left child b	a,c	a	b
left child c	c	b	a

The diagram below shows two computations for the input "bba". The computation on the left rejects the input since the state of the apex is "a"; but the computation on the right accepts the input since the state of the apex is "c". Since some computation results in an accepting state for the apex, the input "bba" is accepted by the NTA. The input "bbb" would be rejected by this NTA since the only computation results in the state "a" for the apex.

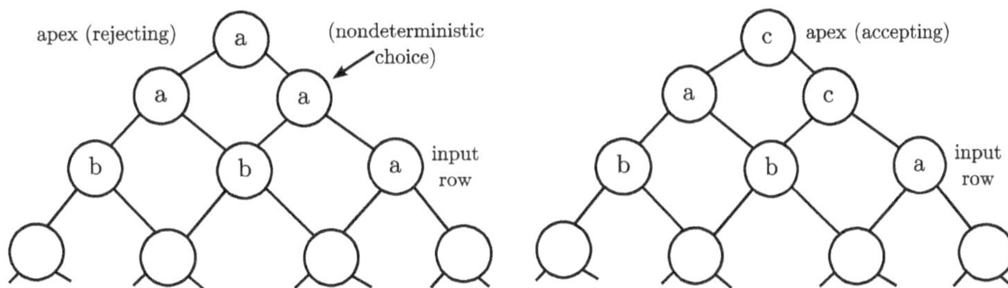

Input

The states (and inputs) of an NTA are consecutive lowercase letters. Thus the states for a 5-state NTA are "a", "b", "c", "d", and "e". Accepting states are grouped at the end of the letters so that if a 5-state NTA has two accepting states, the accepting states are "d" and "e".

The input for your program is a sequence of NTA descriptions and initial configurations. An NTA description is given by the number of states n followed by the number of accepting states on one line separated by whitespace. The $n \times n$ transition table follows in row-major order; each transition string is given on a separate line. Each NTA description is followed by a sequence of initial configurations, one per line. A line of "#" terminates the sequence of initial configurations for that NTA. An NTA description in which the number of states is zero terminates the input for your program. NTAs will have at most 15 states, initial configuration will be at most 15 characters.

Output

For each NTA description, print the number of the NTA (NTA 1, NTA 2, etc.). For each initial configuration of an NTA print the word 'accept' or 'reject' followed by a copy of the initial configuration.

<table>
<tr><td>Sample Input</td><td>Sample Output</td></tr>
<tr><td>

```
3 1
a
a
c
ca
a
b
c
b
a
bba
aaaaa
abab
babbba
a
baaab
abbbaba
baba
bcbab
#
3 2
ab
a
c
a
ab
b
c
b
ab
abc
cbc
#
0 0
```

</td><td>

```
NTA 1
accept   bba
reject   abab
accept   babbba
reject   a
reject   aaaaa
accept   baaab
accept   abbbaba
accept   baba
reject   bcbab

NTA 2
reject   abc
accept   cbc
```

</td></tr>
</table>

G   Trucking

Allied Container Movers (ACM) is a trucking company that provides overnight freight delivery. ACM has a distribution network with several intermediate container processing centers (ICPCs). At an ICPC, an incoming trailer is unloaded at a stripping door. Freight destined for that center is simply acknowledged as received. Onward shipments are distributed to relay doors based on their next destinations, where they are loaded onto waiting trailers.

Each ICPC has several stripping doors for unloading incoming trailers. When the number of trailers to be stripped exceeds the number of stripping doors, incoming trailers are queued until a door is available. A single trailer may have freight for several different ICPCs. Trailers with freight destined only for the local ICPC receive a lower priority for access to a stripping door than trailers with relay freight. In a similar fashion, trailers with relay freight having a closer final destination have lower priority than trailers with relay freight having a distant final destination. The time to unload a container and, if necessary, reload all its shipments onto one or more relay trailers is always 2 hours regardless of the size and number of shipments. A relay trailer is immediately routed to its next destination when it is full or when all shipments for the day expected for that destination have been loaded onto the trailer. Shipments are measured as a percent of a trailer volume and may be subdivided to the nearest percent in order to fill the trailer. There is no delay between a trailer departing and another trailer becoming available at the relay or stripping doors. There is never a shortage of trailers for onward distribution.

In order to help ACM assess the efficiency of their network, you must write a program to determine the average time a trailer waits for access to a stripping door and identify those shipments which will not arrive in their entirety at their intermediate or final destinations on time.

Input

The input describes a possibly disjoint subset of the network's ICPCs and traffic patterns that must be analyzed. The first line of the input contains an integer n which specifies the number of ICPC descriptions to be processed, $1 \leq n \leq 100$. This is followed by n descriptions, each describing one ICPC. Each description begins with a line containing three integers, csd, where c is the center number, $0 \leq c \leq 99$, s is the number of stripping doors at center c, $0 \leq s \leq 10$, and d is the number of relay doors at center c, $0 \leq d \leq 10$. There then follow d lines, one for each relay door. Each of these lines contains three integers, rvl, where r is the relay center's number, $0 \leq r \leq 99$, v is the total volume of shipments to that center for the day expressed as a percentage of trailer volume, $0 \leq v \leq 900$ and l is the latest acceptable time for shipments to arrive at center r, expressed as minutes since the start of the day, $0 \leq l \leq 1440$. ($v > 100$ indicates that more than a single trailer must be used.)

The second part of the input describes some of the day's traffic. This part begins with one integer m on a line by itself indicating the number of trailer arrival records that follow, $1 \leq m \leq 100$. Each record begins with a line containing three integers, acs, where a is the trailer's arrival time expressed as minutes since the start of the day, $0 \leq a \leq 1440$, at center number c, and s is the number of shipments in the trailer, $0 \leq s \leq 10$. Then all s shipments are described by s lines of 5 integers, $iorvt$, representing the shipment identification code i, $0 \leq i \leq 99$, the origin and next relay center numbers o and r respectively, the volume of the shipment v as a percentage of trailer volume and the time t taken to travel from center c to destination r measured in minutes. t is zero if c equals r. Arrival records are in order of ascending values of a. No two records have the same pair (a, c). All center numbers used as values for c and r will have an appropriate corresponding definition in the first part of the input, though the center numbers used for o need not.

Output

For each of the n ICPCs, your program must write out a line describing the average wait time for stripping doors in the appropriate one of these two forms:

```
The average wait for a stripping door at ICPC c is ###.# minutes.
There is no wait for a stripping door at ICPC c.
```

The average wait time is affected only by trailers which wait at least one minute for a stripping door.

Your program should then list all the shipments any part of which will not arrive at their intermediate or final destinations by any of the latest arrival times given along the route. This report should appear in columns headed as shown:

```
The late shipments are:
Id Origin Destination Volume
```

Sample Input

```
2
0 1 1
      8   40   600
8 3 4
      6  115  1200
      2   95  1260
     10  100  1440
      4   55  1380
7
500 0 1
     17   11   8   40     80
700 8 3
     24   11   8   45      0
     18   11   6   40    120
     23   11  10   15    600
720 8 1
     16    3   8  100      0
750 8 2
      4   15   2   50    180
      7   15   6   50    120
760 8 4
     14    3   4   20    300
     27    3   2   20    180
     33    3  10   35    600
     16    3   6   25    120
780 8 2
     12    9   2   25    180
     15    9   4   35    300
800 8 1
     19   18  10   50    600
```

Sample Output

```
There is no wait for a stripping door at ICPC 0.
The average wait for a stripping door at ICPC 8 is 63.3 minutes.

The late shipments are:
Id Origin Destination Volume
17      11            8     40
23      11           10     15
33       3           10     35
19      18           10     50
```

WORLD FINALS 1997

SAN JOSE, CALIFORNIA

World Champion

HARVEY MUDD COLLEGE

Brian Carnes
Brian Johnson
Kevin Watkins
Dominic Mazzoni

Director of Judging
  Dick Rinewalt   *Texas Christian University*

Chief Judge
  Jo Perry   *North Carolina State University*

Judges
  Owen Astrachan   *Duke University*
  David Elizandro   *Tennessee Tech University*
  Robin O'Leary   *Swansea*
  Robert Roos   *Allegheny College*
  Matthias Ruhl   *MIT*
  Patrick Ryan   *TechnoSolutions, Inc.*
  Laurie White   *Mercer University*
  Stanley Wileman, Jr.   *University of Nebraska at Omaha*

UVa Online Judge problem numbers
  506   A   System Dependencies
  507   B   Jill Rides Again
  508   C   Morse Mismatches
  509   D   RAID!
  510   E   Optional Routing
  511   F   Do You Know the Way to San Jose?
  512   G   Spreadsheet Tracking
  513   H   Window Frames

A   System Dependencies

Components of computer systems often have dependencies—other components that must be installed before they will function properly. These dependencies are frequently shared by multiple components. For example, both the TELNET client program and the FTP client program require that the TCP/IP networking software be installed before they can operate. If you install TCP/IP and the TELNET client program, and later decide to add the FTP client program, you do not need to reinstall TCP/IP.

For some components it would not be a problem if the components on which they depended were reinstalled; it would just waste some resources. But for others, like TCP/IP, some component configuration may be destroyed if the component was reinstalled.

It is useful to be able to remove components that are no longer needed. When this is done, components that only support the removed component may also be removed, freeing up disk space, memory, and other resources. But a supporting component, not explicitly installed, may be removed only if all components which depend on it are also removed. For example, removing the FTP client program and TCP/IP would mean the TELNET client program, which was not removed, would no longer operate. Likewise, removing TCP/IP by itself would cause the failure of both the TELNET and the FTP client programs. Also if we installed TCP/IP to support our own development, then installed the TELNET client (which depends on TCP/IP) and then still later removed the TELNET client, we would not want TCP/IP to be removed.

We want a program to automate the process of adding and removing components. To do this we will maintain a record of installed components and component dependencies. A component can be installed explicitly in response to a command (unless it is already installed), or implicitly if it is needed for some other component being installed. Likewise, a component, not explicitly installed, can be explicitly removed in response to a command (if it is not needed to support other components) or implicitly removed if it is no longer needed to support another component. Installing an already implicitly-installed component won't make that component become explicity installed.

Input

The input will contain a sequence of commands (as described below), each on a separate line containing no more than eighty characters. Item names are case sensitive, and each is no longer than ten characters. The command names (DEPEND, INSTALL, REMOVE and LIST) always appear in uppercase starting in column one, and item names are separated from the command name and each other by one or more spaces. All appropriate DEPEND commands will appear before the occurrence of any INSTALL command that uses them. There will be no circular dependencies. The end of the input is marked by a line containing only the word END.

Command Syntax	*Interpretation/Response*
`DEPEND item1 item2 [item3 ...]`	**item1** depends on **item2** (and **item3** ...)
`INSTALL item1`	install **item1** and those on which it depends
`REMOVE item1`	remove **item1**, and those on which it depends, if possible
`LIST`	list the names of all currently-installed components

Output

Echo each line of input. Follow each echoed `INSTALL` or `REMOVE` line with the actions taken in response, making certain that the actions are given in the proper order. Also identify exceptional conditions (see Sample Output, below, for examples of all cases). For the `LIST` command, display the names of the currently installed components in the installation order. No output, except the echo, is produced for a `DEPEND` command or the line containing `END`. There will be at most one dependency list per item.

Sample Input

```
DEPEND   TELNET TCPIP NETCARD
DEPEND TCPIP NETCARD
DEPEND DNS TCPIP NETCARD
DEPEND  BROWSER   TCPIP   HTML
INSTALL NETCARD
INSTALL TELNET
INSTALL foo
REMOVE NETCARD
INSTALL BROWSER
INSTALL DNS
LIST
REMOVE TELNET
REMOVE NETCARD
REMOVE DNS
REMOVE NETCARD
INSTALL NETCARD
REMOVE TCPIP
REMOVE BROWSER
REMOVE TCPIP
END
```

Sample Output

```
DEPEND   TELNET TCPIP NETCARD
DEPEND TCPIP NETCARD
DEPEND DNS TCPIP NETCARD
DEPEND BROWSER   TCPIP  HTML
INSTALL NETCARD
   Installing NETCARD
INSTALL TELNET
   Installing TCPIP
   Installing TELNET
INSTALL foo
   Installing foo
REMOVE NETCARD
   NETCARD is still needed.
INSTALL BROWSER
   Installing HTML
   Installing BROWSER
INSTALL DNS
   Installing DNS
LIST
   NETCARD
   TCPIP
   TELNET
   foo
   HTML
   BROWSER
   DNS
REMOVE TELNET
   Removing TELNET
REMOVE NETCARD
   NETCARD is still needed.
REMOVE DNS
   Removing DNS
REMOVE NETCARD
   NETCARD is still needed.
INSTALL NETCARD
   NETCARD is already installed.
REMOVE TCPIP
   TCPIP is still needed.
REMOVE BROWSER
   Removing BROWSER
   Removing HTML
   Removing TCPIP
REMOVE TCPIP
   TCPIP is not installed.
END
```

B Jill Rides Again

Jill likes to ride her bicycle, but since the pretty city of Greenhills where she lives has grown, Jill often uses the excellent public bus system for part of her journey. She has a folding bicycle which she carries with her when she uses the bus for the first part of her trip. When the bus reaches some pleasant part of the city, Jill gets off and rides her bicycle. She follows the bus route until she reaches her destination or she comes to a part of the city she does not like. In the latter event she will board the bus to finish her trip.

Through years of experience, Jill has rated each road on an integer scale of "niceness." Positive niceness values indicate roads Jill likes; negative values are used for roads she does not like. There are not zero values. Jill plans where to leave the bus and start bicycling, as well as where to stop bicycling and re-join the bus, so that the sum of niceness values of the roads she bicycles on is maximized. This means that she will sometimes cycle along a road she does not like, provided that it joins up two other parts of her journey involving roads she likes enough to compensate. It may be that no part of the route is suitable for cycling so that Jill takes the bus for its entire route. Conversely, it may be that the whole route is so nice Jill will not use the bus at all.

Since there are many different bus routes, each with several stops at which Jill could leave or enter the bus, she feels that a computer program could help her identify the best part to cycle for each bus route.

Input

The input file contains information on several bus routes. The first line of the file is a single integer b representing the number of route descriptions in the file. The identifier for each route (r) is the sequence number within the data file, $1 \leq r \leq b$. Each route description begins with the number of stops on the route: an integer s, $2 \leq s \leq 20,000$ on a line by itself. The number of stops is followed by $s - 1$ lines, each line i $(1 \leq i < s)$ is an integer n_i representing Jill's assessment of the niceness of the road between the two stops i and $i + 1$.

Output

For each route r in the input file, your program should identify the beginning bus stop i and the ending bus stop j that identify the segment of the route which yields the maximal sum of niceness, $m = n_i + n_{i+1} + \ldots + n_{j-1}$. If more than one segment is maximally nice, choose the one with the longest cycle ride (largest $j - i$). To break ties in longest maximal segments, choose the segment that begins with the earliest stop (lowest i). For each route r in the input file, print a line in the form:

`The nicest part of route r is between stops i and j.`

However, if the maximal sum is not positive, your program should print:

`Route r has no nice parts.`

Sample Input

```
3
3
   -1
    6
10
    4
   -5
    4
   -3
    4
    4
   -4
    4
   -5
4
   -2
   -3
   -4
```

Sample Output

```
The nicest part of route 1 is between stops 2 and 3
The nicest part of route 2 is between stops 3 and 9
Route 3 has no nice parts
```

C Morse Mismatches

Samuel F. B. Morse is best known for the coding scheme that carries his name. Morse code is still used in international radio communication. The coding of text using Morse code is straightforward. Each character (case is insignificant) is translated to a predefined sequence of *dits* and *dahs* (the elements of Morse code). Dits are represented as periods ("·") and dahs are represented as hyphens or minus signs ("–"). Each element is transmitted by sending a signal for some period of time. A dit is rather short, and a dah is, in perfectly formed code, three times as long as a dit. A short silent space appears between elements, with a longer space between characters. A still longer space separates words. This dependence on the spacing and timing of elements means that Morse code operators sometimes do not send perfect code. This results in difficulties for the receiving operator, but frequently the message can be decoded depending on context.

In this problem we consider reception of words in Morse code without spacing between letters. Without the spacing, it is possible for multiple words to be coded the same. For example, if the message "dit dit dit" were received, it could be interpreted as "EEE", "EI", "IE" or "S" based on the coding scheme shown in the sample input. To decide between these multiple interpretations, we assume a particular context by expecting each received word to appear in a dictionary.

For this problem your program will read a table giving the encoding of letters and digits into Morse code, a list of expected words (*context*), and a sequence of words encoded in Morse code (*morse*). These morse words may be flawed. For each *morse* word, your program is to determine the matching word from *context*, if any. If multiple words from *context* match *morse*, or if no word matches perfectly, your program will display the best matching word and a mismatch indicator.

If a single word from *context* matches *morse* perfectly, it will be displayed on a single line, by itself. If multiple *context* words match *morse* perfectly, then select the matching word with the fewest characters. If this still results in an ambiguous match, any of these matches may be displayed. If multiple *context* words exist for a given *morse*, the first matching word will be displayed followed by an exclamation point ("!").

We assume only a simple case of errors in transmission in which elements may be either truncated from the end of a *morse* word or added to the end of a *morse* word. When no perfect matches for *morse* are found, display the word from *context* that matches the longest prefix of *morse*, or has the fewest extra elements beyond those in *morse*. If multiple words in *context* match using these rules, any of these matches may be displayed. Words that do not match perfectly are displayed with a question mark ("?") suffixed.

The input data will only contain cases that fall within the preceding rules.

Input

The Morse code table will appear first and consists of lines each containing an uppercase letter or a digit C, zero or more blanks, and a sequence of no more than six periods and hyphens giving the Morse code for C. Blanks may precede or follow the items on the line. A line containing a single asterisk ("*"), possibly preceded or followed by blanks, terminates the Morse code table. You may assume that there will be Morse code given for every character that appears in the *context* section.

The *context* section appears next, with one word per line, possibly preceded and followed by blanks. Each word in *context* will contain no more than ten characters. No characters other than upper case letters and digits will appear. Thered will be at most 100 *context* words. A line containing only a single asterisk ("*"), possibly preceded or followed by blanks, terminates the *context* section.

The remainder of the input contains morse words separated by blanks or end-of-line characters. A line containing only a single asterisk ("*"), possibly preceded or followed by blanks, terminates the input. No *morse* word will have more than eighty (80) elements.

Output

For each input *morse* word, display the appropriate matching word from *context* followed by an exclamation mark ("!") or question mark ("?") if appropriate. Each word is to appear on a separate line starting in column one.

Sample Input

```
A        .-
B        -...
C        -.-.
D        -..
E        .
F        ..-.
G        --.
H        ....
I        ..
J        .---
K        -.-
L        .-..
M        --
N        -.
O        ---
P        .--.
Q        --.-
R        .-.
S        ...
T        -
U        ..-
V        ...-
W        .--
X        -..-
Y        -.--
Z        --..
0        -----
1        .----
2        ..---
3        ...--
4        ....-
5        .....
6        -....
7        --...
```

```
8         ---..
9         ----.
*
AN
EARTHQUAKE
EAT
GOD
HATH
IM
READY
TO
WHAT
WROTH
*
.--....--     .....--....
--.----..    .--.-.----..
.--....--     .--.
..-.-.-....--.-..-.--.-.
..--    .-...--..-.--
----         ..--
*
```

Sample Output

```
WHAT
HATH
GOD
WROTH?
WHAT
AN
EARTHQUAKE
EAT!
READY
TO
EAT!
```

D RAID!

RAID (Redundant Array of Inexpensive Disks) is a technique which uses multiple disks to store data. By storing the data on more than one disk, RAID is more fault tolerant than storing data on a single disk. If there is a problem with one of the disks, the system can still recover the original data provided that the remaining disks do not have corresponding problems.

One approach to RAID breaks data into blocks and stores these blocks on all but one of the disks. The remaining disk is used to store the parity information for the data blocks. This scheme uses *vertical parity* in which bits in a given position in data blocks are exclusive ORed to form the corresponding parity bit. The parity block moves between the disks, starting at the first disk, and moving to the next one in order. For instance, if there were five disks and 28 data blocks were stored on them, they would be arranged as follows:

Disk 1	Disk 2	Disk 3	Disk 4	Disk 5
Parity 1-4	Data block 1	Data block 2	Data block 3	Data block 4
Data block 5	**Parity 5-8**	Data block 6	Data block 7	Data block 8
Data block 9	Data block 10	**Parity 9-12**	Data block 11	Data block 12
Data block 13	Data block 14	Data block 15	**Parity 13-16**	Data block 16
Data block 17	Data block 18	Data block 19	Data block 20	**Parity 17-20**
Parity 21-24	Data block 21	Data block 22	Data block 23	Data block 24
Data block 25	**Parity 25-28**	Data block 26	Data block 27	Data block 28

With this arrangement of disks, a block size of two bits and even parity, the hexadecimal sample data 6C7A79EDFC (01101100 01111010 01111001 11101101 11111100 in binary) would be stored as:

Disk 1	Disk 2	Disk 3	Disk 4	Disk 5
00	01	10	11	00
01	**10**	11	10	10
01	11	**01**	10	01
11	10	11	**11**	01
11	11	11	00	**11**

If a block becomes unavailable, its information can still be retrieved using the information on the other disks. For example, if the first bit of the first block of disk 3 becomes unavailable, it can be reconstructed using the corresponding parity and data bits from the other four disks. We know that our sample system uses even parity:

$$0 \oplus 0 \oplus ? \oplus 1 \oplus 0 = 0$$

So the missing bit must be 1.

An arrangement of disks is invalid if a parity error is detected, or if any data block cannot be reconstructed because two or more disks are unavailable for that block.

Write a program to report errors and recover information from RAID disks.

Input

The input consists of several disk sets.

Each disk set has 3 parts. The first part of the disk set contains three integers on one line: the first integer d, $2 \leq d \leq 6$, is the number of disks, the second integer s, $1 \leq s \leq 64$, is the size of each block in bits, and the third integer b, $1 \leq b \leq 100$, is the total number of data and parity blocks on each disk. The second part of the disk set is a single letter on a line, either "E" signifying even parity or "O" signifying odd parity. The third part of the disk set contains d lines, one for each disk, each holding $s \times b$ characters representing the bits on the disk, with the most significant bits first. Each bit will be specified as "0" or "1" if it holds valid data, or "x" if that bit is unavailable. The end of input will be a disk set with $d = 0$. There will be no other data for this set which should not be processed.

Output

For each disk set in the input, display the number of the set and whether the set is valid or invalid. If the set is valid, display the recovered data bits in hexadecimal. If necessary, add extra "0" bits at the end of the recovered data so the number of bits is always a multiple of 4. All output shall be appropriately labeled.

Sample Input

```
5 2 5
E
0001011111
0110111011
1011011111
1110101100
0010010111
3 2 5
E
0001111111
0111111011
xx11011111
3 5 1
O
11111
11xxx
x1111
0
```

Sample Output

```
Disk set 1 is valid, contents are: 6C7A79EDFC
Disk set 2 is invalid.
Disk set 3 is valid, contents are: FFC
```

E Optimal Routing

Acme Courier Message, Inc. (ACM) is planning to add a service for delivery of documents and small parcels. ACM will group parcels and documents in bags, which will be transported by car among different stations for intermediate handling and routing prior to final delivery. ACM is in the initial stages of determining the workload requirements for transporting bags among stations.

When a driver delivers a bag, she will (if possible) locate and pick up another bag for delivery to another station, continuing in this manner until there are no more deliverable bags. A deliverable bag is one that can be picked up and delivered to its destination by a driver prior to the end of her workday. The total time for a driver's workday begins with the time of pickup of her first bag and includes the time she spends delivering bags, the time in transit, and the time waiting at stations for deliverable bags. ACM would like its drivers to spend the maximum amount of time possible delivering the bags between stations within a normal workday. In addition, ACM wants drivers' final destinations to be the same as the stations where they started whenever possible.

You must write a program to determine optimal driver routes for several ACM scenarios. Each scenario describes bags and stations for a single workday. In this simple version, routes for all drivers will originate from the same station, which we call station A. Optimal routes are subject to the following restrictions.

1. A driver's normal workday will not exceed 10 hours.

2. Drivers will travel from one station to another with one bag, if one is available for pickup. If there are no deliverable bags at a station, the driver will proceed to another station that has a scheduled deliverable bag to continue her route.

3. If several different routes with a final destination of station A are possible, the one requiring the longest cumulative delivery time is optimal. If there are more than one with the longest cumulative delivery time, the one with the shortest total workday time is optimal.

4. Whenever possible, the final destination of a driver is station A. However, if it is impossible to schedule a final destination of station A, then the route requiring the longest cumulative delivery time is optimal. If there are more than one with the longest cumulative delivery time, the one with the shortest total workday time is optimal.

5. Every bag that originates from station A will be delivered. (Some bags originating at other stations will not necessarily be delivered.) No bag will be delivered more than once.

The optimal route for the driver who picks up the first available deliverable bag at station A is completely determined before any consideration of subsequent drivers. The optimal route of the second driver, who picks up the next available deliverable bag at station A that has not already been scheduled for delivery by the first driver, is completely determined next. The optimal route determination continues in this manner until all the bags that can be delivered have been scheduled for delivery. Undeliverable bags will be identified and reported. Throughout the entire process, each driver will be routed according to the bags not already scheduled earlier for delivery. In all scenarios the time to travel from station A to any other station is 10 hours or less.

Input

Input for each scenario comes in two parts: a list of the bags and a table of times required to drive between stations. The first line in each scenario consists of an integer n representing the number of bags to be delivered. The next n lines describe each bag in the following format:

id origin destination time

where *id* is the bag identification number (integer), *origin* and *destination* are the station labels
for the bag's origin and destination (uppercase letters), and *time* is when the bag is available for
transport. The format for *time* is *hhmm*, where *hh* and *mm* are integers representing time on a
24-hour clock varying from 0001 to 2400. Data on a line are separated by single blanks. Each
station is labeled with a unique uppercase letter. Bags may appear in any time order in the list.
The end of input is signified by a scenario for which the number of bags is 0.

Input data for the table of driving times consist of lines of the form:

station1 station2 time

where *station1* and *station2* are uppercase letters and *time* is as described earlier. Transit times
between stations are listed for all stations which are included in the list of bags. Transit times are
bidirectional. Different scenarios are completely unrelated.

Output

Output for each scenario begins by identifying the scenario by number (`Scenario 1`, `Scenario 2`,
etc.). Following that is a listing of each driver's optimal route. Each route begins with the number
of the driver (`Driver 1`, `Driver 2`, etc.) and then a summary of the driver's route including all
transits between stations in the order in which the stations were visited. For transits which deliver
a bag, display the bag identification number and its origin and destination stations. For transits
which do not deliver a bag, display the origin and destinations stations.

Output for each driver is summarized by the total delivery time and the total workday time in
the form *hhmm*, following the time format specified in the input of time values. If two different
routes for a driver are optimal, then output may show either one. The final section of output for a
scenario will include a listing of all undeliverable bags or a statement indicating successful delivery
of all bags. Each section of a scenario and each scenario should be separated by a blank line.

Sample Input   Sample Output

```
7                      Scenario 1
1 A B 0800
3 A C 0850             Driver 1
2 B C 0700               Bag #1 from station A to station B
6 B D 1250               Bag #2 from station B to station C
5 B C 1400               Bag #7 from station C to station A
7 C A 1600               Total delivery time: 0920
8 D C 1130               Total workday time: 0935
A B 0400
A C 0135             Driver 2
A D 0320               Bag #3 from station A to station C
B C 0345                 -->Transit without delivery from station C to station B
B D 0120               Bag #5 from station B to station C
C D 0200               Total delivery time: 0520
0                      Total workday time: 0905

                     Undelivered Bags:
                       Bag #8 remains at station D
                       Bag #6 remains at station B
```

F   Do You Know the Way to San Jose?

The Internet now offers a variety of interactive map facilities, so that users can see either an overview map of a large geographic region or can "zoom in" to a specific street, sometimes even a specific building, on a much more detailed map. For instance, downtown San Jose might appear in a map of California, a map of Santa Clara county, and a detailed street map.

Suppose you have a large collection of rectangular maps and you wish to design a browsing facility that will process a sequence of map requests for locations at various levels of map detail. Locations are expressed using *location names*. Each location name has a unique pair of real coordinates (x, y). Maps are unique, labeled with identifying map names, and defined by two pairs of real coordinates— $(x_1, y_1)(x_2, y_2)$—representing opposite corners of the map. All map edges are parallel to the standard Cartesian x and y axes. A map and a location can have the same name. The *aspect ratio* of a map is the ratio of its height to its width (where width is measured in the x direction and height is measured in the y direction).

The level of detail of a map can be approximated by using the rectangular area represented by the map; i.e., assume that a map covering a smaller area contains more detailed information. Maps can overlap one another. If a location (x, y) lies within two or more maps having equal areas, the preferred map (at that level of detail) is the one in which the location is nearest the center of the map. If the location is equidistant from the centers of two overlapping maps of the same area, then the preferred map (at that level of detail) is the one whose aspect ratio is nearest to the aspect ratio of the browser window, which is 0.75. If this still does not break the tie, then the preferred map is the one in which the location is furthest from the lower right corner of the map (this heuristic is intended to minimize the need for scrolling in the user's browser window). Finally, if there is still a tie, then the preferred map is the one containing the smallest x-coordinate.

The *maximum detail level* available for a given location is the maximal number of maps of different areas that contain the location. Clearly, different locations can have different maximum detail levels. The map at detail i for the location is the map with the ith largest area among a maximal set of maps of the distinct area containing the location. Thus, the map at detail level 1 for the location will be the least detailed (largest area) map containing the location and the map at the maximum detail level will be the most detailed (smallest area) map containing the location.

Input

The input file consists of a set of maps, locations, and requests; it is organized as follows:

- The word "MAPS", in all uppercase letters and on a line by itself, introduces a set of one or more maps. Following the set heading, each map is described by a single line consisting of a map name (an alphabetic string with no leading, trailing, or embedded blanks) and two real coordinate pairs—$x_1\ y_1\ x_2\ y_2$—representing opposite corners of the map.

- The word "LOCATIONS", in all uppercase letters and on a line by itself, introduces a set of one or more locations. Following this heading, each location is described by a line consisting of a location name (an alphabetic string with no leading, trailing, or embedded blanks) and a real coordinate pair—$x\ y$—representing the center of the location.

- The word "REQUESTS", in all uppercase letters and on a line by itself, introduces a set of zero or more requests. Following this heading, each request is described by a line consisting of a location name (an alphabetic string with no leading, trailing, or embedded blanks) followed by a positive integer representing the desired detail level for that location.

- The word "END", in all uppercase and on a line by itself, terminates the file.

All map and location data preceding the requests are valid. There will be no duplicate maps. The result of processing a valid request is the name of the map containing the given location at the given detail level (using the tie-breaking rules described above). Invalid requests can result from requesting unknown location names, locations that do not appear in any map, or detail levels that exceed the number of maps of different areas containing the location.

Output

Each request must be echoed to the output. If the request is valid, display the name of the map satisfying the request. If the location is not on a map, display a message to that effect. If the location is on the map but the detail level is too large, display the name of the map of the smallest available area (largest possible detail level). The sample below illustrates all these definitions.

Sample Input

```
MAPS
BayArea -6.0 12.0 -11.0 5.0
SantaClara 4.0 9.0 -3.5 2.5
SanJoseRegion -3.0 10.0 11.0 3.0
CenterCoast -5.0 11.0 1.0 -8.0
SanMateo -5.5 4.0 -12.5 9.0
NCalif -13.0 -7.0 13.0 15.0
LOCATIONS
Monterey -4.0 2.0
SanJose -1.0 7.5
Fresno 7.0 0.1
SanFrancisco -10.0 8.6
SantaCruz -4.0 2.0
SanDiego 13.8 -19.3
REQUESTS
SanJose 3
SanFrancisco 2
Fresno 2
Stockton 1
SanDiego 2
SanJose 4
SantaCruz 3
END
```

Sample Output

```
SanJose at detail level 3 using SanJoseRegion
SanFrancisco at detail level 2 using BayArea
Fresno at detail level 2 no map at that detail level; using NCalif
Stockton at detail level 1 unknown location
SanDiego at detail level 2 no map contains that location
SanJose at detail level 4 using SantaClara
SantaCruz at detail level 3 no map at that detail level; using CenterCoast
```

G   Spreadsheet Tracking

Data in spreadsheets are stored in cells, which are organized in rows (r) and columns (c). Some operations on spreadsheets can be applied to single cells (r,c), while others can be applied to entire rows or columns. Typical cell operations include inserting and deleting rows or columns and exchanging cell contents.

Some spreadsheets allow users to mark collections of rows or columns for deletion, so the entire collection can be deleted at once. Some (unusual) spreadsheets allow users to mark collections of rows or columns for insertions too. Issuing an insertion command results in new rows or columns being inserted before each of the marked rows or columns. Suppose, for example, the user marks rows 1 and 5 of the spreadsheet on the left for deletion. The spreadsheet then shrinks to the one on the right.

↘	1	2	3	4	5	6	7	8	9
1	22	55	66	77	88	99	10	12	14
2	2	24	6	8	22	12	14	16	18
3	18	19	20	21	22	23	24	25	26
4	24	25	26	67	22	69	70	71	77
5	68	78	79	80	22	25	28	29	30
6	16	12	11	10	22	56	57	58	59
7	33	34	35	36	22	38	39	40	41

↘	1	2	3	4	5	6	7	8	9
1	2	24	6	8	22	12	14	16	18
2	18	19	20	21	22	23	24	25	26
3	24	25	26	67	22	69	70	71	77
4	16	12	11	10	22	56	57	58	59
5	33	34	35	36	22	38	39	40	41

If the user subsequently marks columns 3, 6, 7, and 9 for deletion, the spreadsheet shrinks to this.

↘	1	2	3	4	5
1	2	24	8	22	16
2	18	19	21	22	25
3	24	25	67	22	71
4	16	12	10	22	58
5	33	34	36	22	40

If the user marks rows 2, 3 and 5 for insertion, the spreadsheet grows to the one on the left. If the user then marks column 3 for insertion, the spreadsheet grows to the one in the middle. Finally, if the user exchanges the contents of cell (1,2) and cell (6,5), the spreadsheet looks like the one on the right.

↘	1	2	3	4	5
1	2	24	8	22	16
2					
3	18	19	21	22	25
4					
5	24	25	67	22	71
6	16	12	10	22	58
7					
8	33	34	36	22	40

↘	1	2	3	4	5	6
1	2	24		8	22	16
2						
3	18	19		21	22	25
4						
5	24	25		67	22	71
6	16	12		10	22	58
7						
8	33	34		36	22	40

↘	1	2	3	4	5	6
1	2	22		8	22	16
2						
3	18	19		21	22	25
4						
5	24	25		67	22	71
6	16	12		10	24	58
7						
8	33	34		36	22	40

You must write tracking software that determines the final location of data in spreadsheets that result from row, column, and exchange operations similar to the ones illustrated here.

Input

The input consists of a sequence of spreadsheets, operations on those spreadsheets, and queries about them. Each spreadsheet definition begins with a pair of integers specifying its initial number of rows (r) and columns (c), followed by an integer specifying the number (n) of spreadsheet operations. Row and column labeling begins with 1. The maximum number of rows or columns of each spreadsheet is limited to 50. The following n lines specify the desired operations.

An operation to exchange the contents of cell (r_1, c_1) with the contents of cell (r_2, c_2) is given by:

EX r_1 c_1 r_2 c_2

The four insert and delete commands—DC (delete columns), DR (delete rows), IC (insert columns), and IR (insert rows) are given by:

$< command > A\ x_1\ x_2\ \ldots\ x_A$

where $< command >$ is one of the four commands; A is a positive integer less than 10, and $x_1, \ldots, x_A$ are the labels of the columns or rows to be deleted or inserted before. For each insert and delete command, the order of the rows or columns in the command has no significance. Within a single delete or insert command, labels will be unique.

The operations are followed by an integer which is the number of queries for the spreadsheet. Each query consists of positive integers r and c, representing the row and column number of a cell in the original spreadsheet. For each query, your program must determine the current location of the data that was originally in cell (r, c). The end of input is indicated by a row consisting of a pair of zeros for the spreadsheet dimensions.

Output

For each spreadsheet, your program must output its sequence number (starting at 1). For each query, your program must output the original cell location followed by the final location of the data or the word GONE if the contents of the original cell location were destroyed as a result of the operations. Separate output from different spreadsheets with a blank line.

The data file will not contain a sequence of commands that will cause the spreadsheet to exceed the maximum size.

Sample Input

```
7 9
5
DR   2  1 5
DC  4  3 6 7 9
IC  1  3
IR  2  2 4
EX 1 2 6 5
4
4 8
5 5
7 8
6 5
0 0
```

Sample Output

```
Spreadsheet #1
Cell data in (4,8) moved to (4,6)
Cell data in (5,5) GONE
Cell data in (7,8) moved to (7,6)
Cell data in (6,5) moved to (1,2)
```

H   Window Frames

Elements of graphical user interfaces include such things as buttons, text boxes, scroll bars, drop-down menus and scrollable list boxes. Each is considered to be a special kind of object called a widget. Where these widgets are placed, how much space they are allocated, and how they change size constitutes the geometry of a window.

One geometry management scheme uses special rectangular widgets called *frames* to contain and thus group other widgets. A frame is a *parent* if some or all of its own space is allocated to additional frames, which are its *children*. The frame which has no parent is called the *root frame*; its size is specified by the user (in the input data). This problem requires that you determine the allocation of space to, and the position of frames placed in root frames of various sizes.

The *cavity* in a frame is the space in the frame that is not occupied by its children. When a new child frame is created, it is allocated an entire horizontal strip along the top or bottom edge of the cavity (this is called a *horizontal child*) or an entire vertical strip along the right or left edge of the cavity (this is called a *vertical child*). Thus, as a result of creating a new child, the cavity becomes smaller, but it remains rectangular. The process of placing children inside the enclosing frame is called *packing*. Children are positioned in the cavity according to the order in which they are packed.

The figure below shows the child frames of a parent frame. Frame 1 along the right edge was packed first, then frame 2 along the bottom edge, frame 3 along the left edge, and finally frame 4 along the right edge. The cavity, shown in white, contains available space for packing subsequent child frames.

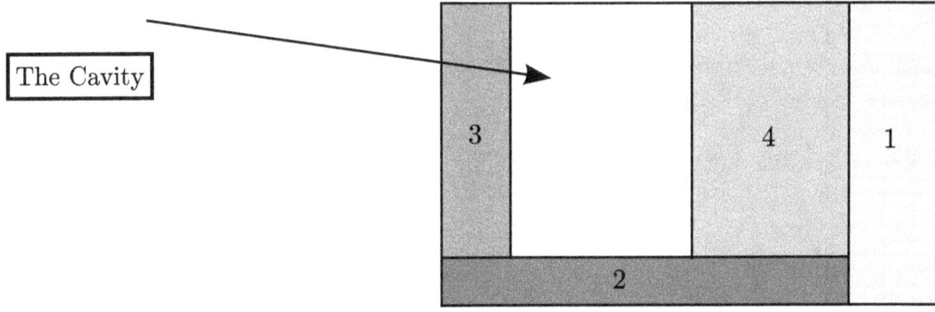

Each frame covers a rectangular grid of pixels. If the root frame covers c columns and r rows of pixels, then the pixel in the top left corner is at coordinate (0,0) and the pixel in the lower right corner is at coordinate $(c-1, r-1)$. The position of a frame is specified by the coordinates of its upper left corner pixel and its lower right corner pixel.

Each frame has minimum dimensions determined by an input parameter d and the minimum dimensions of its children. A frame must be at least large enough to pack all of its children. The minimum dimensions of each frame are determined as follows:

Packing Side	Frame Type	Minimum Width	Minimum Height
Right or left	Vertical	Maximum of d and the width necessary for the frame's children	Maximum of 1 and the height necessary for the frame's children
Bottom or top	Horizontal	Maximum of 1 and the width necessary for the frame's children	Maximum of d and the height necessary for the frame's children

When a frame is larger than the minimum dimensions just specified, the additional interior space is apportioned to its children and/or its cavity. Each frame has an expansion flag (which is an input parameter) that, when set, indicates a vertical frame can grow wider or a horizontal frame can grow taller. For example, a frame with its expansion flag set, allocated space along the top of the cavity, can grow taller, with the extra height extending downward.

The distribution of additional horizontal space in a frame is handled as follows. Let x be the number of horizontal pixels by which the parent frame exceeds its minimum width. If n, the number of the vertical children in the frame with their expansion flags set, is non-zero, then the x pixels are distributed among the n vertical children. If q is the quotient of x divided by n and r is the remainder, then each of the n vertical frames grows wider by q pixels and the first r of them that were packed in the frame grow wider by 1 pixel in addition to the q. If n is zero, then none of the vertical children grow wider, and the x pixels are added to the width of the cavity. In either case, the horizontal children in the enlarged frame become wider, if necessary, in such a manner as to ensure the single cavity remains rectangular.

The distribution of additional vertical space in a parent frame to its children and/or its cavity is handled in a manner similar to that used to distribute additional horizontal space, with the appropriate change in direction of growth. Only the horizontal children with their expansion flags set grow taller to utilize the additional vertical pixels, and if none of the horizontal children have their expansion flags set, the additional pixels are added to the height of the cavity. As expected, the vertical children also become taller, if necessary, to ensure the rectangular and uniqueness properties of the cavity.

In the next illustration, the root frame on the left has been enlarged to yield the one on the right. Frames 6 and 7 are horizontal and vertical children, respectively, of frame 5. Only frames 4, 6 and 7 have their expansion flags set. In the frame on the right, the additional horizontal and vertical space has been distributed to the children so as to result in the growth indicated by the arrows. Note that frame 7 does not change size because no room is available for expansion in its parent, frame 5. Frame 6 does not change size for the same reason.

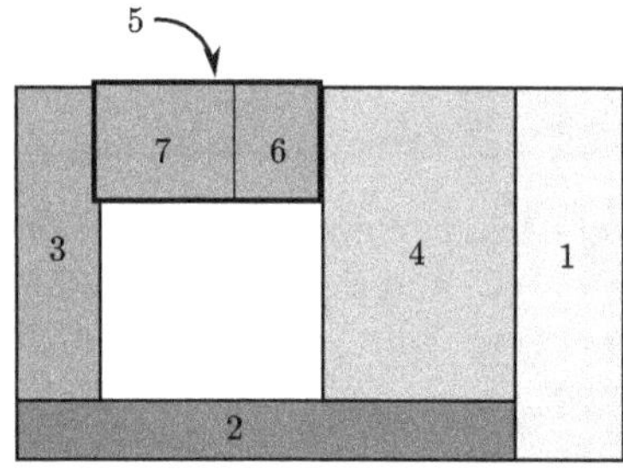
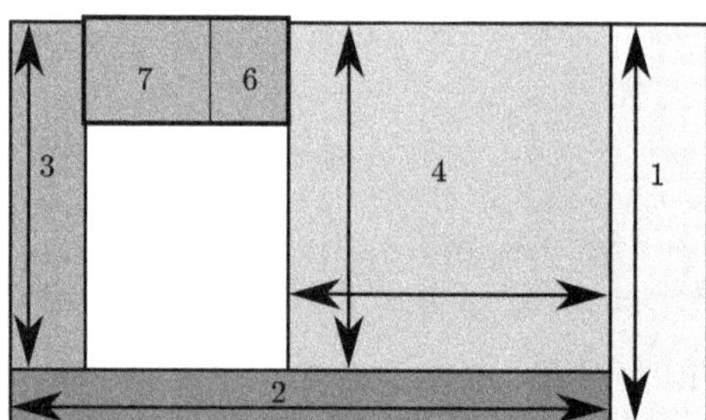

Input

The input consists of a sequence of root frames, their descendants, and different potential root frame sizes. Each item in the sequence corresponding to a single root has the following format:

M N   *M* is the total number of frames excluding the root.
          N is the number of different root sizes (both are positive integers).

followed by M lines of the form:

$n\ p\ s\ d\ e$

where: n is the name of the frame (a positive integer);
        p is the name of the parent (where 0 is the root frame);
        s is one of the characters "L", "R", "T", and "B" indicating packing side;
        d is the minimum dimension (a positive integer); and
        e is 0 or 1, where 0 means the expansion flag is cleared, 1 means it is set;

followed by N lines of the form:

$c\ r$ where c is the number of columns of pixels, and
          r is the number of rows of pixels in the root frame (both positive integers).

Root frames are not listed. Frame numbers for a given root are distinct. Children of a frame will not appear in the input before their parents. Frames are packed in the order in which they appear in the input. The end of input is signified by a line with M and N both 0.

Output

Begin the output of each root by writing its record number (1 for the first, 2 for the second, etc.). For each size corresponding to that root, write the size (rows × columns) and then list the name of each frame along with the coordinates of its upper left and lower right corners. List the frames in the order in which they are packed in their parents, with the root's first child and its descendants first, the second child and its descendants second, and so on. If the root size is too small to pack its frames, print the message "is too small" instead of attempting to list the frames. Separate output for different root sizes by a line of dashes.

Sample Input

```
7 1
1 0 R 50 0
2 0 B 10 0
3 0 L 40 0
4 0 R 20 1
5 0 T 30 0
6 5 R 20 0
7 5 L 10 1
1000 1000
2 2
1 0 R 100 1
2 0 T 30 1
100 50
200 100
0 0
```

Sample Output

```
Root Frame #1
------------------------------------------------
  Display: 1000 X 1000
    Frame:  1   (950,0)    (999,999)
    Frame:  2   (0,990)    (949,999)
    Frame:  3   (0,0)    (39,989)
    Frame:  4   (70,0)    (949,989)
    Frame:  5   (40,0)    (69,29)
    Frame:  6   (50,0)    (69,29)
    Frame:  7   (40,0)    (49,29)
------------------------------------------------


Root Frame #2
------------------------------------------------
  Display: 100 X 50 is too small
------------------------------------------------
  Display: 200 X 100
    Frame:  1   (1,0)    (199,99)
    Frame:  2   (0,0)    (0,99)

------------------------------------------------
```

WORLD FINALS 1998

ATLANTA, GEORGIA

World Champion

CHARLES UNIVERSITY PRAGUE

Jiri Hajek
Pavel Machek
Martin Mares

Director of Judging
Dick Rinewalt   *Texas Christian University*

Chief Judge
Jo Perry   *North Carolina State University*

Judges
Owen Astrachan	*Duke University*
Don Chamberlin	*IBM Almaden Research Center*
David Elizandro	*Tennessee Tech University*
Robert Roos	*Allegheny College*
Matthias Ruhl	*MIT*
Patrick Ryan	*TechnoSolutions, Inc.*
Laurie White	*Mercer University*
Stanley Wileman, Jr.	*University of Nebraska at Omaha*

UVa Online Judge problem numbers
800	A	Crystal Clear
801	B	Flight Planning
802	C	Lead or Gold
803	D	Page Selection by Keyword Matching
804	E	Petri Net Simulation
805	F	Polygon Intersections
806	G	Spatial Structures
807	H	Towers of Powers

A   Crystal Clear

A new high technology company has developed a material that it hopes to market as an insulator. The material consists of crystals and the square lattice on which the crystals are grown. The points on the lattice are at 1 centimeter intervals. The crystals are formed from seeds that are planted at the lattice points. Each crystal grows into a circle of diameter 1 centimeter.

Using this material in applications will require cutting the lattice into pieces. One of the problems in cutting the lattice is that some crystals will be sliced in the process. Slicing a crystal other than through the center completely destroys that crystal's insulation properties. (A cut touching a crystal tangentially does not destroy that crystal's insulation property.)

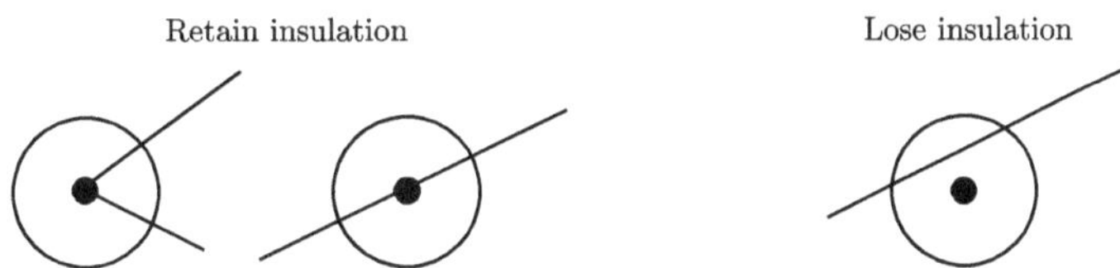

The insulation capacity of a piece is directly proportional to the total area of the insulating crystals (or parts of crystals) that are on the piece. The following figure shows a polygonal piece with its insulating crystals shaded.

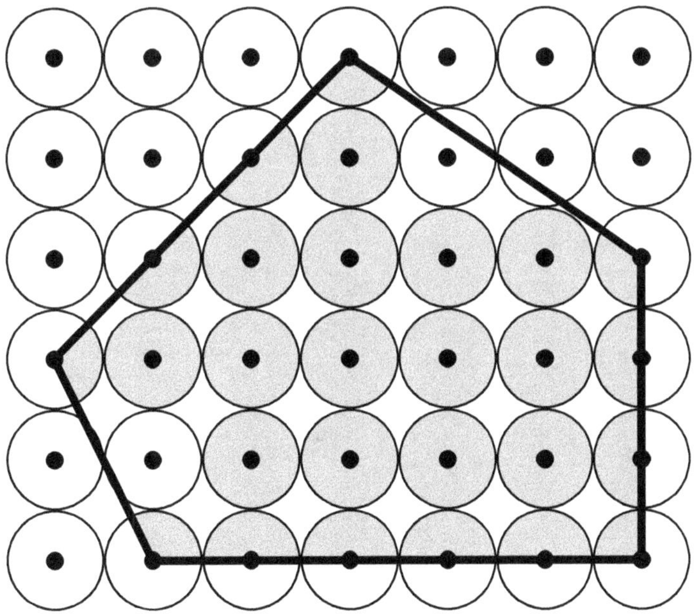

Your job is to determine the insulating capacity of such polygonal pieces by computing the total area of the insulating crystals in it.

Input

The input consists of a sequence of polygon descriptions. Each description consists of a positive integer n ($3 \leq n \leq 25$) representing the number of vertices, followed by n pairs of integers. Each pair is the x and y coordinates of one vertex of the polygon. (The coordinate system is aligned with the lattice such that the integer coordinates are precisely the lattice points.)

Vertices of each polygon are given in clockwise order. No polygon will be degenerate. No coordinate will be larger than 250 in absolute value.

The input is terminated by zero for the value of n.

Output

For each polygon, first print its number ('Shape 1', 'Shape 2', etc.) and then the area of the insulating crystals in `cm^2`, exact to three digits to the right of the decimal point.

The following sample corresponds to the previous illustration.

Sample Input

```
5
0 2
3 5
6 3
6 0
1 0
0
```

Sample Output

```
Shape 1
Insulating area = 15.315 cm^2
```

B Flight Planning

Your job is to write a program that plans airplane flights. Each flight consists of a series of one or more legs. Your program must choose the best altitude for each leg to minimize the amount of fuel consumption during the trip.

The airplane has a fixed airspeed, given by the constant VCRUISE, and a most-efficient cruising altitude, AOPT. When flying at altitude AOPT, fuel consumption in gallons per hour is given by GPHOPT. When flying at an altitude that is different from AOPT, fuel consumption increases by GPHEXTRA for each 1000 feet above or below AOPT. The flight starts and finishes at an altitude of 0. Each 1000 foot climb burns an extra amount of fuel given by CLIMBCOST (there is no reduction in fuel consumption when you descend). Make the approximation that all climbing and descending is done in zero time at the beginning of each flight leg. Thus each leg is flown at a constant airspeed and altitude. For this problem, the airplane characteristics are given by the following constants:

VCRUISE	400	knots (a knot is one nautical mile per hour)
AOPT	30,000	feet
GPHOPT	2,000	gallons per hour
GPHEXTRA	10	gallons per hour for each 1,000 feet
CLIMBCOST	50	gallons per 1,000 feet of climb

Before each flight, you are given the length of each leg and the tailwind expected for each leg. A positive tailwind increases the airplane's speed over the ground, and a negative tailwind decreases its speed over the ground. For example, if airspeed is 400 knots and the tailwind is -50 knots, speed over the ground is 350 knots.

By policy, altitude for each leg must be some integer multiple of 1,000 feet, between 20,000 and 40,000 feet, inclusive. Your program must compute the best altitude for each leg to minimize overall fuel consumption for the trip, and must compute the fuel required for the trip.

Input

The first line contains an integer N, representing the number of flights you are required to plan. Each flight consists of the following input lines:

- The first input line in a flight contains an integer K ($0 < K < 10$), representing the number of legs in the flight.

- The next K input lines each contain the following three integers:

  1. The length of the leg, in nautical miles

  2. The expected tailwind at 20,000 feet, in knots

  3. The expected tailwind at 40,000 feet, in knots

The expected tailwind at altitudes between 20,000 and 40,000 feet is computed by linear interpolation. For example, the expected tailwind at 30,000 feet is halfway between the expected tailwind at 20,000 feet and the expected tailwind at 40,000 feet.

Output

Your program must produce one output line for each flight. The output line must contain the flight number (counting from the beginning of the problem), the chosen altitude for each leg (in thousands of feet), and the fuel required for the trip (in gallons, to the nearest gallon).

Sample Input

```
2
2
1500 -50 50
1000 0 0
3
1000 50 0
2000 0 20
1800 50 100
```

Sample Output

```
Flight 1: 35 30 13985
Flight 2: 20 30 40 23983
```

C Lead or Gold

How to make gold from lead has baffled alchemists for centuries. At the last Alchemists Club Meeting (ACM), a sensational breakthrough was announced. By mixing the three chemicals Algolene, Basicine and Cobolase in the correct ratio, one can create a mixture that transforms lead into gold. Since Algolene, Basicine and Cobolase (or A, B, C for short) are generally not sold individually, but rather mixed into solutions, this may not be easy as it seems.

Consider the following example. Two mixtures of Algolene, Basicine and Cobolase are available, in ratios of 1:2:3 and 3:7:1, respectively. By mixing these solutions in a ratio of 1:2 we obtain a solution of A, B, C with ratio 7:16:5. But there is no way to combine these mixtures into a new one with ratio 3:4:5. If we additionally had a solution of ratio 2:1:2, then a 3:4:5 mixture would be possible by combining eight parts of 1:2:3, one part of 3:7:1 and five parts of 2:1:2.

Determining which mixing ratios we can obtain from a given set of solutions is no trivial task. But, as the ACM has shown, it is possibly a very profitable one. You must write a program to find mixing ratios.

Input

The input file contains several test cases. The first line of each test case contains an integer n ($0 \leq n < 100$) that represents the number of mixtures in the test case. The next n lines each contain three non-negative integers a_i, b_i, c_i, specifying the ratio $a_i : b_i : c_i$ in which A, B, C occur in the i-th mixture. At least one of these integers is positive for each mixture.

Finally, there is one line containing three non-negative integers a, b, c, which specify the ratio $a : b : c$ in the desired solution. At least one of these integers is positive.

The input file is terminated with the integer '0' on a line by itself following the last test case.

Output

For each test case, output the word 'Mixture', followed by the ordinal number of the test case. On the next line, if it is possible to obtain the desired solution by mixing the input solutions, output the word 'Possible'. Otherwise, output the word 'Impossible'.

Sample Input

```
2
1 2 3
3 7 1
3 4 5
3
1 2 3
3 7 1
2 1 2
3 4 5
0
```

Sample Output

```
Mixture 1
Impossible

Mixture 2
Possible
```

D Page Selection by Keyword Matching

Anyone who has used the World Wide Web is familiar with search engines used to find pages matching a user- generated query. Many of these engines are quite sophisticated, using advanced algorithms and parallel searching techniques to provide fast, accurate responses.

This problem is somewhat simpler. A group of web pages has been classified by associating a list of keywords, given in decreasing order of relevance, with each page (i.e., the order of keywords is from the most specific keyword to the least specific). For example, a page on programming in Smalltalk has the keywords Smalltalk, programming, and computers in that order; the most relevant keyword is Smalltalk.

Queries also include a list of keywords, again from most to least relevant. For example, in a query consisting of the keyword Smalltalk followed by the keyword computers, Smalltalk is more important than computers.

In this problem you are to determine the top five (or fewer) pages that match each of an arbitrary number of queries. To determine the strength of the relationship between a query and a web page, assume the keywords for each page and each query are assigned integer weights, in descending order, starting with N, where N is the maximum number of keywords allowed for a web page and query. The strength of the relationship is the sum of the products of the weights associated with each keyword that appears both in the web page list and the query list. For example, assume the following web pages and keyword lists:

Page 1: Smalltalk, programming, computers

Page 2: computers, programming

Page 3: computers, Smalltalk

For N equal 8, a query with keywords Smalltalk and programming in that order yields a strength rating of 113 for Page 1 (8*8 + 7*7), 49 for Page 2 (7*7), and 56 for Page 3 (8*7). A query with keywords Smalltalk and computers yields a strength rating of 106 for Page 1 (8*8 + 7*6), 56 for Page 2 (7*8), and 112 for Page 3 (8*7 + 7*8).

Input

Input data consist of one line for each web page and query. A line consists of a code letter followed by a list of keywords. Code letters P, Q, and E denote a page, a query, and the end of file respectively. Code letters and keywords are separated by at least one space. P's and Q's may occur in any order. Pages are added sequentially starting with one. Each page has at least one but no more than 8 keywords. Each word consists of no more than 20 alphabetic characters. The case of characters in the keywords is not significant. There will be a maximum of 25 pages in the input.

Each query also has of a list of between one and eight keywords. Again, a keyword has no more than 20 alphabetic characters, case being insignificant. Number the queries sequentially starting with one.

Output

For each query, identify the 5 (or fewer) pages read so far that are most relevant to the query. Print a single line containing the query identifier, a colon, and the page identifiers of the five most relevant pages in the decreasing order of relevance. Page identifiers consist of the letter 'P' followed by the page number. Query identifiers consist of the letter 'Q' followed by the query number. If several pages have the same relevance, list them by increasing page number. Do not list pages that have no relationship (zero strength), even if fewer than five pages are identified.

Sample Input

```
P Smalltalk programming computers
P computers programming
P computers Smalltalk
P FORTRAN programming
P COBOL programming
P programming
Q Smalltalk
Q programming
Q computers
Q Smalltalk computers
Q Smalltalk programming
Q cooking French
E
```

Sample Output

```
Query    Pages
Q1:      P1 P3
Q2:      P6 P1 P2 P4 P5
Q3:      P2 P3 P1
Q4:      P3 P1 P2
Q5:      P1 P3 P6 P2 P4
Q6:
```

E   Petri Net Simulation

A Petri net is a computational model used to illustrate concurrent activity. Each Petri net contains some number of places (represented by circles), transitions (represented by black rectangles), and directed edges used to connect places to transitions, and transitions to places. Each place can hold zero or more tokens (represented by black dots). Here are two examples:

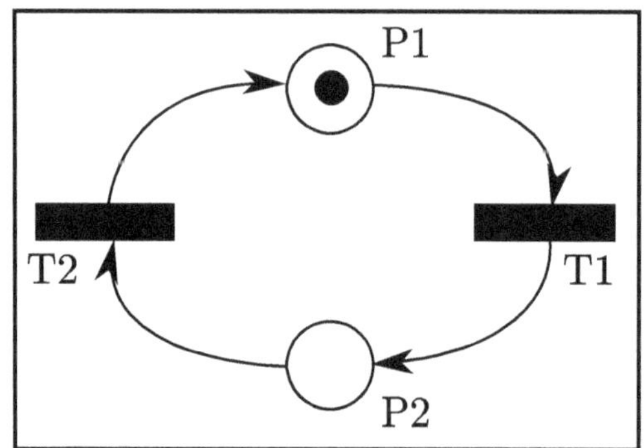

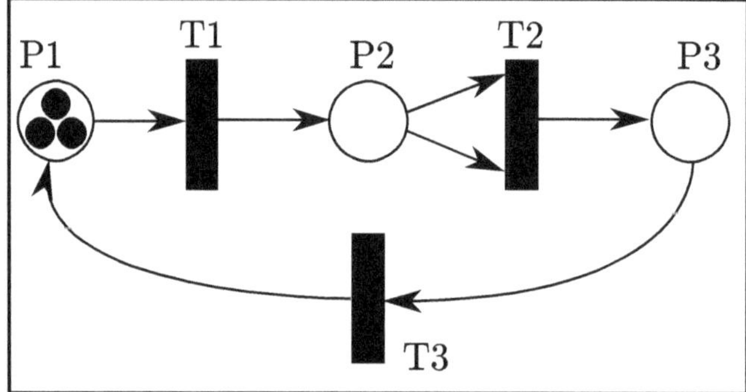

In the first Petri net above, there are two places (P1 and P2) and two transitions (T1 and T2). P1 initially has one token; P2 has none. P1 is an input place for transition T1, and P2 is an output place for T1. In the second example there are three places and three transitions, with three tokens in P1. T2 has two input places, both of which are P2.

Operation of a Petri Net:

Each transition in a Petri net is either enabled or disabled. A transition is enabled if there is at least one token in each of its input places. Any transition can fire whenever it is enabled. If multiple transitions are enabled, any one of them may fire. When a transition fires, one token is removed from each of the input places, and one token is added to each of the output places; this is effectively done atomically, as one action. When there are no enabled transitions, a Petri net is said to be dead.

In the top example only T1 is enabled. When it fires one token is removed from P1, and one token is added to P2. Then T2 is enabled. When it fires one token is removed from P2, and one token is added to P1. Clearly this Petri net will repeat this cycle forever.

The bottom example is more interesting. T1 is enabled and fires, effectively moving a token to P2. At this point T1 is still the only enabled transition (T2 requires that P2 have two tokens before it is enabled). T1 fires again, leaving one token in P1 and two tokens in P2. Now both T1 and T2 are enabled. Assume T2 fires, removing two tokens from P2 and adding one token to P3.

Now T1 and T3 are enabled. Continuing until no more transitions are enabled, you should see that only one token will be left in P2 after 9 transition firings. (Note that if T1 had fired instead of T2 when both were enabled, this result would have been the same after 9 firings.)

In this problem you will be presented with descriptions of one or more Petri nets. For each you are to simulate some specified number of transition firings, NF, and then report the number of tokens remaining in the places. If the net becomes dead before NF transition firings, you are to report that fact as well.

Input

Each Petri net description will first contain an integer NP ($0 < NP < 100$) followed by NP integers specifying the number of tokens initially in each of the places numbered $1, 2, \ldots, NP$. Next there will appear an integer NT ($0 < NT < 100$) specifying the number of transitions. Then, for each transition (in increasing numerical order $1, 2, \ldots, NT$) there will appear a list of integers terminated by zero.

The negative numbers in the list will represent the input places, so the number $-n$ indicates there is an input place at n. The positive numbers in the list will indicate the output places, so the number p indicates an output place at p. There will be at least one input place and at least one output place for each transition. Finally, after the description of all NT transitions, there will appear an integer indicating the maximum number of firings you are to simulate, NF. The input will contain one or more Petri net descriptions followed by a zero.

Output

For each Petri net description in the input display three lines of output. On the first line indicate the number of the input case (numbered sequentially starting with 1) and whether or not NF transitions were able to fire. If so, indicate the net is still live after NF firings. Otherwise indicate the net is dead, and the number of firings which were completed. In either case, on the second line give the identities of the places which contain one or more tokens after the simulation, and the number of tokens each such place contains. This list should be in ascending order. The third line of output for each set should be blank.

The input data will be selected to guarantee the uniqueness of the correct output displays.

Sample Input

```
2
1 0
2
-1 2 0
-2 1 0
100
3
3 0 0
3
-1 2 0
-2 -2 3 0
-3 1 0
100
0
```

Sample Output

```
Case 1: still live after 100 transitions
Places with tokens: 1 (1)

Case 2: dead after 9 transitions
Places with tokens: 2 (1)
```

F   Polygon Intersections

Most drawing or illustration programs have simple tools for creating polygon objects. The better ones can find the regions that are the intersections of two polygons. The picture below shows two polygons, one is a pentagon and the other is a triangle. Their intersection consists of the two dark regions.

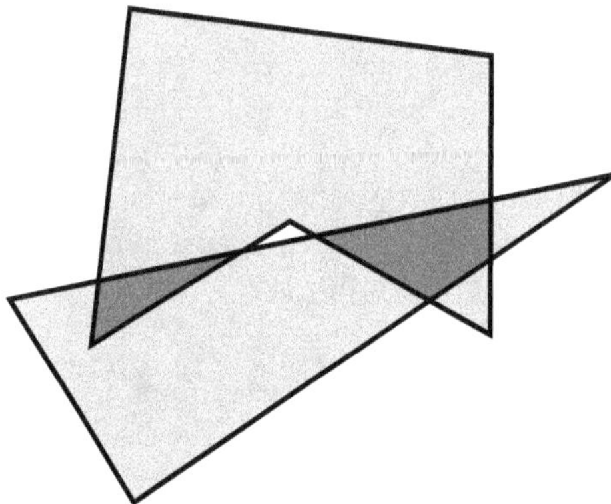

IBM has just hired you as a member of a programming team that will create a very sophisticated drawing/illustration program. Your task is to write the part of the program that deals with polygon intersections. Your boss has told you to delay work on the user interface and focus only on the geometric representations of the intersections.

A polygon in the Cartesian plane can be represented by a sequence of points that are its vertices. The vertices in the sequence appear in the order in which they are visited when traveling clockwise around the polygon's boundary; so any two adjacent vertices in the sequence are the endpoints of a line segment that is one of the polygon's sides. The last and the first vertices in the sequence are also endpoints of a side. Vertices are identified by their x- and y- coordinates. Assume the following about each polygon.

- No point will occur as a vertex (on the same polygon) more than once.

- Two sides can intersect only at a common endpoint (vertex).

- The angle between any two sides with a common vertex has a measure that is greater than 0 and less than 360.

- The polygon has at least 3 vertices.

The intersection of two polygons consists of 0 or more connected regions. Your problem is to take two polygons and determine the regions of their intersection that are polygons satisfying the criteria above.

Input

The input contains several data sets, each consisting of two polygons. Each polygon appears as a sequence of numbers:

$$n\ x_1\ y_1\ x_2\ y_2 \ldots x_n\ y_n$$

where the integer n is the number of vertices of the polygon, and the real coordinates (x_1, y_1) through (x_n, y_n) are the boundary vertices. The end of input is indicated by two 0's for the values of n. These two 0's merely mark the end of data and should not be treated as an additional data set.

Output

For each data set, your program should output its number ('Data set 1', 'Data set 2', etc.), and the number of regions in the intersection of its two polygons. Label each region in the data set ('Region 1', 'Region 2', etc.) and list its vertices in the order they appear when they are visited going either clockwise or counterclockwise around the boundary of the region. The first vertex printed should be the vertex with the smallest x-coordinate (to break ties, use the smallest y-coordinate). No region may include degenerate parts (consisting of adjacent sides whose angle of intersection is 0). If the three endpoints of two adjacent sides are collinear, the two sides should be merged into a single side. Print each vertex in the standard form (x, y), where x and y have two digits to the right of the decimal.

The following sample input contains exactly one data set. (The data set corresponds to the illustration at the beginning of this problem description.)

Sample Input

```
3 2 1 0.5 3.5 8 5
5 1.5 3 2 7 6.5 6.5 6.5 3.25 4 4.5
0
0
```

Sample Output

```
Data Set 1
Number of intersection regions: 2
Region 1:(1.50,3.00)(1.59,3.72)(3.25,4.05)
Region 2:(4.43,4.29)(6.50,4.70)(6.50,4.00)(5.86,3.57)
```

G Spatial Structures

Computer graphics, image processing, and GIS (geographic information systems) all make use of a data structure called a quadtree. Quadtrees represent regional or block data efficiently and support efficient algorithms for operations like the union and intersection of images.

A quadtree for a black and white image is constructed by successively dividing the image into four equal quadrants. If all the pixels in a quadrant are the same color (all black or all white) the division process for that quadrant stops. Quadrants that contain both black and white pixels are subdivided into four equal quadrants and this process continues until each subquadrant consists of either all black or all white pixels. It is entirely possible that some subquadrants consist of a single pixel.

For example, using 0 for white and 1 for black, the region on the left below is represented by the matrix of zeros and ones in the middle. The matrix is divided into subquadrants as shown on the right where gray squares represent subquadrants that consist entirely of black pixels.

```
0 0 0 0 0 0 0 0
0 0 0 0 0 0 0 0
0 0 0 0 1 1 1 1
0 0 0 0 1 1 1 1
0 0 0 1 1 1 1 1
0 0 1 1 1 1 1 1
0 0 1 1 1 1 0 0
0 0 1 1 1 0 0 0
```

A quadtree is constructed from the block structure of an image. The root of the tree represents the entire array of pixels. Each non-leaf node of a quadtree has four children, corresponding to the four subquadrants of the region represented by the node. Leaf nodes represent regions that consist of pixels of the same color and thus are not subdivided. For example, the image shown above, with the block structure on the right, is represented by the quadtree below.

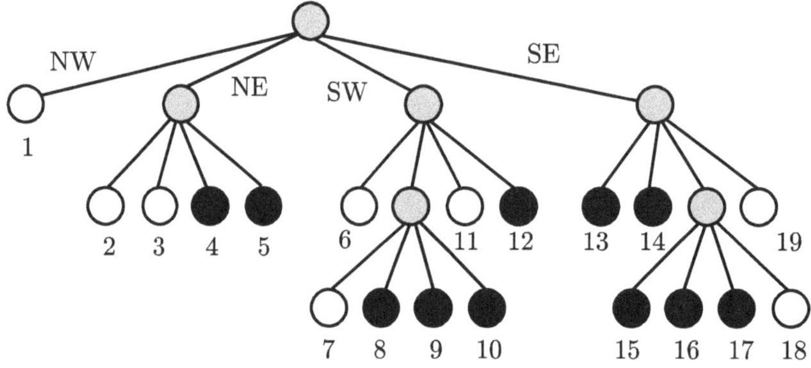

Leaf nodes are white if they correspond to a block of all white pixels, and black if they correspond to a block of all black pixels. In the tree, each leaf node is numbered corresponding to the block it represents in the diagram above. The branches of a non-leaf node are ordered from left-to-right as shown for the northwest, northeast, southwest, and southeast quadrants (or upper-left, upper-right, lower-left, lower-right).

A tree can be represented by a sequence of numbers representing the root-to-leaf paths of black nodes. Each path is a base five number constructed by labeling branches with 1, 2, 3, or 4 with $NW = 1$, $NE = 2$, $SW = 3$, $SE = 4$, and with the least significant digit of the base five number corresponding to the branch from the root. For example, the node labeled 4 has path NE, SW which is 32_5 (base 5) or 17_{10} (base 10); the node labeled 12 has path SW, SE or $43_5 = 23_{10}$; and the node labeled 15 has path SE, SW, NW or $134_5 = 44_{10}$. The entire tree is represented by the sequence of numbers (in base 10)

$$9\ 14\ 17\ 22\ 23\ 44\ 63\ 69\ 88\ 94\ 113$$

Write a program that converts images into root-to-leaf paths and converts root-to-leaf paths into images.

Input

The input contains one or more images. Each image is square, and the data for an image starts with an integer n, where $|n|$ is the length of a side of the square (always a power of two, with $|n| < 64$) followed by a representation of the image. A representation is either a sequence of n^2 zeros and ones comprised of $|n|$ lines of $|n|$ digits per line, or the sequence of numbers that represent the root-to-leaf paths of each black node in the quadtree that represents the image.

If n is positive, the zero/one representation follows; if n is negative, the sequence of black node path numbers (in base 10) follows. The sequence is terminated by the number '-1'. A one-node tree that represents an all-black image is represented by the number '0'. A one-node tree that represents an all-white image is represented by an empty sequence (no numbers).

The end of data is signaled by a value of '0' for n.

Output

For each image in the input, first output the number of the image, as shown in the sample output. Then output the alternate form of the image.

If the image is represented by zeros and ones, the output consists of root-to-leaf paths of all black nodes in the quadtree that represents the image. The values should be base 10 representations of the base 5 path numbers, and the values should be printed in sorted order. If there are more than 12 black nodes, print a newline after every 12 nodes. The total number of black nodes should be printed after the path numbers.

If the image is represented by the root-to-leaf paths of black nodes, the output consists of an ASCII representation of the image with the character '.' used for white/zero and the character '*' used for black/one. There should be n characters per line for an $n \times n$ image.

Sample Input

```
8
00000000
00000000
00001111
00001111
00011111
00111111
00111100
00111000
-8
9 14 17 22 23 44 63 69 88 94 113 -1
2
00
00
-4
0 -1
0
```

Sample Output

```
Image 1
9 14 17 22 23 44 63 69 88 94 113
Total number of black nodes = 11

Image 2
. . . . . . . .
. . . . . . . .
. . . . ****
. . . . ****
. . . *****
. . ******
. . ****. .
. . ***. . .

Image 3
Total number of black nodes = 0

Image 4
****
****
****
****
```

H Towers of Powers

One of the many problems in computer-generated graphics is realistically modeling the "orderly randomness" of things like mountain ranges and city skylines. A new student intern at a graphics company had an idea—use fluctuations in number representations to model height. In this problem you will compute several such number representations and show the "skylines" they produce.

Let n be any positive integer, and let b be an integer greater than or equal to 2. The *completebase* − *bexpansionofn* is obtained as follows. First write the usual base-b expansion of n, which is just a sum of powers of b, each multiplied by a coefficient between 1 and $b − 1$, omitting terms with zero coefficients. For example, if $n = 20000$ and $b = 3$, the base-3 expansion of 20000 is given by

$$20000 = 3^9 + 3^5 + 2 \times 3^3 + 2 \times 3^2 + 2$$

To obtain the *complete* base-b expansion, we apply the same procedure to the exponents until all numbers are represented in base b. For $n = 20000$ and $b = 3$ we would have

$$20000 = 3^{3^2} + 3^{3+2} + 2 \times 3^3 + 2 \times 3^2 + 2$$

As another example, consider $n = 16647$ and $b = 2$. The resulting expansion is

$$16647 = 2^{2^{2+1}+2^2+2} + 2^{2^{2+1}} + 2^2 + 2 + 1$$

The rising and falling heights of the numbers form the number's "skyline."

For each pair of integers n and b in the input, display the complete base-b representation of n. Your display should use multiple output lines for different exponent heights. The display must begin with $n =$, followed by the expansion. Answers should use an asterisk (∗) as the multiplication symbol between coefficients and powers of b. Zero terms must not be printed, and unnecessary coefficients and exponents must not be shown (for example, display 1 instead of b^0, b^2 instead of $1 * b^2$ and b instead of b^1). To assist in accurately viewing the skyline of the number, the display must show one character (either a digit, +, or ∗) per column of the multi-line display; there must be no unnecessary spaces. The correct format is illustrated in the sample output shown below.

Answers must be displayed using no more than 80 columns. Expansions requiring more than 80 columns must be split between terms, and a second set of display lines used to show the remaining portion of the expansion. The second part of the answer must begin in the same column as the previous part of the answer. See the sample output for an example.

Input

Input is a sequence of pairs of integers, n and b, followed by a pair of zeroes. Each value for n will be positive, and each value for b will be greater than or equal to 2. No value will exceed the maximum signed integer size for the machine.

Output

For each input pair, n and b, print the complete base-b expansion of n as described above. Print a line containing

n `in complete base` b:

preceding each expansion. Separate the output for consecutive pairs by a line of hyphens. All coefficients, bases, and exponents are to be displayed as standard base 10 integers. The expansion for each input pair will require at most two standard screen widths, allowing for indentation and splitting between terms of the expansion.

Sample Input

```
20000 3
16647 2
1000 12
85026244 3
0 0
```

Sample Output

```
20000 in complete base 3:

          2
      3    3+2     3     2
20000 = 3   +3    +2*3 +2*3 +2
--------------------------------------------------------
16447 in complete base 2:

          2+1   2       2+1
      2     +2 +2  2       2
16647 = 2           +2     +2 +2+1
--------------------------------------------------------
1000 in complete base 12:

            2
1000 = 6*12 +11*12+4
--------------------------------------------------------
85026244 in complete base 3:

              2         2        2        2        2       2        2
          3 +2*3+1     3 +2*3    3 +3+2    3 +3+1   3 +2    3 +1     3
85026244 = 3          +2*3      +2*3      +2*3     +2*3    +2*3     +2*3


            2*3+2  2*3+1     3
          +2*3     +3      +2*3 +3+1
```

WORLD FINALS 1999

EINDHOVEN, THE NETHERLANDS

World Champion

UNIVERSITY OF WATERLOO

Ondrej Lhotak

Viet-Trung Luu

David Kennedy

Director of Judging
Dick Rinewalt   *Texas Christian University*

Chief Judge
Jo Perry   *North Carolina State University*

Judges
Don Chamberlin   *IBM Almaden Research Center*
David Elizandro   *Tennessee Tech University*
Peter Kluit   *Delft University of Technology*
Ron Pacheco   *Perficio, LLC*
Robert Roos   *Allegheny College*
Matthias Ruhl   *MIT*
Laurie White   *Mercer University*
Stanley Wileman, Jr.   *University of Nebraska at Omaha*

UVa Online Judge problem numbers
808 A Bee Breeding
809 B Bullet Hole
810 C A Dicey Problem
811 D The Fortified Forest
812 E Trade on Verweggistan
813 F Robot
814 G The Letter Carrier's Rounds
815 H Flooded!

A Bee Breeding

Professor B. Heif is conducting experiments with a species of South American bees that he found during an expedition to the Brazilian rain forest. The honey produced by these bees is of superior quality compared to the honey from European and North American honey bees. Unfortunately, the bees do not breed well in captivity. Professor Heif thinks the reason is that the placement of the different maggots (for workers, queens, etc.) within the honeycomb depends on environmental conditions, which are different in his laboratory and the rain forest.

As a first step to validate his theory, Professor Heif wants to quantify the difference in maggot placement. For this he measures the distance between the cells of the comb into which the maggots are placed. To this end, the professor has labeled the cells by marking an arbitrary cell as number 1, and then labeling the remaining cells in a clockwise fashion, as shown in the following figure.

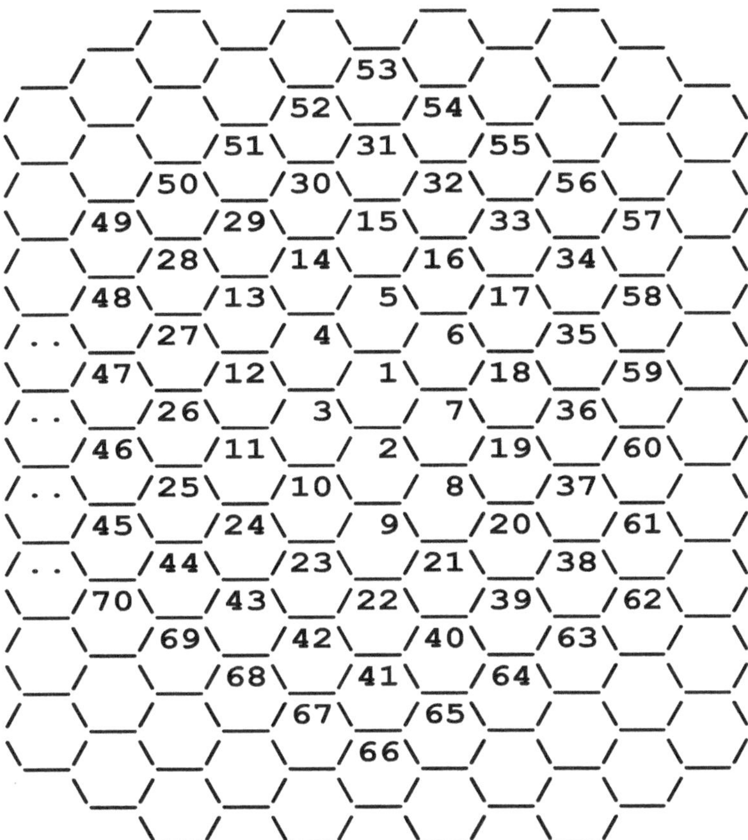

For example, two maggots in cells 19 and 30 are 5 cells apart. One of the shortest paths connecting the two cells is via the cells 19 - 7 - 6 - 5 - 15 - 30, so you must move five times to adjacent cells to get from 19 to 30.

Professor Heif needs your help to write a program that computes the distance, defined as the number of cells in a shortest path, between any pair of cells.

Input

The input consists of several lines, each containing two integers a and b ($a, b \leq 10000$), denoting numbers of cells. The integers are always positive, except in the last line where $a = b = 0$ holds. This last line terminates the input and should not be processed.

Output

For each pair of numbers (a, b) in the input file, output the distance between the cells labeled a and b. The distance is the minimum number of moves to get from a to b.

Sample Input

```
19 30
0 0
```

Sample Output

```
The distance between cells 19 and 30 is 5.
```

B Bullet Hole

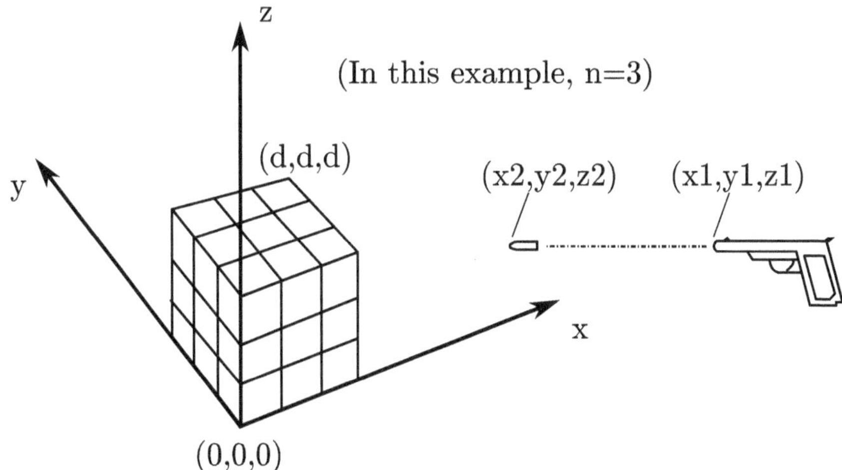

A cube is suspended in space. A Cartesian coordinate system is defined with its origin at one of the bottom corners of the cube, as shown in the figure. The cube has side dimension d, so its opposite corners are at coordinates $(0, 0, 0)$ and (d, d, d). The positive z-direction of the coordinate system is "up" with respect to gravity.

The interior of the cube contains partitions with uniform spacing in each dimension, so that the cube is partitioned into n^3 mini-cubes of equal size. The partitions are thin and watertight, and each mini-cube is filled with water. The total volume of water in all the minicubes is d^3 .

A gun fires a bullet which may hit the cube. The muzzle of the gun is at the point (x_1, y_1, z_1). The point (x_2, y_2, z_2) is a point on the bullet's path that defines the direction of the bullet. The bullet does not shatter the cube, but wherever the bullet touches a side or interior partition of the cube, it makes a small hole. Bullet holes may be made in the sides, edges, or corners of the interior mini-cubes. Water, influenced by gravity, may leak through these small holes. All the water that leaks out of the large cube is collected and measured.

Input

The input data set consists of several trials. Each trial is described by eight integers. The first integer is n $(n \le 50)$, as described above. The second integer is d $(d \le 100)$. The remaining six integers—$x_1, y_1, z_1, x_2, y_2, z_2$—represent the origin and a point on the path of the bullet $(-100 \le x_1, y_1, z_1, x_2, y_2, z_2 \le 100)$. The origin and the point on the path of the bullet are not the same. The origin may be inside the cube. After the last trial, the integer '0' terminates the data set.

Output

Your program must compute the total volume of water that leaks out of the large cube. For each trial, print the trial number, the notation 'Volume =', and the total volume of water accurate to two digits to the right of the decimal point.

Print a blank line between trials.

Note: In this problem, two real numbers are considered equal if they are less than 10^{-6} apart.

Sample Input

```
 5    25       5   15    0       5   15 100
 3    30       0  -35    0       3  -25    3
10    16       8   17   11      12   19    6
 0
```

Sample Output

```
Trial 1, Volume = 2500.00

Trial 2, Volume = 1950.00

Trial 3, Volume = 0.00
```

C   A Dicey Problem

The three-by-three array in Figure 1 is a maze. A standard six-sided die is needed to traverse the maze (the layout of a standard six–sided die is shown in Figure 2). Each maze has an initial position and an initial die configuration. In Figure 1, the starting position is row 1, column 2—the "2" in the top row of the maze—and the initial die configuration has the "5" on top of the die and the "1" facing the player (assume the player is viewing the maze from the bottom edge of the figure).

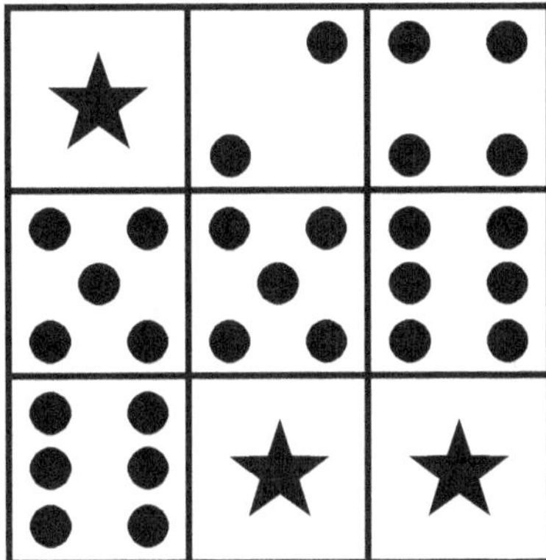

Figure 1: Sample Dice Maze

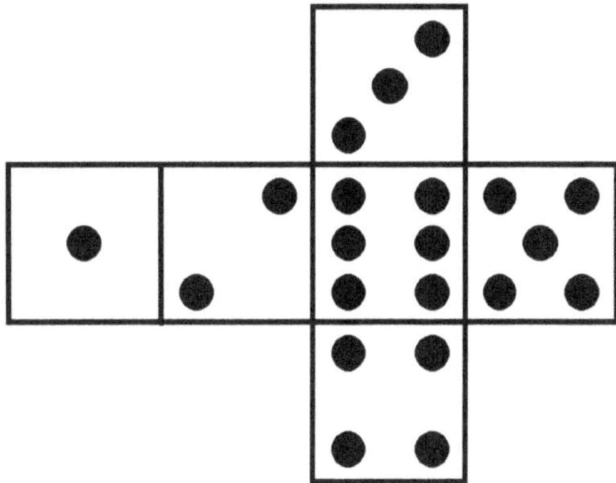

Figure 2: Standard Layout of Six-Sided Dice

To move through the maze you must tip the die over on an edge to land on an adjacent square, effecting horizontal or vertical movement from one square to another. However, you can only move onto a square that contains the same number as the number displayed on the top of the die before the move, or onto a "wild" square which contains a star. Movement onto a wild square is always allowed regardless of the number currently displayed on the top of the die. The goal of the maze is to move the die off the starting square and to then find a way back to that same square.

For example, at the beginning of the maze there are two possible moves. Since the 5 is on top of the die, it is possible to move down one square, and since the square to the left of the starting position is wild it is also possible to move left. If the first move chosen is to move down, this brings the 6 to the top of the die and moves are now possible both to the right and down. If the first move chosen is instead to the left, this brings the 3 to the top of the die and no further moves are possible.

If we consider maze locations as ordered pairs of row and column numbers $(row, column)$ with row indexes starting at 1 for the top row and increasing toward the bottom, and column indexes starting at 1 for the left column and increasing to the right, the solution to this simple example maze can be specified as: (1,2), (2,2), (2,3), (3,3), (3,2), (3,1), (2,1), (1,1), (1,2). A bit more challenging example maze is shown in Figure 3.

The goal of this problem is to write a program to solve dice mazes. The input file will contain several mazes for which the program should search for solutions. Each maze will have either a unique solution or no solution at all. That is, each maze in the input may or may not have a solution, but those with a solution are guaranteed to have only one unique solution. For each input maze, either a solution or a message indicating no solution is possible will be sent to the output.

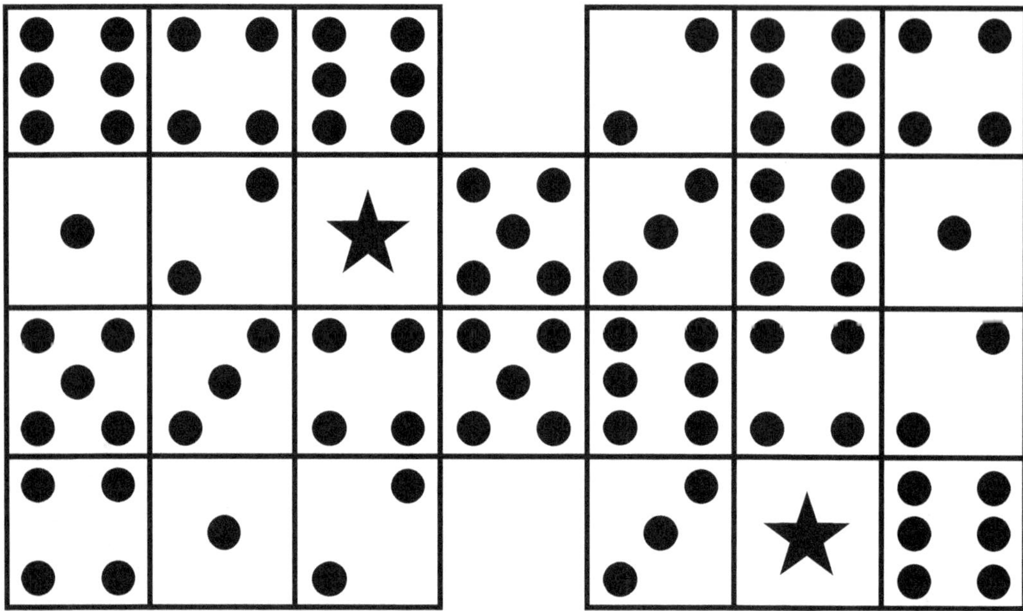

Figure 3: Start at (2,6) with the 3 on top and the 6 facing you.

Input

The input file begins with a line containing a string of no more than 20 non-blank characters that names the first maze. The next line contains six integers delimited by single spaces. These integers are, in order, the number of rows in the maze (an integer from 1 to 10, call this value R), the number of columns in the maze (an integer from 1 to 10, call this value C), the starting row, the starting column, the number that should be on top of the die at the starting position, and finally the number that should be facing you on the die at the starting position. The next R lines contain C integers each, again delimited by single spaces. This $R \times C$ array of integers defines the maze. A value of zero indicates an empty location in the maze (such as the two empty squares in the center column of the maze in Figure 3), and a value of '-1' indicates a wild square.

This input sequence is repeated for each maze in the input. An input line containing only the word 'END' (without the quotes) as the name of the maze marks the end of the input.

Output

The output should contain the name of each maze followed by its solution or the string 'No Solution Possible' (without the quotes). All lines in the output file except for the maze names should be indented exactly two spaces. Maze names should start in the leftmost column.

Solutions should be output as a comma-delimited sequence of the consecutive positions traversed in the solution, starting and ending with the same square (the starting square as specified in the input). Positions should be specified as ordered pairs enclosed in parentheses. The solution should list 9 positions per line (with the exception of the last line of the solution for which there may not be a full 9 positions to list), and no spaces should be present within or between positions.

Sample Input

```
DICEMAZE1
3 3 1 2 5 1
-1 2 4
5 5 6
6 -1 -1
DICEMAZE2
4 7 2 6 3 6
6 4 6 0 2 6 4
1 2 -1 5 3 6 1
5 3 4 5 6 4 2
4 1 2 0 3 -1 6
DICEMAZE3
3 3 1 1 2 4
2 2 3
4 5 6
-1 -1 -1
END
```

Sample Output

```
DICEMAZE1
  (1,2),(2,2),(2,3),(3,3),(3,2),(3,1),(2,1),(1,1),(1,2)
DICEMAZE2
  (2,6),(2,5),(2,4),(2,3),(2,2),(3,2),(4,2),(4,1),(3,1),
  (2,1),(2,2),(2,3),(2,4),(2,5),(1,5),(1,6),(1,7),(2,7),
  (3,7),(4,7),(4,6),(3,6),(2,6)
DICEMAZE3
  No Solution Possible
```

D   The Fortified Forest

Once upon a time, in a faraway land, there lived a king. This king owned a small collection of rare and valuable trees, which had been gathered by his ancestors on their travels. To protect his trees from thieves, the king ordered that a high fence be built around them. His wizard was put in charge of the operation.

Alas, the wizard quickly noticed that the only suitable material available to build the fence was the wood from the trees themselves. In other words, it was necessary to cut down some trees in order to build a fence around the remaining trees. Of course, to prevent his head from being chopped off, the wizard wanted to minimize the value of the trees that had to be cut. The wizard went to his tower and stayed there until he had found the best possible solution to the problem. The fence was then built and everyone lived happily ever after.

You are to write a program that solves the problem the wizard faced.

Input

The input contains several test cases, each of which describes a hypothetical forest. Each test case begins with a line containing a single integer n, $2 \leq n \leq 15$, the number of trees in the forest. The trees are identified by consecutive integers 1 to n. Each of the subsequent lines contains 4 integers x_i, y_i, v_i, l_i that describe a single tree. (x_i, y_i) is the position of the tree in the plane, v_i is its value, and l_i is the length of fence that can be built using the wood of the tree. v_i and l_i are between 0 and 10,000.

The input ends with an empty test case ($n = 0$).

Output

For each test case, compute a subset of the trees such that, using the wood from that subset, the remaining trees can be enclosed in a single fence. Find the subset with a minimum value. If more than one such minimum-value subset exists, choose one with the smallest number of trees. For simplicity, regard the trees as having zero diameter.

Display, as shown below, the test case numbers (1, 2, ...), the identity of each tree to be cut, and the length of the excess fencing (accurate to two fractional digits).

Display a blank line between test cases.

Sample Input

```
6
 0  0  8  3
 1  4  3  2
 2  1  7  1
 4  1  2  3
 3  5  4  6
 2  3  9  8
3
 3  0 10  2
 5  5 20 25
 7 -3 30 32
0
```

Sample Output

```
Forest 1
Cut these trees: 2 4 5
Extra wood: 3.16

Forest 2
Cut these trees: 2
Extra wood: 15.00
```

E   Trade on Verweggistan

Since the days of Peter Stuyvesant and Abel Tasman, Dutch merchants have been traveling all over the world to buy and sell goods. Once there was some trade on Verweggistan, but it ended after a short time. After reading this story you will understand why.

At that time Verweggistan was quite popular, because it was the only place in the world where people knew how to make a 'prul'. The end of the trade on Verweggistan meant the end of the trade in pruls (or 'prullen', as the Dutch plural said), and very few people nowadays know what a prul actually is.

Pruls were manufactured in workyards. Whenever a prul was finished it was packed in a box, which was then placed on top of the pile of previously produced pruls. On the side of each box the price was written. The price depended on the time it took to manufacture the prul. If all went well, a prul would cost one or two florins, but on a bad day the price could easily rise to 15 florins or more. This had nothing to do with quality; all pruls had the same value.

In those days pruls sold for 10 florins each in Holland. Transportation costs were negligible since the pruls were taken as extra on ships that would sail anyway. When a Dutch merchant went to Verweggistan, he had a clear purpose: buy pruls, sell them in Holland, and maximize his profits. Unfortunately, the Verweggistan way of trading pruls made this more complicated than one would think.

One would expect that merchants would simply buy the cheapest pruls, and the pruls that cost more than 10 florins would remain unsold. Unfortunately, all workyards on Verweggistan sold their pruls in a particular order. The box on top of the pile was sold first, then the second one from the top, and so on. So even if the fifth box from the top was the cheapest one, a merchant would have to buy the other four boxes above to obtain it.

As you can imagine, this made it quite difficult for the merchants to maximize their profits by buying the right set of pruls. Not having computers to help with optimization, they quickly lost interest in trading pruls at all.

In this problem, you are given the description of several workyard piles. You have to calculate the maximum profit a merchant can obtain by buying pruls from the piles according to the restrictions given above. In addition, you have to determine the number of pruls he has to buy to achieve this profit.

Input

The input describes several test cases. The first line of input for each test case contains a single integer w, the number of workyards in the test case ($1 \leq w \leq 50$).

This is followed by w lines, each describing a pile of pruls. The first number in each line is the number b of boxes in the pile ($0 \leq b \leq 20$). Following it are b positive integers, indicating the prices (in florins) of the pruls in the stack, given from top to bottom.

The input is terminated by a description starting with $w = 0$. This description should not be processed.

Output

For each test case, print the case number (1, 2, ...). Then print two lines, the first containing the maximum profit the merchant can achieve. The second line should specify the number of pruls the merchant has to buy to obtain this profit. If this number is not uniquely determined, print the possible values in increasing order. If there are more than ten possible values, print only the 10 smallest. Display a blank line between test cases.

Sample Input

```
1
6 12 3 10 7 16 5
2
5 7 3 11 9 10
9 1 2 3 4 10 16 10 4 16
0
```

Sample Output

```
Workyards 1
Maximum profit is 8.
Number of pruls to buy: 4

Workyards 2
Maximum profit is 40.
Number of pruls to buy: 6 7 8 9 10 12 13
```

F Robot

A robot arm used in an automated factory consists of N connected links: $link_1$ which is connected to $link_2$, ..., and $link_{N-1}$ which is connected to $link_N$. Each link is a straight rod of a specified length, $len_1, len_2, \ldots, len_N$. Between each pair of connected links is a servo, $servo_2$ (between $link_1$ and $link_2$), ..., and $servo_N$ (between $link_{N-1}$ and $link_N$) that can be activated to adjust the angle between the connected links. $Link_1$ is also connected by a servo, $servo_1$, to the factory floor (at the point $x = 0, y = 0, z = 0$ in a Cartesian coordinate system). At the free (unconnected) end of the last link ($link_N$) is a "hand" that can be used to grasp objects.

In the initial setting of the robot arm, each servo is set to no rotation (0 degrees), and the links in the robot arm coincide with the z-axis. The xy plane is horizontal (the factory floor), and the entire robot arm is initially pointing up, vertically. From this initial setting, each servo can effect a rotation of up to 90 degrees in either of two directions. $Servo_1$ moves the entire robot arm in the xz plane by rotation about the y-axis. $Servo_2$ moves the arm (except $link_1$) in the (perhaps rotated) yz plane by rotation about the x-axis. In a similar manner, each odd-numbered servo can rotate the remaining part of the arm in the (perhaps rotated) xz plane, and each even-numbered servo can rotate the remaining part of the arm in the (perhaps rotated) yz plane. In effect, the servos rotate the links about the y and x-axes of coordinate systems fixed to the end of each link. Counterclockwise rotations about a coordinate axis are produced with positive rotation angles, if we are looking along the positive half of the axis toward the coordinate origin. The sample data has been carefully chosen to illustrate the effects of these rotations.

There are two restrictions on the final positioning of the robot's arm. No part of the arm can be below the factory floor, and the links in the robot's arm cannot intersect with each other (except where they are connected by the servos).

You should check only the final position of the arm.

Given the number of links in a robot's arm, their lengths, and the proposed settings of the servos, first determine if the proposed positioning of the arm is allowable. If the arm can be positioned as proposed, then determine the coordinates of the robot's hand, accurate to three fractional digits. Otherwise identify the first (smallest numbered) servo that has an inappropriate setting, and why that setting is inappropriate. Links are assumed to intersect if they come within 0.001 length units of each other.

Input

The input data will contain multiple test cases. Each test case includes, in order, the number of links, N, their lengths, $len_1, len_2, \ldots, len_N$, and the proposed angles to which the servos (starting with $servo_1$) are to be set. The lengths and servo angles are real numbers, and the number of links is an integer. There will be no more than 10 links in any robot arm. The last test case is followed by a negative integer.

Output

For each test case, display the test case number (starting with 1). Then, if the proposed setting is allowable, display the position of the robot's hand in the original (factory floor) coordinate system (with three fractional digits). Otherwise display the identity of the first servo with an inappropriate setting and why that setting is inappropriate. An output format similar to that shown below is acceptable.

Sample Input

```
2 25 15 0 90.0
1 1.0 45.0
2 1 1 0 45
4 1 2 3 4 90 0 0 0
3 1 1 1 0 90 90
2 1 1 45.0 45
4 1 1 1 2 0 90 0 90
8 10 1 1 1 1 1 1 2
   0 0 90 0 90 0 90 0
-1
```

Sample Output

```
Case 1: robot's hand is at (0.000,-15.000,25.000)
Case 2: robot's hand is at (0.707,0.000,0.707)
Case 3: robot's hand is at (0.000,-0.707,1.707)
Case 4: robot's hand is at (10.000,0.000,0.000)
Case 5: robot's hand is at (1.000,-1.000,1.000)
Case 6: robot's hand is at (1.207,-0.707,1.207)
Case 7: servo 4 attempts to move arm below floor
Case 8: servo 8 causes link collision
```

G The Letter Carrier's Rounds

For an electronic mail application you are to describe the SMTP-based communication that takes place between pairs of MTAs. The sender's User Agent gives a formatted message to the sending Message Transfer Agent (MTA). The sending MTA communicates with the receiving MTA using the Simple Mail Transfer Protocol (SMTP). The receiving MTA delivers mail to the receiver's User Agent. After a communication link is initialized, the sending MTA transmits command lines, one at a time, to the receiving MTA, which returns a three-digit coded response after each command is processed. The sender commands are shown below in the order sent for each message. There is more than one RCPT TO line when the same message is sent to several users at the same MTA. A message to users at different MTAs requires separate SMTP sessions.

`HELO` *myname*	Identifies the sender to the receiver (yes, there is only one L)
`MAIL FROM:`$< sender >$	Identifies the message sender
`RCPT TO:`$< user >$	Identifies one recipient of the message
`DATA`	Followed by an arbitrary number of lines of text comprising the message body, ending with a line containing a period in column one.
`QUIT`	Terminates the communication.

The following response codes are sent by the receiving MTA:

221 Closing connection (after QUIT)

250 Action was okay (after MAIL FROM and RCPT TO specifying an acceptable user, or completion of a message)

354 Start sending mail (after DATA)

550 Action not taken; no such user here (after RCPT TO with unknown user)

Input

The input contains descriptions of MTAs followed by an arbitrary number of messages. Each MTA description begins with the MTA designation and its name (1 to 15 alphanumeric characters). Following the MTA name is the number of users that receive mail at that MTA and a list of the users (1 to 15 alphanumeric characters each). The MTA description is terminated by an asterisk in column 1. Each message begins with the sending user's name and is followed by a list of recipient identifiers. Each identifier has the form *user@mtaname*. The message (each line containing no more than 72 characters) begins and terminates with an asterisk in column 1. A line with an asterisk in column 1 instead of a sender and recipient list indicates the end of the entire input.

Output

For each message, show the communication between the sending and receiving MTAs. Every MTA mentioned in a message is a valid MTA; however, message recipients may not exist at the destination MTA. The receiving MTA rejects mail for those users by responding to the RCPT TO command with the 550 code. A rejection will not affect delivery to authorized users at the same MTA. If there is not at least one authorized recipient at a particular MTA, the DATA is not sent. Only one SMTP session is used to send a message to users at a particular MTA. For example, a message to 5 users at the same MTA will have only one SMTP session. Also a message is addressed

to the same user only once. The order in which receiving MTAs are contacted by the sender is
the same as in the input file. As shown in the sample output, prefix the communication with the
communicating MTA names, and indent each communication line. No innecessary spaces should
be printed.

Sample Input

```
MTA London 4 Fiona Paul Heather Nevil
MTA SanFrancisco 3 Mario Luigi Shariff
MTA Paris 3 Jacque Suzanne Maurice
MTA HongKong 3 Chen Jeng Hee
MTA MexicoCity 4 Conrado Estella Eva Raul
MTA Cairo 3 Hamdy Tarik Misa
*
Hamdy@Cairo Conrado@MexicoCity Shariff@SanFrancisco Lisa@MexicoCity
*
Congratulations on your efforts !!
--Hamdy
*
Fiona@London Chen@HongKong Natasha@Paris
*
Thanks for the report!  --Fiona
*
*
```

Sample Output

```
Connection between Cairo and MexicoCity
     HELO Cairo
     250
     MAIL FROM:<Hamdy@Cairo>
     250
     RCPT TO:<Conrado@MexicoCity>
     250
     RCPT TO:<Lisa@MexicoCity>
     550
     DATA
     354
     Congratulations on your efforts !!
     --Hamdy
     .
     250
     QUIT
     221
Connection between Cairo and SanFrancisco
     HELO Cairo
     250
     MAIL FROM:<Hamdy@Cairo>
     250
```

```
    RCPT TO:<Shariff@SanFrancisco>
    250
    DATA
    354
    Congratulations on your efforts !!
    --Hamdy
    .
    250
    QUIT
    221
Connection between London and HongKong
    HELO London
    250
    MAIL FROM:<Fiona@London>
    250
    RCPT TO:<Chen@HongKong>
    250
    DATA
    354
    Thanks for the report!  --Fiona
    .
    250
    QUIT
    221
Connection between London and Paris
    HELO London
    250
    MAIL FROM:<Fiona@London>
    250
    RCPT TO:<Natasha@Paris>
    550
    QUIT
    221
```

H   Flooded!

To enable homebuyers to estimate the cost of flood insurance, a real-estate firm provides clients with the elevation of each 10-meter by 10-meter square of land in regions where homes may be purchased. Water from rain, melting snow, and burst water mains will collect first in those squares with the lowest elevations, since water from squares of higher elevation will run downhill. For simplicity, we also assume that storm sewers enable water from high-elevation squares in valleys (completely enclosed by still higher elevation squares) to drain to lower elevation squares, and that water will not be absorbed by the land.

From weather data archives, we know the typical volume of water that collects in a region. As prospective homebuyers, we wish to know the elevation of the water after it has collected in low-lying squares, and also the percentage of the region's area that is completely submerged (that is, the percentage of 10-meter squares whose elevation is strictly less than the water level). You are to write the program that provides these results.

Input

The input consists of a sequence of region descriptions. Each begins with a pair of integers, m and n, each less than 30, giving the dimensions of the rectangular region in 10-meter units. Immediately following are m lines of n integers giving the elevations of the squares in row-major order. Elevations are given in meters, with positive and negative numbers representing elevations above and below sea level, respectively. The final value in each region description is an integer that indicates the number of cubic meters of water that will collect in the region. A pair of zeroes follows the description of the last region.

Output

For each region, display the region number (1, 2, ...), the water level (in meters above or below sea level) and the percentage of the region's area under water, each on a separate line. The water level and percentage of the region's area under water are to be displayed accurate to two fractional digits. Follow the output for each region with a blank line.

Sample Input

```
3 3
25 37 45
51 12 34
94 83 27
10000
0 0
```

Sample Output

```
Region 1
Water level is 46.67 meters.
66.67 percent of the region is under water.
```

WORLD FINALS 2000

ORLANDO, FLORIDA

World Champion

ST. PETERSBURG STATE UNIVERSITY

Nikolai Durov
Andrei Lopatine
Oleg Eterevsky

Director of Judging
Dick Rinewalt   *Texas Christian University*

Chief Judge
Jo Perry   *North Carolina State University*

Judges
Don Chamberlin   *IBM Almaden Research Center*
David Elizandro   *Tennessee Tech University*
Peter Kluit   *Delft University of Technology*
Ron Pachcco   *Perficio, LLC*
Robert Roos   *Allegheny College*
Matthias Ruhl   *MIT*
Laurie White   *Mercer University*
Stanley Wileman, Jr.   *University of Nebraska at Omaha*

UVa Online Judge problem numbers
816   A   Abbott's Revenge
817   B   According to Bartjens
818   C   Cutting Chains
819   D   Gifts Large and Small
820   E   Internet Bandwidth
821   F   Page Hopping
822   G   Queue and A
823   H   Stopper Stumper

A Abbott's Revenge

The 1999 World Finals Contest included a problem based on a "dice maze." At the time the problem was written, the judges were unable to discover the original source of the dice maze concept. Shortly after the contest, however, Mr. Robert Abbott, the creator of numerous mazes and an author on the subject, contacted the contest judges and identified himself as the originator of dice mazes. We regret that we did not credit Mr. Abbott for his original concept in last year s problem statement. But we are happy to report that Mr. Abbott has offered his expertise to this year s contest with his original and unpublished "walk-through arrow mazes."

As are most mazes, a walk-through arrow maze is traversed by moving from intersection to intersection until the goal intersection is reached. As each intersection is approached from a given direction, a sign near the entry to the intersection indicates in which directions the intersection can be exited. These directions are always left, forward or right, or any combination of these.

Figure 1 illustrates a walk-through arrow maze. The intersections are identified as "(row, column)" pairs, with the upper left being (1,1). The "Entrance" intersection for Figure 1 is (3,1), and the "Goal" intersection is (3,3). You begin the maze by moving north from (3,1). As you walk from (3,1) to (2,1), the sign at (2,1) indicates that as you approach (2,1) from the south (traveling north) you may continue to go only forward. Continuing forward takes you toward (1,1). The sign at (1,1) as you approach from the south indicates that you may exit (1,1) only by making a right. This turns you to the east now walking from (1,1) toward (1,2). So far there have been no choices to be made. This is also the case as you continue to move from (1,2) to (2,2) to (2,3) to (1,3). Now, however, as you move west from (1,3) toward (1,2), you have the option of continuing straight or turning left. Continuing straight would take you on toward (1,1), while turning left would take you south to (2,2). The actual (unique) solution to this maze is the following sequence of intersections: (3,1) (2,1) (1,1) (1,2) (2,2) (2,3) (1,3) (1,2) (1,1) (2,1) (2,2) (1,2) (1,3) (2,3) (3,3).

You must write a program to solve valid walk-through arrow mazes. Solving a maze means (if possible) finding a route through the maze that leaves the Entrance in the prescribed direction, and ends in the Goal. This route should not be longer than necessary, of course.

Input

The input file will consist of one or more arrow mazes. The first line of each maze description contains the name of the maze, which is an alphanumeric string of no more than 20 characters. The next line contains, in the following order, the starting row, the starting column, the starting direction, the goal row, and finally the goal column. All are delimited by a single space. The maximum dimensions of a maze for this problem are 9 by 9, so all row and column numbers are single digits from 1 to 9. The starting direction is one of the characters N, S, E or W, indicating north, south, east and west, respectively.

All remaining input lines for a maze have this format: two integers, one or more groups of characters, and a sentinel asterisk, again all delimited by a single space. The integers represent the row and column, respectively, of a maze intersection. Each character group represents a sign at that intersection. The first character in the group is N, S, E or W to indicate in what direction of travel the sign would be seen. For example, S indicates that this is the sign that is seen when travelling south. (This is the sign posted at the north entrance to the intersection.) Following this first direction character are one to three arrow characters. These can be L, F or R indicating left, forward, and right, respectively.

The list of intersections is concluded by a line containing a single zero in the first column. The next line of the input starts the next maze, and so on. The end of input is the word END on a single line by itself.

Output

For each maze, the output file should contain a line with the name of the maze, followed by one or more lines with either a solution to the maze or the phrase "No Solution Possible". Maze names should start in column 1, and all other lines should start in column 3, i.e., indented two spaces. Solutions should be output as a list of intersections in the format "(R,C)" in the order they are visited from the start to the goal, should be delimited by a single space, and all but the last line of the solution should contain exactly 10 intersections.

The first maze in the following sample input is the maze in figure below.

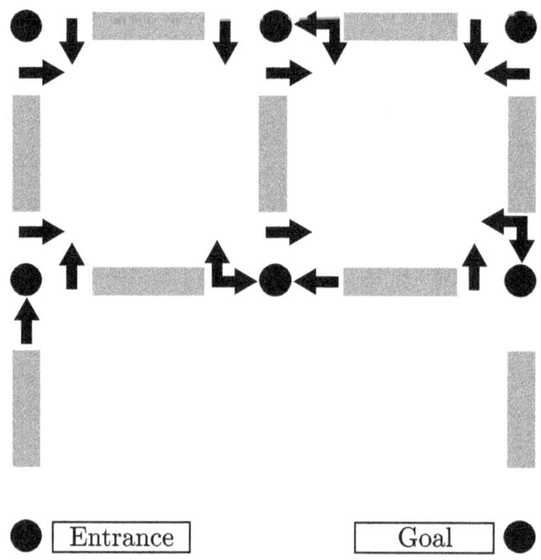

Sample Input

```
SAMPLE
3 1 N 3 3
1 1 WL NR *
1 2 WLF NR ER *
1 3 NL ER *
2 1 SL WR NF *
2 2 SL WF ELF *
2 3 SFR EL *
0
NOSOLUTION
3 1 N 3 2
1 1 WL NR *
1 2 NL ER *
2 1 SL WR NFR *
2 2 SR EL *
0
END
```

Sample Output

```
SAMPLE
  (3,1) (2,1) (1,1) (1,2) (2,2) (2,3) (1,3) (1,2) (1,1) (2,1)
  (2,2) (1,2) (1,3) (2,3) (3,3)
NOSOLUTION
  No Solution Possible
```

B According to Bartjens

The wide dissemination of calculators and computers has its disadvantages. Even students in technical disciplines tend to exhibit a surprising lack of calculating ability. Accustomed to the use of calculators and computers, many of them are unable to make calculations like $7 * 8$ mentally or like $13 * 17$ using pencil and paper. We all know, but who cares?

Professor Bartjens[1] cares. Professor Bartjens is a bit old fashioned. He decided to give his students some training in calculating without electronic equipment by creating a collection of calculation problems, (like $2100 - 100 = \ldots$). To simplify grading the problems, he constructed them so that almost all of them had 2000 as an answer. Not all of them, of course. His students would be smart enough to recognize the pattern, and fill in 2000 everywhere without further thinking. Unfortunately Professor Bartjens' printer driver turned out to be even more old-fashioned than the professor himself, and it could not interface with his new printer. Inspecting the printed problems, he soon recognized the pattern: *none of the operations was transmitted to the printer.* A problem like:

```
2100-100=
```

was printed as:

```
2100100=
```

Fortunately, all the digits and the equal sign were still printed. To make this bad situation much worse, Professor Bartjens' source file had disappeared. So Professor Bartjens has another problem: what were his original problems? Given the fact that the answer (most likely) should be 2000, the line `2100100=` could have been any one of the lines:

```
2100-100=
2*100*10+0=
2*100*10-0=
2*10*0100=
2*-100*-10+0=
```

Professor Bartjens does remember a few things about how he wrote the problems:

- He is sure that whenever he wrote down a number (other than 0), it would not start with a zero. So `2*10*0100=` could **not** have been one of his problems.

- He also knows he never wrote the number zero as anything but 0. So he would **not** have a problem like `2*1000+000=`.

- He used only binary operators, not the unary minus or plus, so `2*-100*-10+0=` was **not** an option either.

- He used the operators +, – and * only, avoiding the operator / (after all, they were first year students).

- He knew all problems followed the usual precedence and associativity rules.

You are to help Professor Bartjens recover his problem set by writing a program that when given a row of digits, insert one or more of the operators +, – and * in such a way that the value of the resulting expression equals 2000.

---

[1] Willem Bartjens (1569-1638) was the author of Cijferinge, a much used Dutch textbook on arithmetic. The phrase "...according to Bartjens" (uttered following a calculation) made his name immortal.

Input

The input consists of one or more test cases. Each test case is a single line containing n digits ('0'...'9'), $1 \leq n \leq 9$, followed by an equal sign. There will not be any blanks embedded in the input, but there may be some after the equal sign.

The last test case is followed by a line containing only the equal sign. This line should not be processed.

Output

For each test case, print the word 'Problem', then the number of the case, then all possible ways of inserting operators in the row of digits such that the resulting expression has the value 2000, subject to Professor Bartjens' memory of how he wrote the problems. Use the format shown below. If there is more than one possible problem, they may be written in any order, but no problem may appear more than once in the list. Each possible problem should be on a new line, indented 2 spaces. If there is no solution the answer 'IMPOSSIBLE' should be printed, indented 2 spaces.

Sample Input

```
2100100=
77=
=
```

Sample Output

```
Problem 1
  2100-100=
  2*100*10+0=
  2*100*10-0=
Problem 2
  IMPOSSIBLE
```

C   Cutting Chains

What a find! Anna Locke has just bought several links of chain some of which may be connected. They are made from zorkium, a material that was frequently used to manufacture jewelry in the last century, but is not used for that purpose anymore. It has its very own shine, incomparable to gold or silver, and impossible to describe to anyone who has not seen it first hand.

Anna wants the pieces joined into a single end-to-end strand of chain. She takes the links to a jeweler who tells her that the cost of joining them depends on the number of chain links that must be opened and closed. In order to minimize the cost, she carefully calculates the minimum number of links that have to be opened to rejoin all the links into a single sequence. This turns out to be more difficult than she at first thought. You must solve this problem for her.

Input

The input consists of descriptions of sets of chain links, one set per line. Each set is a list of integers delimited by one or more spaces. Every description starts with an integer n, which is the number of chain links in the set, where $1 \le n \le 15$. We will label the links $1, 2, \ldots, n$. The integers following n describe which links are connected to each other. Every connection is specified by a pair of integers i, j where $1 \le i, j \le n$ and $i \ne j$, indicating that chain links i and j are connected, i.e., one passes through the other. The description for each set is terminated by the pair '-1 -1', which should not be processed.

The input is terminated by a description starting with $n = 0$. This description should not be processed and will not contain data for connected links.

Output

For each set of chain links in the input, output a single line which reads

Set N: Minimum links to open is M

where N is the set number and M is the minimal number of links that have to be opened and closed such that all links can be joined into one single chain.

Sample Input

```
5 1 2 2 3 4 5 -1 -1
7 1 2 2 3 3 1 4 5 5 6 6 7 7 4 -1 -1
4 1 2 1 3 1 4 -1 -1
3 1 2 2 3 3 1 -1 -1
3 1 2 2 1 -1 -1
0
```

Sample Output

```
Set 1: Minimum links to open is 1
Set 2: Minimum links to open is 2
Set 3: Minimum links to open is 1
Set 4: Minimum links to open is 1
Set 5: Minimum links to open is 1
```

D   Gifts Large and Small

WrapIt.com specializes in wrapping gifts. Started several years ago as a service offered to local department stores and malls, today WrapIt serves customers world-wide and boasts that it can package anything from half-carat diamonds to whole apartment blocks.

WrapIt has found that some customers prefer their gifts to be wrapped in the smallest possible packages, whereas others prefer large packages that make their gifts seem larger than they really are.

The company needs a program that computes the smallest and largest rectangular package into which a gift can be "tightly" wrapped. Since this is a difficult problem, the company will initially settle for a two-dimensional version of the program.

Each gift is approximated as a simple polygon, and all packages are represented by rectangles. A gift is said to "fit tightly" in a package if the gift touches all four sides of the package. The figure below shows how a triangular gift might fit tightly in two packages of different sizes. For each gift, your program must compute the areas of the smallest and largest packages into which the gift can fit tightly.

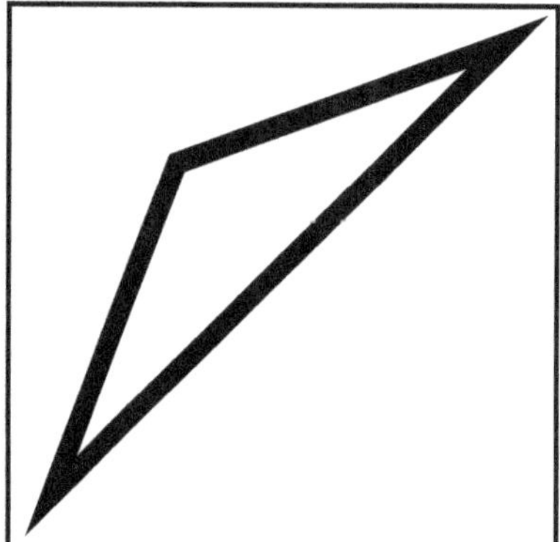

Input

The input contains several gift descriptions. Each description begins with a line containing an integer n ($3 \leq n \leq 100$), which is the number of vertices in the polygon that represents the gift. The following n lines contain pairs of integers that represent the coordinates of the polygon vertices, in clockwise order. Each polygon will have a non-zero area and will not intersect itself.

The input is terminated by a line containing the integer 0.

Output

For each gift, first print the number of the gift. Then on separate lines, print the minimum and maximum areas of the packages into which the gift fits tightly, using the format in the sample output. Print a blank line after each test case.

The computed areas should be exact to three digits to the right of the decimal point.

Sample Input

```
3
-3 5
7 9
17 5
4
10 10
10 20
20 20
20 10
0
```

Sample Output

```
Gift 1
Minimum area = 80.000
Maximum area = 200.000

Gift 2
Minimum area = 100.000
Maximum area = 200.000
```

E Internet Bandwidth

On the Internet, machines (nodes) are richly interconnected, and many paths may exist between a given pair of nodes. The total message-carrying capacity (bandwidth) between two given nodes is the maximal amount of data per unit time that can be transmitted from one node to the other. Using a technique called packet switching, this data can be transmitted along several paths at the same time.

For example, the following figure shows a network with four nodes (shown as circles), with a total of five connections among them. Every connection is labeled with a bandwidth that represents its data-carrying capacity per unit time.

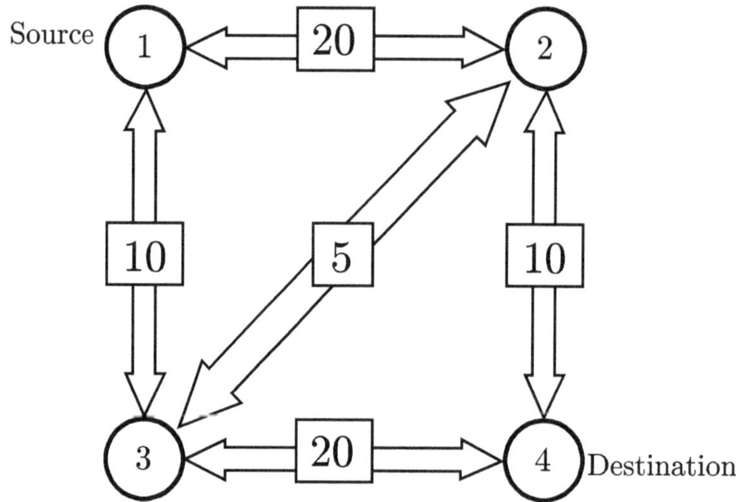

In our example, the bandwidth between node 1 and node 4 is 25, which might be thought of as the sum of the bandwidths 10 along the path 1-2-4, 10 along the path 1-3-4, and 5 along the path 1-2-3-4. No other combination of paths between nodes 1 and 4 provides a larger bandwidth.

You must write a program that computes the bandwidth between two given nodes in a network, given the individual bandwidths of all the connections in the network. In this problem, assume that the bandwidth of a connection is always the same in both directions (which is not necessarily true in the real world).

Input

The input file contains descriptions of several networks. Every description starts with a line containing a single integer n ($2 \leq n \leq 100$), which is the number of nodes in the network. The nodes are numbered from 1 to n. The next line contains three numbers s, t, and c. The numbers s and t are the source and destination nodes, and the number c is the total number of connections in the network. Following this are c lines describing the connections. Each of these lines contains three integers: the first two are the numbers of the connected nodes, and the third number is the bandwidth of the connection. The bandwidth is a non-negative number not greater than 1000.

There might be more than one connection between a pair of nodes, but a node cannot be connected to itself. All connections are bi-directional, i.e. data can be transmitted in both directions along a connection, but the sum of the amount of data transmitted in both directions must be less than the bandwidth.

A line containing the number 0 follows the last network description, and terminates the input.

Output

For each network description, first print the number of the network. Then print the total bandwidth between the source node s and the destination node t, following the format of the sample output. Print a blank line after each test case.

Sample Input

```
4
1 4 5
1 2 20
1 3 10
2 3 5
2 4 10
3 4 20
0
```

Sample Output

```
Network 1
The bandwidth is 25.
```

F Page Hopping

It was recently reported that, on the average, only 19 clicks are necessary to move from any page on the World Wide Web to any other page. That is, if the pages on the web are viewed as nodes in a graph, then the average path length between arbitrary pairs of nodes in the graph is 19.

Given a graph in which all nodes can be reached from any starting point, your job is to find the average shortest path length between arbitrary pairs of nodes. For example, consider the following graph. Note that links are shown as directed edges, since a link from page a to page b does not imply a link from page b to page a.

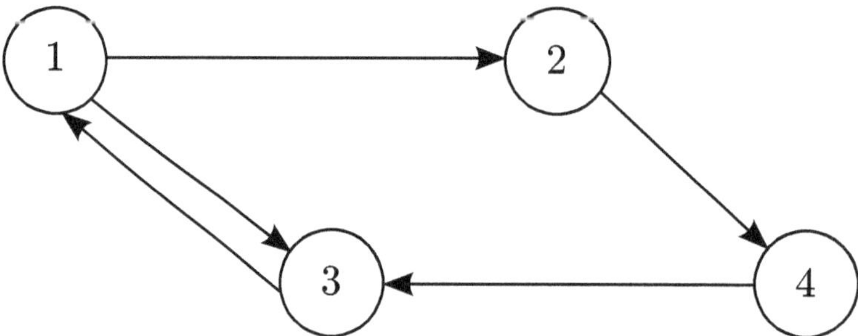

The length of the shortest path from node 1 to nodes 2, 3, and 4 is 1,1, and 2 respectively. From node 2 to nodes 1, 3 and 4, the shortest paths have lengths of 3, 2, and 1. From node 3 to nodes 1, 2, and 4, the shortest paths have lengths of 1, 2, and 3. Finally, from node 4 to nodes 1, 2, and 3 the shortest paths have lengths of 2, 3, and 1. The sum of these path lengths is $1 + 1 + 2 + 3 + 2 + 1 + 1 + 2 + 3 + 2 + 3 + 1 = 22$. Since there are 12 possible pairs of nodes to consider, we obtain an average path length of $22/12$, or 1.833 (accurate to three fractional digits).

Input

The input data will contain multiple test cases. Each test case will consist of an arbitrary number of pairs of integers, a and b, each representing a link from a page numbered a to a page numbered b. Page numbers will always be in the range 1 to 100. The input for each test case will be terminated with a pair of zeroes, which are not to be treated as page numbers. An additional pair of zeroes will follow the last test case, effectively representing a test case with no links, which is not to be processed. The graph will not include self-referential links (that is, there will be no direct link from a node to itself), and at least one path will exist from each node in the graph to every other node in the graph.

Output

For each test case, determine the average shortest path length between every pair of nodes, accurate to three fractional digits. Display this length and the test case identifier (they're numbered sequentially starting with 1) in a form similar to that shown in the sample output below.

Sample Input

```
1 2   2 4   1 3   3 1   4 3   0 0
1 2   1 4   4 2   2 7   7 1   0 0
0 0
```

Sample Output

```
Case 1: average length between pages = 1.833 clicks
Case 2: average length between pages = 1.750 clicks
```

G Queue and A

The customer support group of Contest.com receives and responds to requests for technical support via e-mail. Requests may begin arriving when the office opens at 8:00 a.m. and all requests must be serviced by the end of the day.

As requests are received, they are classified according to a predetermined list of topics. Each member of the support staff has responsibility for one or more of these topics and each topic has one or more support personnel assigned to it. Because staff members have different levels of expertise, each staff member has a prioritized list of topics that he or she can handle. Staff personnel are not permitted to handle requests outside their specified areas.

As staff members become available, they select from the pool of waiting requests according to their priority list of topics. All requests arriving at time t are available for allocation at time t. If two staff members are simultaneously available, scheduling preference is given to the one whose most recent job was scheduled earliest. If there is still a tie, scheduling preference is given to the person whose id number appears earlier in the input list of staff people. At the opening of business, all personnel are available to handle requests.

You have been asked to perform a preliminary analysis of the technical support environment based on a number of different scenarios. For each scenario, information will be given about the mix of requests and the division of labor among the staff. For each topic, you will given the average number of requests per day for that topic, the average elapsed time before the first of these requests is received, the average time between requests for this topic, and the average time needed to service the request. All times are given in minutes. You will also be given a list of support personnel and, for each one, a list of the topics for which he or she has responsibility. (Since data are based on estimates, factors such as coffee breaks, lunch, computer failures, etc., can be ignored.)

Input

Input consists of a number of scenarios.

Each scenario begins with the number of request topics, a positive integer no larger than 20. This is followed by a description of each topic. Each description consists of five integer values: a unique topic identifier, the number of requests for that topic, the elapsed time before the first request for that topic is received, the time needed to service a request, and the time between successive requests. All but the third of these values are positive integers; the elapsed time until the first request could be zero. Following this, the number of personnel is given. This will be a positive integer not to exceed 5. Finally, a description of each person is given in the form of three or more positive integer values: a unique identifying number for the person, the number of topics covered by this person, and a list of the topic identifiers arranged from highest priority to lowest priority for that person.

A zero follows the last scenario.

Output

For each scenario, the output consists of the scenario number followed by the statement,

`All requests are serviced within` m `minutes.`

where m is the number of minutes from the start of the business day until the last request is serviced.

Sample Input

```
3
128 20 0 5 10
134 25 5 6 7
153 30 10 4 5
4
10 2 128 134
11 1 134
12 2 128 153
13 1 153
0
```

Sample Output

```
Scenario 1: All requests are serviced within 195 minutes.
```

H   Stopper Stumper

Stephen Stepper's Supply Store sells stoppersrubber corks for sealing jars, bottles, and other containers that have round openings. A stopper is shaped like two concentric cylinders, each of height 1.5 centimeters, glued together. Figure 1 shows two stoppers of different sizes.

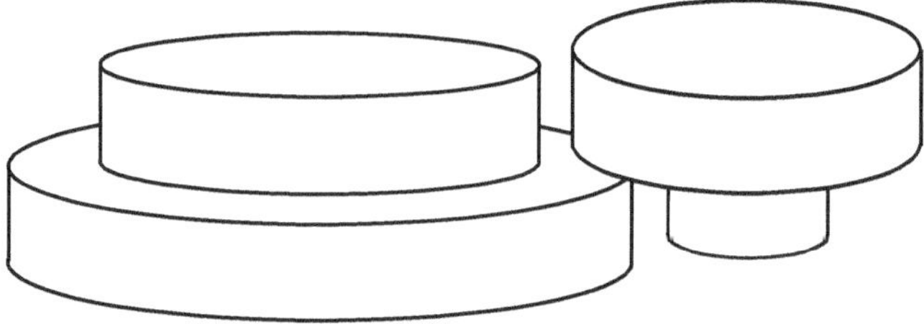

Figure 1. Two stoppers

When Stephen packages an order to be shipped by mail, he tries to use space efficiently to conserve packing material. Since stoppers are the smallest items in his store, he packs them last, and finds that he must often pack several stoppers into small triangular gaps at the top of the shipping carton. Stoppers must inserted in one of the two orientations shown in Figure 1. The triangular spaces are only 3 cm deep, so stoppers cannot be placed on top of one another; however, the large cylinder of one stopper is permitted to overlap the large cylinder of another inverted stopper as shown in Figures 1 and 2. Your job is to help Stephen decide what collections of stoppers will fit into a triangular space.

For instance, suppose a triangular space with side lengths 8, 7, and 10 were available, and we had to fit three stoppers in it with inside/outside diameters of 2cm/3cm, 1.5cm/3cm, and 1cm/3cm. One way to pack them is as shown in Figure 2. (The dotted circle indicates that the smaller cylinder of one of the stoppers is underneath the larger one.) The only packing Stephen will consider has the larger cylinder of each stopper touching two sides of the triangle, with no two larger cylinders touching the same pair of sides.

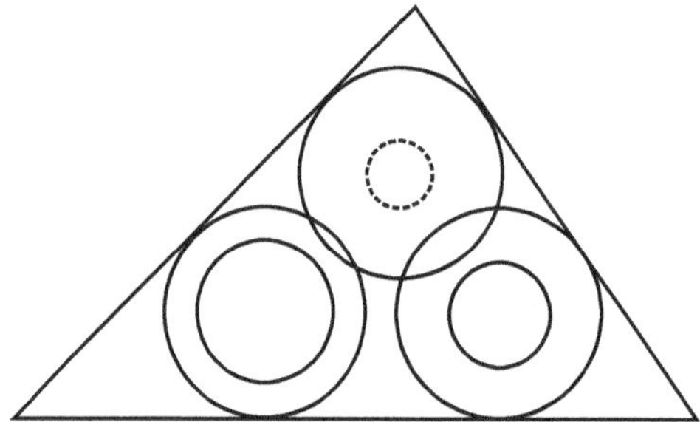

Figure 2: Three stoppers packed inside a triangle

Input

The input consists of a sequence of triangle specifications and descriptions of three stoppers for each triangle. Each triangular space is specified by three positive integers representing the lengths of the three sides; only valid triangles will appear in the input. A pair of positive real numbers represents each stopper. The first number in the pair represents the diameter of the smaller cylinder, and the second represents the diameter of the larger cylinder. The final line of the input file contains zeros for all the data values.

Output

For each triangle, print a line identifying its sequence number in the input data and a line indicating whether or not the stoppers can be packed into the triangular space. Separate the output for each triangle with a blank line. Do not print anything for the final line of zeros in the input. Imitate the sample output as closely as possible.

Sample Input

```
 6  6  6    0.5  1.0    0.3  2.0    0.4  1.0
10 10 10    2.0  3.0    1.0  2.0    1.5  3.5
20  6 20    3.0  4.5    0.5  1.0    4.0  5.0
 8  7 10    2.0  3.0    1.5  3.0    1.0  3.0
 8  7 10    2.0  3.0    2.5  3.0    2.0  3.0
 0  0  0    0.0  0.0    0.0  0.0    0.0  0.0
```

Sample Output

```
Triangle number 1:
All three stoppers will fit in the triangular space

Triangle number 2:
All three stoppers will fit in the triangular space

Triangle number 3:
Stoppers will not fit in the triangular space

Triangle number 4:
All three stoppers will fit in the triangular space

Triangle number 5:
Stoppers will not fit in the triangular space
```

WORLD FINALS 2001

VANCOUVER, CANADA

World Champion

ST. PETERSBURG STATE UNIVERSITY

Nikolai Durov
Andrei Lopatine
Victor Petrov

Director of Judging
Dick Rinewalt   *Texas Christian University*

Chief Judge
Jo Perry   *North Carolina State University*

Judges
Don Chamberlin   *IBM Almaden Research Center*
David Elizandro   *Tennessee Tech University*
Peter Kluit   *Delft University of Technology*
Robert Roos   *Allegheny College*
Matthias Ruhl   *MIT*
Laurie White   *Mercer University*
Stanley Wileman, Jr.   *University of Nebraska at Omaha*

CLI Live Archive problem numbers

2232	A	Airport Configuration
2233	B	Say Cheese
2234	C	Crossword Puzzle
2235	D	Can't Cut Down the Forest for the Trees
2236	E	The Geoduck GUI
2237	F	A Major Problem
2238	G	Fixed Partition Memory Management
2239	H	Professor Monotonic's Networks
2240	I	A Vexing Problem

A   Airport Configuration

ACM Airlines is a regional airline with von Neumann Airport as its home port. For many passengers, von Neumann Airport is not the start of their trip, nor their final destination, so many transfer passengers pass through the airport.

The von Neumann Airport has a corridor layout. Arrival gates are located, equally spaced, at the north side of the corridor. Departure gates are at the south side of the corridor, equally spaced as well. The distance between two adjacent gates equals the width of the corridor. Each arrival gate is assigned to exactly one city, and the same holds for the departure gates. Passengers arrive at the arrival gate assigned to their city of origin and exit the terminal or proceed to a connecting flight at a gate assigned to their destination city. For this problem, only passengers with connecting flights are considered.

Transferring passengers generate a lot of traffic in the corridor. The average number of people traveling between cities is known beforehand. Using this information, it should be possible to reduce the traffic. If transfers from city Cx to city Cy occur very frequently, it may help to locate the gates assigned to these cities near or even directly opposite each other.

Due to the presence of shops and gardens it is not possible to cross the corridor diagonally, so the distance between arriving gate G1 and departing gate G3 (see diagram) equals $1 + 2 = 3$.

You must assess total traffic load for several different configurations. The traffic load between an origin and destination gate is defined as the number of origin to destination passengers multiplied by the distance between the arriving and departing gate. The total traffic load is the sum of the traffic loads for all origin-destination pairs.

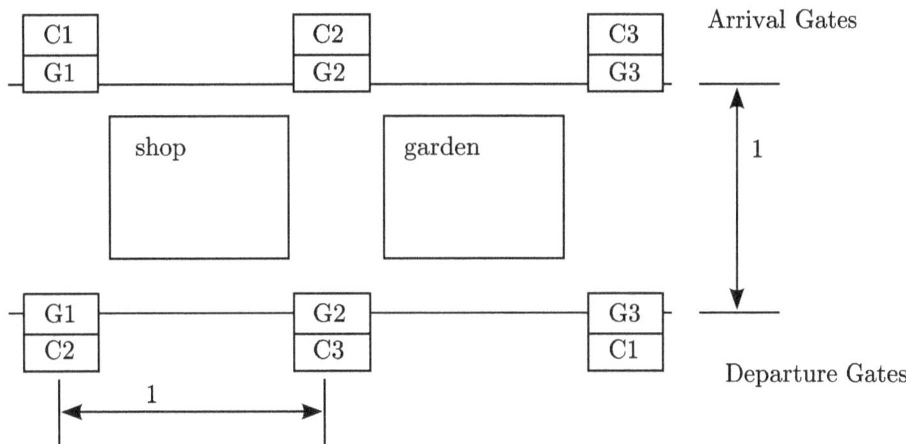

Input

The input file contains several test cases. The last test case in the input file is followed by a line containing the number 0.

Each test case has two parts: first the traffic data, then the configuration section.

The traffic data starts with an integer N $(1 < N < 25)$, representing the number of cities. The following N lines each represent traffic data for one city. Each line with traffic data begins with an integer in the range $1..N$ identifying the city of origin. This is followed by k pairs of integers, one pair for every destination city. Each pair identifies the destination city and the number of passengers (at most 500) traveling from the city of origin to this destination city.

The configuration section consists of one or more (at most 20) configurations and ends with a line containing the number 0.

A configuration consists of 3 lines. The first line contains a positive number identifying the configuration. The next line contains a permutation of the cities, as they are assigned to the arrival gates: the first number represents the city assigned to the first gate, and so on. The next line in the same way represents the cities as they are assigned to the departure gates.

Output

For each test case, the output contains a table presenting the configuration numbers and total traffic load, in ascending order of traffic load. If two configurations have the same traffic load, the one with the lowest configuration number should go first. Follow the output format shown in the sample below.

Sample Input

```
3
1   2   2 10   3 15
2   1   3 10
3   2   1 12   2 20
1
1 2 3
2 3 1
2
2 3 1
3 2 1
0
2
1   1   2 100
2   1   1 200
1
1 2
1 2
2
1 2
2 1
0
0
```

Sample Output

```
Configuration  Load
      2          119
      1          122
Configuration  Load
      2          300
      1          600
```

B Say Cheese

Once upon a time, in a giant piece of cheese, there lived a cheese mite named Amelia Cheese Mite. Amelia should have been truly happy because she was surrounded by more delicious cheese than she could ever eat. Nevertheless, she felt that something was missing from her life.

One morning, her dreams about cheese were interrupted by a noise she had never heard before. But she immediately realized what it was - the sound of a male cheese mite, gnawing in the same piece of cheese! (Determining the gender of a cheese mite just by the sound of its gnawing is by no means easy, but all cheese mites can do it. That's because their parents could.)

Nothing could stop Amelia now. She had to meet that other mite as soon as possible. Therefore she had to find the fastest way to get to the other mite. Amelia can gnaw through one millimeter of cheese in ten seconds. But it turns out that the direct way to the other mite might not be the fastest one. The cheese that Amelia lives in is full of holes. These holes, which are bubbles of air trapped in the cheese, are spherical for the most part. But occasionally these spherical holes overlap, creating compound holes of all kinds of shapes. Passing through a hole in the cheese takes Amelia essentially zero time, since she can fly from one end to the other instantly. So it might be useful to travel through holes to get to the other mite quickly.

For this problem, you have to write a program that, given the locations of both mites and the holes in the cheese, determines the minimal time it takes Amelia to reach the other mite. For the purposes of this problem, you can assume that the cheese is infinitely large. This is because the cheese is so large that it never pays for Amelia to leave the cheese to reach the other mite (especially since cheese-mite eaters might eat her). You can also assume that the other mite is eagerly anticipating Amelia's arrival and will not move while Amelia is underway.

Input

The input file contains descriptions of several cheese mite test cases. Each test case starts with a line containing a single integer n ($0 \leq n \leq 100$), the number of holes in the cheese. This is followed by n lines containing four integers x_i, y_i, z_i, r_i each. These describe the centers (x_i, y_i, z_i) and radii r_i ($r_i > 0$) of the holes. All values here (and in the following) are given in millimeters.

The description concludes with two lines containing three integers each. The first line contains the values x_A, y_A, z_A, giving Amelia's position in the cheese, the second line containing x_O, y_O, z_O, gives the position of the other mite.

The input file is terminated by a line containing the number -1.

Output

For each test case, print one line of output, following the format of the sample output. First print the number of the test case (starting with 1). Then print the minimum time in seconds it takes Amelia to reach the other mite, rounded to the closest integer. The input will be such that the rounding is unambiguous.

Sample Input

```
1
20 20 20 1
0 0 0
0 0 10
1
5 0 0 4
0 0 0
10 0 0
-1
```

Sample Output

```
Cheese 1: Travel time = 100 sec
Cheese 2: Travel time = 20 sec
```

C   Crossword Puzzle

Your brilliant but absent-minded uncle believes he has solved a difficult crossword puzzle but has misplaced the solution. He needs your help to reconstruct the solution from a list that contains all the words in the solution, plus one extra word that is not part of the solution. Your program must solve the puzzle and print the extra word.

The crossword puzzle is represented by a grid with ten squares on each side. Figure 1 shows the top left corner of a puzzle. The puzzle has a certain number of "slots" where a word can be placed. Each slot is represented by the row and column number of the square where the slot begins, and the direction in which the slot extends from its initial square ("across" or "down"). The length of each slot is not specified. The puzzle has a list of candidate words, all but one of which is used in solving the puzzle.

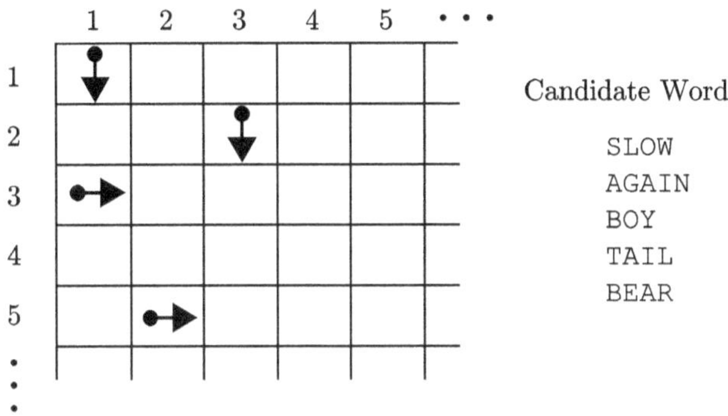

Figure 1: Corner of Example Puzzle

Figure 2 shows a solution to the example puzzle in Figure 1. In a valid solution, each slot is filled with a candidate word. Every maximal horizontal or vertical sequence of two or more letters must be a word in the input. Any candidate word can be used in any slot as long as the word fits in the puzzle and does not conflict with any other word. In the example, all the candidate words are used except the word "BOY".

Figure 2: Example Solution

Input

The input data consist of one or more test cases each describing a puzzle trial. The first input line in each test case contains a positive integer N that represents the number of slots in the puzzle. This line is followed by N lines, each containing the row number and column number of a square where a slot begins, followed by the letter 'A' (if the slot is "Across") or 'D' (if the slot is "Down"). The next $N + 1$ input lines contain candidate words that can be used in the puzzle solution.

The final test case is followed by a line containing the number zero.

Output

For each trial, print the trial number followed by the word that is not used in the puzzle solution, using the format in the example output. Observe the following rules:

1. Print a blank line after each trial.

2. If your uncle has made a mistake and the puzzle has no solution using the given words, print the word "Impossible". For example, if Trial 2 has no solution, you should print "Trial 2: Impossible".

3. If the puzzle can be solved in more than one way, print each word that can be omitted from a valid solution. The words can be printed in any order but each word must be printed only once. For example, if Trial 3 has a solution that omits the word DOG and two solutions that omit the word CAT, you should print "Trial 3: DOG CAT" or "Trial 3: CAT DOG".

Sample Input

```
4
1    1    D
2    3    D
3    1    A
5    2    A
SLOW
AGAIN
BOY
TAIL
BEAR
0
```

Sample Output

```
Trial 1: BOY
```

D Can't Cut Down the Forest for the Trees

Once upon a time, in a country far away, there was a king who owned a forest of valuable trees. One day, to deal with a cash flow problem, the king decided to cut down and sell some of his trees. He asked his wizard to find the largest number of trees that could be safely cut down.

All the king's trees stood within a rectangular fence, to protect them from thieves and vandals. Cutting down the trees was difficult, since each tree needed room to fall without hitting and damaging other trees or the fence. Each tree could be trimmed of branches before it was cut. For simplicity, the wizard assumed that when each tree was cut down, it would occupy a rectangular space on the ground, as shown below. One of the sides of the rectangle is a diameter of the original base of the tree. The other dimension of the rectangle is equal to the height of the tree.

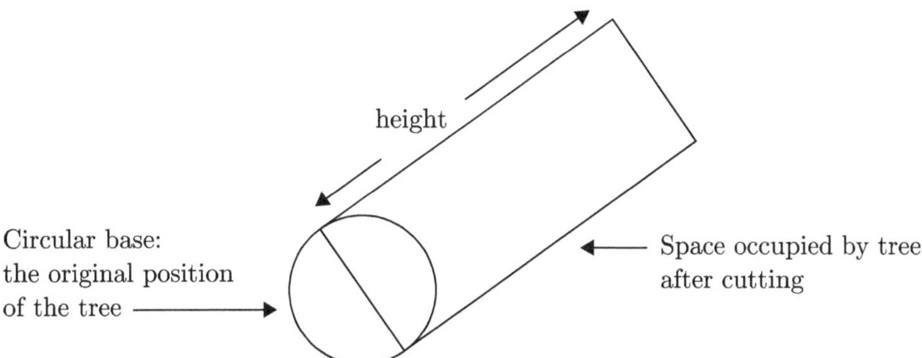

Many of the king's trees were located near other trees (that being one of the tell-tale signs of a forest.) The wizard needed to find the maximum number of trees that could be cut down, one after another, in such a way that no fallen tree would touch any other tree or the fence. As soon as each tree falls, it is cut into pieces and carried away so it does not interfere with the next tree to be cut.

Input

The input consists of several test cases each describing a forest. The first line of each description contains five integers, $xmin$, $ymin$, $xmax$, $ymax$, and n. The first four numbers represent the minimal and maximal coordinates of the fence in the x- and y-directions ($xmin < xmax, ymin < ymax$). The fence is rectangular and its sides are parallel to the coordinate axes. The fifth number n represents the number of trees in the forest ($1 \le n \le 100$).

The next n lines describe the positions and dimensions of the n trees. Each line contains four integers, x_i, y_i, d_i, and h_i, representing the position of the tree's center (x_i, y_i), its base diameter d_i, and its height h_i. No tree bases touch each other, and all the trees are entirely inside the fence, not touching the fence at all.

The input is terminated by a test case with $xmin = ymin = xmax = ymax = n = 0$. This test case should not be processed.

Output

For each test case, first print its number. Then print the maximum number of trees that can be cut down, one after another, such that no fallen tree touches any other tree or the fence. Follow the format in the sample output given below. Print a blank line after each test case.

Sample Input

```
0  0  10  10  3
3  3  2  10
5  5  3  1
2  8  3  9
0  0  0  0  0
```

Sample Output

```
Forest 1
2 tree(s) can be cut
```

E The Geoduck GUI

Researchers at the Association for Computational Marinelife in Vancouver have been working for several years to harness various forms of aquatic life with the goal of constructing an underwater computer that can be seen from outer space. The current research focus is a breed of clam known as the geoduck (pronounced "GOOEY duck"), scientific name *Panope abrupta*. Geoducks can be as heavy as ten pounds and as long as 1 meter with their siphons or "necks" fully extended. Because of their life expectancy (up to 150 years), they seem to be good agents for manipulating a large-scale oceanic graphical user interface-hence, the "geoduck GUI" project.

Current research examines pairs of trained geoducks each starting in a distinct corner of a rectangular grid. They crawl across the grid spreading luminescent chemicals from containers attached to their shells. Geoducks are trained to move one grid unit horizontally or vertically per time unit to approximate a direction vector (each geoduck has a unique vector). If a move takes a geoduck off the edge of the grid, a trained dolphin immediately transports it to the cell on the opposite edge of the grid, effectively providing a "wraparound" mechanism. The entry point in the opposite edge cell is horizontally or vertically aligned with the exit point of the cell departed and the geoduck trajectory is maintained. Geoduck moves are synchronized; however, a geoduck halts when it enters a cell that it has previously visited. If two geoducks move into the same cell at the same time, they halt in that cell. If two geoducks attempt to move into each other's cells at the same time, then they halt. A geoduck is initially placed at a grid corner so that its direction vector points "in" to the grid (e.g., if the x-component is positive and the y-component is negative, the starting position is at the minimum x-value and the maximum y-value in the grid).

Both geoducks begin at time t=1 in their respective (distinct) starting corners. A geoduck follows its vector as if the vector starting point were anchored to the center of geoduck's initial cell position in the grid. It always moves to the next cell that is divided into regions by the vector (or its extension), with one exception. If the vector passes through a corner of the grid, the geoduck moves horizontally and then vertically to reach the next cell divided by the vector. Figure 1 shows several geoduck paths. The numbers in the cells indicate elapsed time. Grid cells are numbered from the lower left starting at zero in both the x and y directions. If the two geoducks in Figure 1 start at the same time in the same 6 by 5 grid, they each halt after 5 time units with a total of 10 cells illuminated.

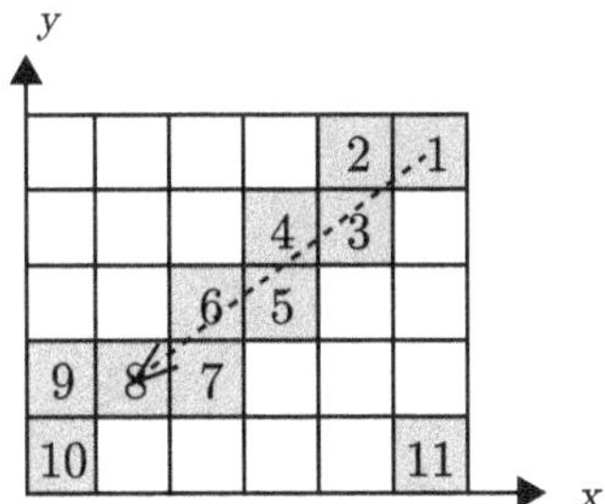

A geoduck with vector (-4,-3) moving in a 6 by 5 grid starting at cell (5,4). At step 12 it halts, since it revisits (5,4).

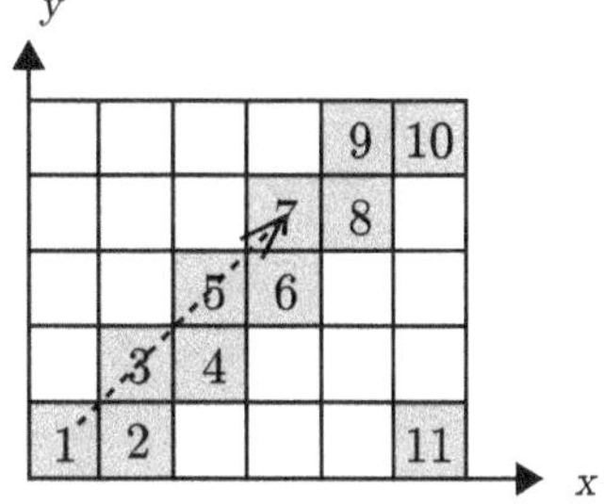

A geoduck with vector (1,1) moving in a 6 by 5 grid starting at cell (0,0). At time step 12 it halts, since it revisits (0,0).

Figure 1: Sample geoduck paths

You must write a program to select pairs of geoducks that illuminate the maximum number of grid cells on the screen in the least amount of time. Repeat your calculations for various grid sizes and comb inations of geoducks.

Input

Input consists of a sequence of test cases each beginning with a line containing two integers m and n, $1 \leq m,n \leq 50$, where m and n are not both 1. These are x and y dimensions of the grid. The second line of each test case contains an integer k, $2 \leq k \leq 10$, representing the number of geoducks. At least one pair of geoducks will have distinct starting points. The next k lines each contain a pair of non-zero integers representing the x and y components of the k geoduck direction vectors.

The final test case is followed by two zeros.

Output

For each test case, print the test case number, the maximum number of illuminated cells, the minimum number of time units required to illuminate that number of cells, and the sequence numbers of each pair of geoducks that achieve these values. Print all pairs of geoducks that achieve maximum illumination in minimum time. The order of printing does not matter; however, do not print any pair twice for the same test case. Imitate the sample output shown below.

Sample Input

```
6 5
3
-4 3
1 1
1 -1
0 0
```

Sample Output

```
Case 1   Cells Illuminated: 10   Minimum Time: 5
   Geoduck IDs:  1  2
   Geoduck IDs:  1  3
```

F   A Major Problem

In western music, the 12 notes used in musical notation are identified with the capital letters A through G, possibly followed by a sharp '#' or flat 'b' character, and are arranged cyclically as shown below. A slash is used to identify alternate notations of the same note.

C/B# C#/Db D D#/Eb E/Fb F/E# F#/Gb G G#/Ab A A#/Bb B/Cb C/B# ...

Any two adjacent notes in the above list are known as a semitone. Any two notes that have exactly one note separating them in the above list are known as a tone. A major scale is composed of eight notes; it begins on one of the above notes and follows the progression tone-tone-semitone-tone-tone-tone-semitone. For example, the major scales starting on C and Db, respectively, are made up of the following notes:

C D E F G A B C
Db Eb F Gb Ab Bb C Db

The following rules also apply to major scales:

1. The scale will contain each letter from A to G once and only once, with the exception of the first letter of the scale, which is repeated as the last letter of the scale.

2. The scale may not contain a combination of both flat and sharp notes.

The note that begins a major scale is referred to as the key of the scale. For example, the scales above are the scales for the major keys of C and Db, respectively. Transposing notes from one scale to another is a simple matter of replacing a note in one scale with the note in the corresponding position of another scale. For example, the note F in the major key of C would transpose to the note Gb in the major key of Db since both notes occupy the same position in their respective scales.

You must write a program to transpose notes from one major scale to another.

Input

The input consists of multiple test cases, with one test case per line. Each line starts with a source key, followed by a target key, and then followed by a list of notes to be transposed from the major scale of the source key to the major scale of the target key. Each list is terminated by a single asterisk character. All notes on a line and the terminating asterisk are delimited by a single space.

The final line of the input contains only a single asterisk which is not to be processed as a test case.

Output

Each test case produces one or more lines of output. If the source and target keys are valid, then the first output line for each input line should read "`Transposing from X to Y:`" where X is the source key and Y is the target key. If either the source or target key is not valid a line which reads "`Key of X/Y is not a valid major key`", where X/Y is the key that is not valid, should be output and the remainder of the input for that line skipped. If both the source and target key are not valid, report only the source key.

For test cases that contain valid source and target keys, the first output line will be followed by one output line for each note to be transposed. If the note is a valid note in the major scale of the source key then the output line should read "M `transposes to` N" where M is the note in the source key and N is the corresponding note in the target key. If the input note is not a valid note in the major scale of the source key then the output line should read "M `is not a valid note in the X major scale`" where M is the input note and X is the source key. For either valid or non-valid notes, the output line should be indented in a consistent manner.

The output data for each input line should be delimited by a single blank line. The format of your output should be similar to the output shown below.

Sample Input

```
C Db F *
Db C Gb *
C B# A B *
C D A A# B Bb C *
A# Bb C *
*
```

Sample Output

```
Transposing from C to Db:
  F transposes to Gb

Transposing from Db to C:
  Gb transposes to F

Key of B# is not a valid major key

Transposing from C to D:
  A transposes to B
  A# is not a valid note in the C major scale
  B transposes to C#
  Bb is not a valid note in the C major scale
  C transposes to D

Key of A# is not a valid major key
```

G   Fixed Partition Memory Management

A technique used in early multiprogramming operating systems involved partitioning the available primary memory into a number of regions with each region having a fixed size, different regions potentially having different sizes. The sum of the sizes of all regions equals the size of the primary memory.

Given a set of programs, it was the task of the operating system to assign the programs to different memory regions, so that they could be executed concurrently. This was made difficult due to the fact that the execution time of a program might depend on the amount of memory available to it. Every program has a minimum space requirement, but if it is assigned to a larger memory region its execution time might increase or decrease.

In this program, you have to determine optimal assignments of programs to memory regions. Your program is given the sizes of the memory regions available for the execution of programs, and for each program a description of how its running time depends on the amount of memory available to it. Your program has to find the execution schedule of the programs that minimizes the average turnaround time for the programs. An execution schedule is an assignment of programs to memory regions and times, such that no two programs use the same memory region at the same time, and no program is assigned to a memory region of size less than its minimum memory requirement. The turnaround time of the program is the difference between the time when the program was submitted for execution (which is time zero for all programs in this problem), and the time that the program completes execution.

Input

The input data will contain multiple test cases. Each test case begins with a line containing a pair of integers m and n. The number m specifies the number of regions into which primary memory has been partitioned ($1 \leq m \leq 10$), and n specifies the number of programs to be executed ($1 \leq n \leq 50$).

The next line contains m positive integers giving the sizes of the m memory regions. Following this are n lines, describing the time-space tradeoffs for each of the n programs. Each line starts with a positive integer k ($k \leq 10$), followed by k pairs of positive integers $s_1, t_1, s_2, t_2, \ldots, s_k, t_k$, that satisfy $s_i < s_{i+1}$ for $1 \leq i < k$. The minimum space requirement of the program is s_1, i.e. it cannot run in a partition of size less than this number. If the program runs in a memory partition of size s, where $s_i \leq s < s_{i+1}$ for some i, then its execution time will be t_i. Finally, if the programs runs in a memory partition of size s_k or more, then its execution time will be t_k.

A pair of zeroes will follow the input for the last test case.

You may assume that each program will execute in exactly the time specified for the given region size, regardless of the number of other programs in the system. No program will have a memory requirement larger than that of the largest memory region.

Output

For each test case, first display the case number (starting with 1 and increasing sequentially). Then print the minimum average turnaround time for the set of programs with two digits to the right of the decimal point. Follow this by the description of an execution schedule that achieves this average turnaround time. Display one line for each program, in the order they were given in the input, that identifies the program number, the region in which it was executed (numbered in the order given in the input), the time when the program started execution, and the time when the program completed execution. Follow the format shown in the sample output, and print a blank line after each test case.

If there are multiple program orderings or assignments to memory regions that yield the same minimum average turnaround time, give one of the schedules with the minimum average turnaround time.

Sample Input

```
2 4
40 60
1 35 4
1 20 3
1 40 10
1 60 7
3 5
10 20 30
2 10 50 12 30
2 10 100 20 25
1 25 19
1 19 41
2 10 18 30 42
0 0
```

Sample Output

```
Case 1
Average turnaround time = 7.75
Program 1 runs in region 1 from 0 to 4
Program 2 runs in region 2 from 0 to 3
Program 3 runs in region 1 from 4 to 14
Program 4 runs in region 2 from 3 to 10

Case 2
Average turnaround time = 35.40
Program 1 runs in region 2 from 25 to 55
Program 2 runs in region 2 from 0 to 25
Program 3 runs in region 3 from 0 to 19
Program 4 runs in region 3 from 19 to 60
Program 5 runs in region 1 from 0 to 18
```

H Professor Monotonic's Networks

Professor Monotonic has been experimenting with comparison networks, each of which includes a number of two-input, two-output comparators. A comparator, as illustrated below, will compare the values on its inputs, i_1 and i_2, and place them on the outputs, o_1 and o_2, so that $o_1 \leq o_2$ regardless of the relationship between the input values.

A comparison network has n inputs $a_1, a_2, \ldots, a_n$ and n outputs $b_1, b_2, \ldots, b_n$. Each of the two inputs to a comparator is either connected to one of the network's n inputs or connected to the output of another comparator. Each of the two outputs from a comparator is either connected to one of the network's n outputs or is connected to the input of another comparator. A graph of the interconnections of comparators must be acyclic. The illustration below shows a comparison network with four inputs, four outputs, and five comparators.

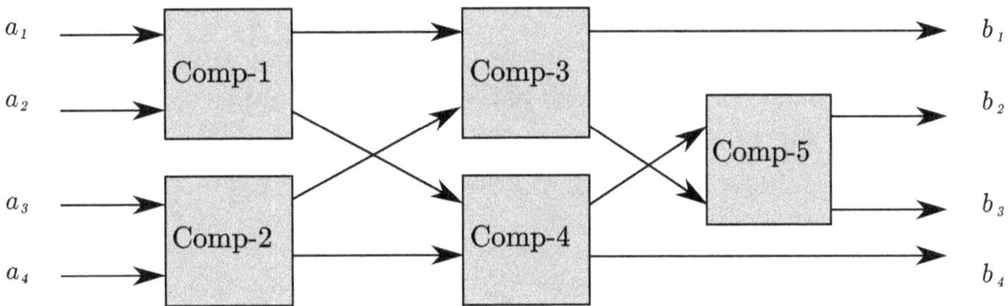

In operation, the network's inputs are applied and the comparators perform their functions. Of course a comparator cannot operate until both of its inputs are available. Assuming a comparator requires one unit of time to operate, this sample network will require three units of time to produce its outputs. Comp-1 and Comp-2 operate in parallel, as do Comp-3 and Comp-4. Comp-5 cannot operate until Comp-3 and Comp-4 have comp leted their work.

Professor Monotonic needs help in determining which proposed comparison networks are also sorting networks, and how long they will take to perform their task. A sorting network is a comparison network for which the outputs are monotonically increasing regardless of the input values. The example above is a sorting network, since for all possible input values the output values will have the relation $b_1 \leq b_2 \leq b_3 \leq b_4$.

Input

The professor will provide a description of each comparison network to be examined. Each description will begin with a line containing values for n (the number of inputs) and k (the number of comparators). These values satisfy $1 \leq n \leq 12$ and $0 \leq k \leq 150$. This is followed by zero or more non-empty lines, each containing at most 15 pairs of comparator inputs. The source of the input to each comparator is given by a pair of integers i and j. Each of these specifies either the subscript of a network input that is input to the comparator (that is, a_i or a_j), or the corresponding output of a preceding comparator.

The outputs of a comparator are numbered the same as its inputs (in other words, if the comparator's inputs are i and j, the corresponding outputs are also labeled i and j). The order in which these pairs appear is significant, and affects the order in which the comparators operate. If two pairs contain an integer in common, the order of the corresponding comparators in the network is determined by the order of the pairs in the list. For example, consider the input data for the example shown:

```
4  5
1  2    3  4    1  3
2  4    2  3
```

This indicates there will be four input values and five comparators in the network. The first comparator (Comp-1) will receive its input values from network inputs a_1 and a_2. The second comp arator (Comp-2) will receive its input values from network inputs a_3 and a_4. The third comparator (Comp-3) will receive its first input from the first output of Comp-1, and will receive its second input from the first output of Comp-2. Similarly, the fourth comparator (Comp-4) will receive its first input from the second output of Comp-1, and will receive its second input from the second output of Comp-2. Finally, the fifth comparator (Comp-5) will receive its first input from the first output of Comp-4, and will receive its second input from the second output of Comp-3. The outputs $b_1, b_2, \ldots, b_n$ are taken from the first output of Comp-3, the first output of Comp-5, the second output of Comp-5, and the second output of Comp-4, respectively.

A pair of zeros will follow the input data for the last network.

Output

For each input case, display the case number (cases are numbered sequentially starting with 1), an indication of whether the network is a sorting network or not, and the number of time units required for the network to operate (regardless of whether it is a sorting network or not).

Sample Input

```
4  5
1  2    3  4    1  3
2  4    2  3
8  0
3  3
1  2    2  3    1  2
0  0
```

Sample Output

```
Case 1 is a sorting network and operates in 3 time units.
Case 2 is not a sorting network and operates in 0 time units.
Case 3 is a sorting network and operates in 3 time units.
```

I A Vexing Problem

The game Vexed is a Tetris-like game created by James McCombe. The game consists of a board and blocks that are arranged in stacks. If the space to the immediate left or right of a block is open (that is, it contains no other block nor any part of the game board "wall"), then that block can be moved in that direction. Only blocks that are not part of the game board wall can be moved; "wall" blocks are stationary in all events. After a block is moved, if it or any other block no longer has anything under it, those blocks fall until they land on another block. After all blocks have landed, if any two or more identically-marked pieces are in contact horizontally and/or vertically, then those blocks are removed as a group. If multiple such groups result, then all groups are removed simultaneously. After all such groups are removed, all blocks again fall to resting positions (again, wall blocks do not move). This might then result in more groups being removed, more blocks falling, and so on, until a stable state is reached. The goal of the game is to remove all the movable blocks from the board.

Consider the simple example shown here. For reference purposes, number the rows of the board from top to bottom starting with an index value of zero, and number the columns from the left to right, also with a starting index value of zero. Board positions can be therefore be referenced as ordered (row, column) pairs. By additionally using an "L" or "R" to refer to a left or right push respectively, we can also use the ordered triple (row, column, direction) to indicate moves.

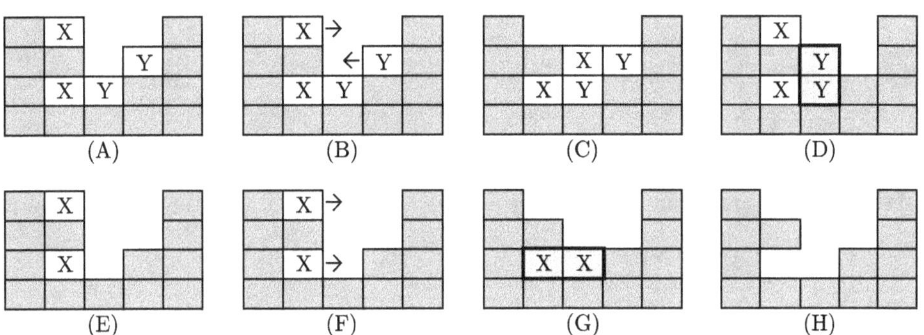

In (A) we have two choices for moves as shown in (B). These moves are (0,1,R) and (1,3,L) using the identification scheme defined above. Note that if we try (0,1,R), the resulting board state as shown in (C) is a dead end; no further moves are possible and blocks still remain on the board. If we choose the other move, however, the blocks at (1,2) and (2,2) are now in vertical contact, so they form a group that should be removed as shown by (D). The resulting board state is shown in (E), leaving the two moves shown by (F). Note that either move would eventually allow a solution, but (0,1,R) leads to a two move solution, whereas (2,1,R) leads to a three move solution. (G) and (H) show the final steps if we choose (0,1,R).

There are often many ways to solve a particular Vexed puzzle. For this problem, only solutions with a minimum number of moves are of interest. The minimum number of moves can sometimes be surprising. Consider another example.

In this example there are ten possible first moves, and there are in fact several ways to arrive at a solution. There is only one move in (A), however, that allows us to achieve a solution with the minimum number of moves. Observe the sequence of events shown if (3,1,R) is chosen as the first move.

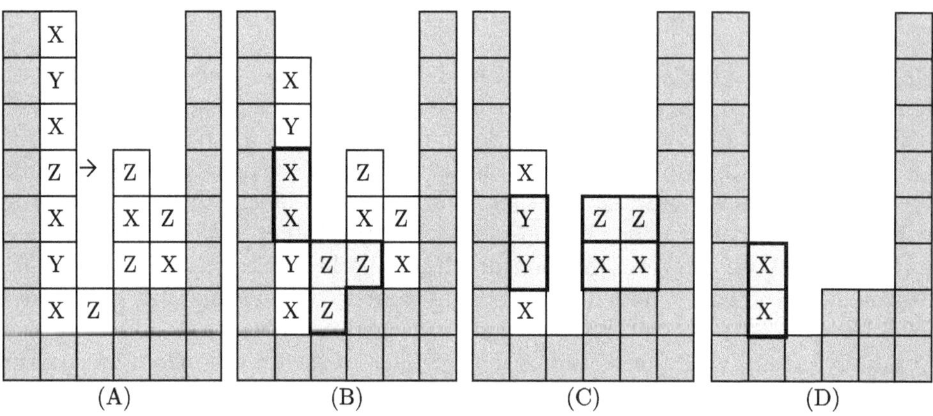

Input

The input will consist of several puzzles. Each begins with a line containing integers giving the number of rows (NR) and columns (NC) in the puzzle, and a string of characters (terminated by the end of line) giving the name of the puzzle; these items are separated by one or more spaces. This line is followed by an NR by NC array of characters defining the puzzle itself; an end of line will follow the last character in each row. NR and NC will each be no larger than 9. The "outer walls" (in addition to "inner wall" blocks) on the left, right, and bottom will always be included as part of the puzzle input, and are represented as hash mark (#) characters. Moveable blocks are represented by capital letters which indicate the marking on the block. To avoid possible ambiguities, open spaces in the puzzle are represented in the input by a hyphen (-) rather than by spaces. Other than the outer walls, wall blocks and moveable blocks may be arranged in any stable pattern. Every input puzzle is guaranteed to have a solution requiring 11 or fewer moves.

A puzzle with zero dimensions marks the end of the input and should not be processed.

Output

For each input puzzle, display a minimum length solution formatted as shown in the sample output. In the event that there are multiple solutions of minimum length, display one of them.

Sample Input	Sample Output
``` 4 5 SAMPLE-01 #A--# ##-B# #AB## ##### 6 7 SAMPLE-02 #--Y--# #-ZX-X# #-##-## #-XZ--# ####YZ# ####### 0 0 END ```	``` SAMPLE-01: Minimum solution length = 2 (B,1,3,L) (A,0,1,R) SAMPLE-02: Minimum solution length = 9 (Y,0,3,R) (Z,4,5,L) (X,1,3,R) (Z,1,2,R) (Z,1,3,R) (X,3,4,R) (X,3,2,R) (X,4,5,L) (X,1,5,L) ```

WORLD FINALS 2002

HONOLULU, HAWAII

World Champion

SHANGHAI JIAOTONG UNIVERSITY

Chenxi Lin
Jian Zhou
Jing Lu

Director of Judging
Dick Rinewalt   *Texas Christian University*

Chief Judge
Jo Perry   *North Carolina State University*

Judges
Osman Ay   *Zambak Publishing*
John Bonomo   *Westminster College*
Don Chamberlin   *IBM Almaden Research Center*
David Elizandro   *Tennessee Tech University*
Peter Kluit   *Delft University of Technology*
Lavon Page   *TogetherSoft Corporation*
Robert Roos   *Allegheny College*
Matthias Ruhl   *Google*
Stanley Wileman, Jr.   *University of Nebraska at Omaha*

CLI Live Archive problem numbers

2474	A	Balloons in a Box
2475	B	Undecodable Codes
2476	C	Crossing the Desert
2477	D	Ferries
2478	E	Island Hoping
2479	F	Toil for Oil
2480	G	Partitions
2481	H	Silly Sort
2482	I	Merrily, We Roll Along!

A Balloons in a Box

You must write a program that simulates placing spherical balloons into a rectangular box.

The simulation scenario is as follows. Imagine that you are given a rectangular box and a set of points. Each point represents a position where you might place a balloon. To place a balloon at a point, center it at the point and inflate the balloon until it touches a side of the box or a previously placed balloon. You may not use a point that is outside the box or inside a previously placed balloon. However, you may use the points in any order you like, and you need not use every point. Your objective is to place balloons in the box in an order that maximizes the total volume occupied by the balloons.

You are required to calculate the volume within the box that is not enclosed by the balloons.

Input

The input consists of several test cases. The first line of each test case contains a single integer n that indicates the number of points in the set ($1 \le n \le 6$). The second line contains three integers that represent the (x, y, z) integer coordinates of a corner of the box, and the third line contains the (x, y, z) integer coordinates of the opposite corner of the box. The next n lines of the test case contain three integers each, representing the (x, y, z) coordinates of the points in the set. The box has non-zero length in each dimension and its sides are parallel to the coordinate axes.

The input is terminated by the number zero on a line by itself.

Output

For each test case print one line of output consisting of the test case number followed by the volume of the box not occupied by balloons. Round the volume to the nearest integer. Follow the format in the sample output given below.

Place a blank line after the output of each test case.

Sample Input

```
2
0 0 0
10 10 10
3 3 3
7 7 7
0
```

Sample Output

```
Box 1: 774
```

B   Undecodable Codes

Phil Oracle has a unique ability that makes him indispensable at the National Spying Agency. His colleagues can bring him any new binary code and he can tell them immediately whether the code is uniquely decodable or not. A code is the assignment of a unique sequence of characters (a codeword) to each character in an alphabet. A binary code is one in which the codewords contain only zeroes and ones.

For example, here are two possible binary codes for the alphabet {a,c,j,l,p,s,v}.

	Code 1	Code 2
a	1	010
c	01	01
j	001	001
l	0001	10
p	00001	0
s	000001	1
v	0000001	101

The encoding of a string of characters from an alphabet (the *cleartext*) is the concatenation of the codewords corresponding to the characters of the cleartext, in order, from left to right. A code is uniquely decodable if the encoding of every possible cleartext using that code is unique. In the example above, Code 1 is uniquely decodable, but Code 2 is not. For example, the encodings of the cleartexts "`pascal`" and "`java`" are both '001010101010'.

Even shorter encodings that are not uniquely decodable are '01' and '10'.

While the agency is very proud of Phil, he unfortunately gives only "yes" or "no" answers. Some members of the agency would prefer more tangible proof, especially in the case of codes that are not uniquely decodable. For this problem you will deal only with codes that are *not* uniquely decodable. For each of these codes you must determine the single encoding having the minimum length (measured in bits) that is ambiguous because it can result from encoding each of two or more different cleartexts. In the case of a tie, choose the encoding which comes first lexicographically.

Input

One or more codes are to be tested. The input for each code begins with an integer m, $1 \le m \le 20$, on a line by itself, where m is the number of binary codewords in the code. This is followed by m lines each containing one binary codeword string, with optional leading and trailing whitespace. No codeword will contain more than 20 bits.

The input is terminated by the number zero on a line by itself.

Output

For each code, display the sequential code number (starting with 1), the length of the shortest encoding that is not uniquely decodable, and the shortest encoding itself, with ties broken as previously described. The encoding must be displayed with 20 bits on each line except the last, which may contain fewer than 20 bits. Place a blank line after the output for each code. Use the format shown in the samples below.

Sample Input

```
3
  0
  01
  10
5
 0110
  00
    111
  001100
      110
5
  1
  001
  0001
  00000000000000000001
  10000000000000000000
0
```

Sample Output

```
Code 1: 3 bits
010

Code 2: 9 bits
001100110

Code 3: 21 bits
10000000000000000000
1
```

C Crossing the Desert

In this problem, you will compute how much food you need to purchase for a trip across the desert on foot. At your starting location, you can purchase food at the general store and you can collect an unlimited amount of free water. The desert may contain oases at various locations. At each oasis, you can collect as much water as you like and you can store food for later use, but you cannot purchase any additional food. You can also store food for later use at the starting location. You will be given the coordinates of the starting location, all the oases, and your destination in a two-dimensional coordinate system where the unit distance is one mile.

For each mile that you walk, you must consume one unit of food and one unit of water. Assume that these supplies are consumed continuously, so if you walk for a partial mile you will consume partial units of food and water. You are not able to walk at all unless you have supplies of both food and water. You must consume the supplies while you are walking, not while you are resting at an oasis. Of course, there is a limit to the total amount of food and water that you can carry. This limit is expressed as a carrying capacity in total units. At no time can the sum of the food units and the water units that you are carrying exceed this capacity. You must decide how much food you need to purchase at the starting location in order to make it to the destination. You need not have any food or water left when you arrive at the destination. Since the general store sells food only in whole units and has only one million food units available, the amount of food you should buy will be an integer greater than zero and less than or equal to one million.

Input

The first line of input in each trial data set contains n ($2 \leq n \leq 20$), which is the total number of significant locations in the desert, followed by an integer that is your total carrying capacity in units of food and water. The next n lines contain pairs of integers that represent the coordinates of the n significant locations. The first significant location is the starting point, where your food supply must be purchased; the last significant location is the destination; and the intervening significant locations (if any) are oases. You need not visit any oasis unless you find it helpful in reaching your destination, and you need not visit the oases in any particular order.

The input is terminated by a pair of zeroes.

Output

For each trial, print the trial number followed by an integer that represents the number of units of food needed for your journey. Use the format shown in the example. If you cannot make it to the destination under the given conditions, print the trial number followed by the word 'Impossible'.

Place a blank line after the output of each test case.

Sample Input

```
4 100
10  -20
-10  5
30  15
15  35
2  100
0  0
100  100
0 0
```

Sample Output

```
Trial 1: 136 units of food

Trial 2: Impossible
```

D Ferries

Millions of years ago massive fields of ice carved deep grooves in the mountains of Norway. The sea filled these grooves with water. The Norwegian people call them fjords. This landscape of mountains and water is beautiful, but it makes traveling difficult. The usual scheme is: drive some kilometers, wait for a ferry, cross a fjord with the ferry, drive some more kilometers, and so on until the destination has been reached. To reach a destination as early as possible, most people have the following strategy: drive as fast as allowed (the maximum speed is 80 km/h) to the next ferry, and wait until it goes. Repeat until the destination has been reached.

Since driving fast requires more fuel than driving slow, this strategy is both expensive and harmful to the environment. The new generation of cruise control systems is designed to help. Given the route you want to go, these systems will gather information about the ferries involved, calculate the earliest possible time of arrival at the final destination, and calculate a driving scheme that avoids driving faster than needed. The systems will calculate your road speed so that you board the next ferry the moment it leaves.

Given a route (a sequence of road-pieces and crossings with ferries), you must write a program to calculate the minimal time it takes to complete this route. Moreover, your program must find a driving scheme such that the maximal driving speed at any point during the trip is as small as possible.

Input

The input file contains one or more test cases. Each test case describes a route. A route consists of several sections, each section being either a piece of road or a crossing. The first line in the description contains a single number s ($s > 0$), which is the number of sections in the route. The next s lines contain the descriptions of the sections. Every line describing a section starts with two names: the place of departure and the place of arrival, followed by either the word 'road' or the word 'ferry' indicating what kind of section it is. If the section is a road, its length (a positive integer) is given in km. For example:

```
Dryna Solholmen road 32
```

Lines describing ferry sections have more information. Following the word 'ferry', the duration of the ferry crossing, in minutes (a positive integer) is given. This is followed by the frequency f ($f > 0$) of the ferry, that is, the number of times the ferry departs in a single hour. The next f integers give the departure times of the ferry, in ascending order. For example:

```
Manhiller Fodnes ferry 20 2 15 35
```

The ferry travels from Manhiller to Fodnes in 20 minutes, and it leaves twice an hour (on 0h15, 0h35, 1h15, 1h35,...). The beginning of the entire trip always starts at a full hour. The sections in a route are consecutive, that is, if a section goes from A to B then the next section starts at B. Every route in the input can be traveled in no more than 10 hours.

The input is terminated by the number zero on a line by itself.

Output

Output for each test case is a single line containing three items. The first item is the test case number. The second is the total travel time for an optimal scheme in the form *hh:mm:ss*. The third item is the maximal road speed in an optimal scheme rounded to two digits to the right of the decimal point.

Place a blank line after the output of each test case.

Sample Input

```
1
Bygd Bomvei road 7
2
Ferje Overfarten ferry 20 2 5 25
Overfarten Havneby ferry 30 3 10 30 50
5
Begynnelse Brygge road 30
Brygge Bestemmelse ferry 15 4 10 25 40 55
Bestemmelse Veiskillet road 20
Veiskillet Grusvei road 25
Grusvei Slutt ferry 50 1 10
0
```

Sample Output

```
Test Case 1: 00:05:15 80.00

Test Case 2: 01:00:00 0.00

Test Case 3: 03:00:00 45.00
```

E Island Hopping

The company Pacific Island Net (PIN) has identified several small island groups in the Pacific that do not have a fast internet connection. PIN plans to tap this potential market by offering internet service to the island inhabitants. Each groups of islands already has a deep-sea cable that connects the main island to the closest internet hub on the mainland (be it America, Australia or Asia). All that remains to be done is to connect the islands in a group to each other. You must write a program to help them determine a connection procedure.

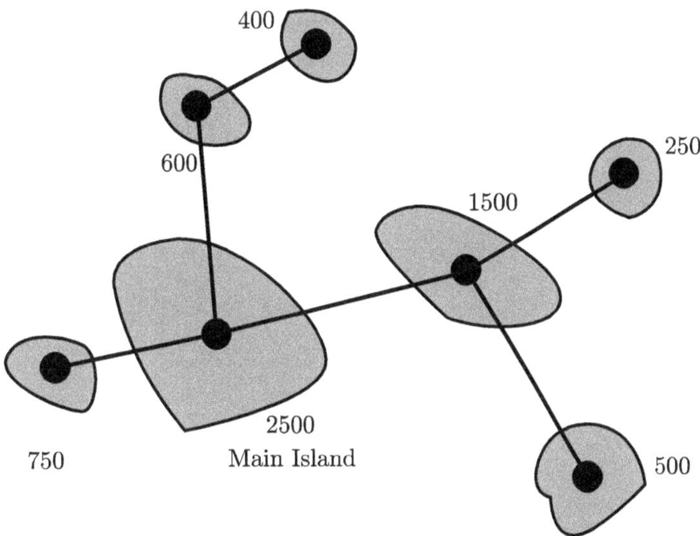

For each island, you are given the position of its router and the number of island inhabitants. In the figure, the dark dots are the routers and the numbers are the numbers of inhabitants. PIN will build connections between pairs of routers such that every router has a path to the main island. PIN has decided to build the network such that the total amount of cable used is minimal. Under this restriction, there may be several optimal networks. However, it does not matter to PIN which of the optimal networks is built.

PIN is interested in the average time required for new customers to access the internet, based on the assumption that construction on all cable links in the network begins at the same time. Cable links can be constructed at a rate of one kilometer of cable per day. As a result, shorter cable links are completed before the longer links. An island will have internet access as soon as there is a path from the island to the main island along completed cable links. If m_i is the number of inhabitants of the ith island and t_i is the time when the island is connected to the internet, then the average connection time is:

$$\frac{\sum t_i * m_i}{\sum m_i}$$

Input

The input consists of several descriptions of groups of islands. The first line of each description contains a single positive integer n, the number of islands in the group ($n \leq 50$). Each of the next n lines has three integers x_i, y_i, m_i, giving the position of the router (x_i, y_i) and number of inhabitants m_i $(m_i > 0)$ of the islands. Coordinates are measured in kilometers. The first island in this sequence is the main island. The input is terminated by the number zero on a line by itself.

Output

For each group of islands in the input, output the sequence number of the group and the average number of days until the inhabitants are connected to the internet. The number of days should have two digits to the right of the decimal point. Use the output format in the sample given below.

Place a blank line after the output of each test case.

Sample Input

```
7
11 12 2500
14 17 1500
9 9 750
7 15 600
19 16 500
8 18 400
15 21 250
0
```

Sample Output

```
Island Group: 1  Average 3.20
```

F   Toil for Oil

Prospecting for new sources of oil has become a high-technology industry. With improved drilling technology it has become economically viable to seek out ever smaller and harder to reach deposits of oil. However, using exploratory drilling to locate these deposits is not cost-efficient, so researchers have developed methods to detect oil indirectly.

One such method to detect oil is sonar, which uses reflected sound waves to locate caves in underground rock formations. Determining how much oil can be contained in such a cave is a difficult problem.

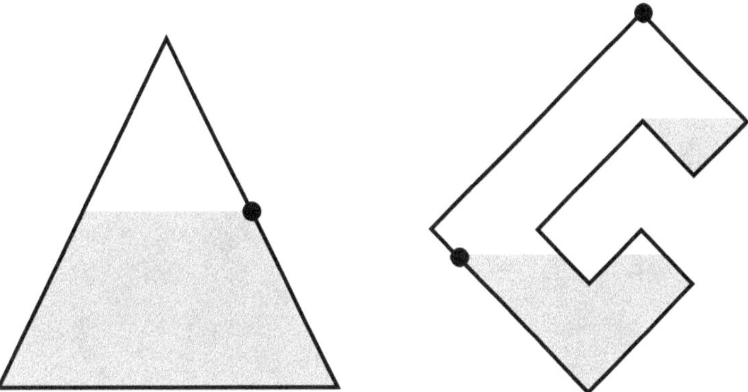

In this problem, you will be given some cross-sections of underground caves, represented by polygons such as the ones shown in the figure. Some of the points bounding the polygon may be holes through which oil can seep out into the surrounding rock (represented by black circles in the figure). Given the polygonal shape of the cave and the positions of the holes, you must compute the maximum amount of oil that could be in the cave (shown as gray shaded areas in the figure). This amount is limited by the fact that, in any connected body of oil, the oil level can never be above a hole, since it would drain into the surrounding rock instead.

Input

The input contains several cave descriptions, each in the form of a polygon that specifies a cross-section of a cave. The first line of each description contains a single integer n, representing the number of points on the polygon ($3 \le n \le 100$).

Each of the following n lines contains three integers x_i, y_i, h_i. The values (x_i, y_i) give the positions of the points on the boundary of the polygon in counterclockwise order. The polygon is simple-that is, it does not cross or touch itself. The value of hi is equal to 1 if the point is a hole through which oil can seep out, and 0 otherwise. The "upward" direction in each case is the positive y-axis.

The input is terminated by a zero on a line by itself.

Output

For each cave description, print its sequence number (starting with 1) followed by its oil capacity. Approximate the oil capacity by the area within the given cross-section that may contain oil, rounded to the nearest integer. Use the format in the example output given below. Place a blank line after each test case.

Sample Input

```
4
10  0  0
5   10  1
0   20  0
-10  0  0
11
0  6  0
1  5  1
6  0  0
10  4  0
8  6  0
6  4  0
4  6  0
8  10  0
10  8  0
12  10  0
8  14  1
0
```

Sample Output

```
Cave 1: Oil capacity = 150

Cave 2: Oil capacity = 27
```

G Partitions

A *partition* of a rectangle is a subdivision of the rectangle into a set of smaller, non-overlapping sub-rectangles. Figure 1 shows several examples of partitions.

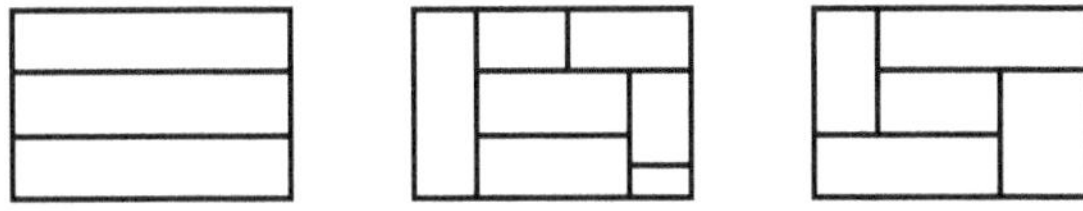

Figure 1

Figure 2 shows three equal sized rectangles, partitioned into sub-rectangles. Partition B is obtained from partition A by partitioning two of the sub-rectangles of A. Generally, if a partition B is obtained from A by partitioning one or more of its sub-rectangles, we say that B is *finer* than A, or that A is *coarser* than B. This relation is partial: partition C is neither coarser nor finer than A or B.

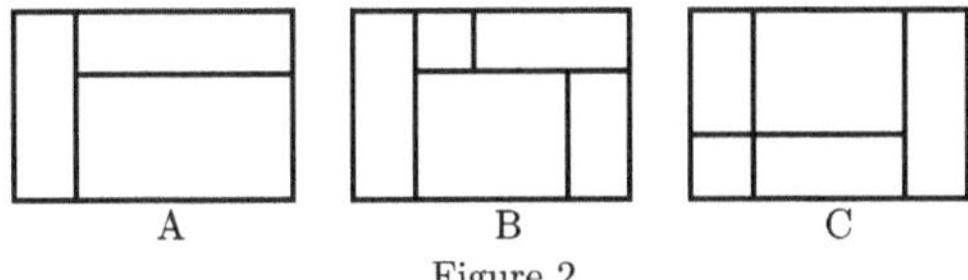

Figure 2

Given two partitions D and E of the same rectangle, infinitely many partitions exist that are finer than both D and E. In Figure 3 both F and G are finer than D and E. Among the partitions that are finer than both D and E, a unique one exists that is *coarsest*. This partition is called the *infimum* of D and E. In Figure 3, partition F is the infimum of D and E.

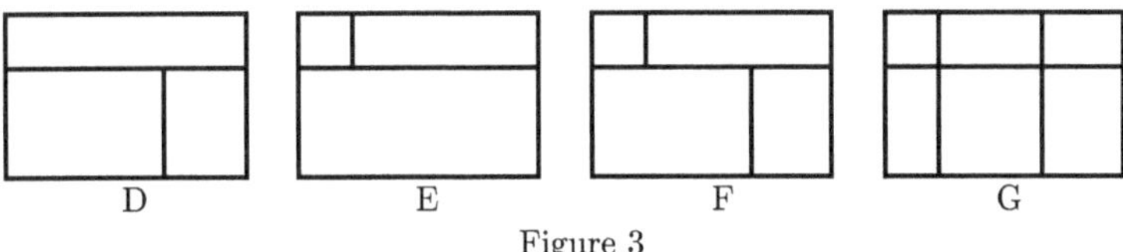

Figure 3

In Figure 4, both H and J are coarser than D and E. Here J is the finest partition that is coarser than D and E. Then J is the *supremum* of D and E.

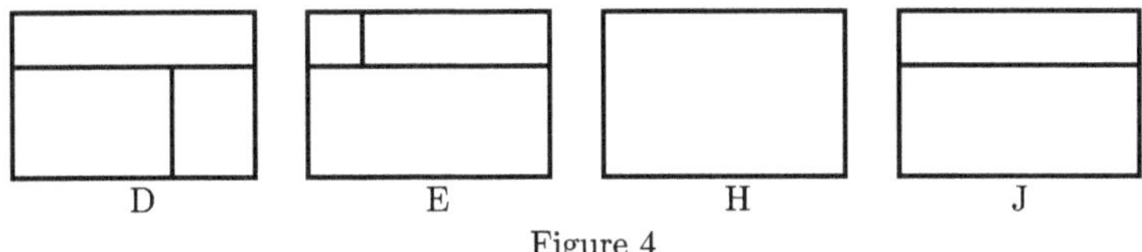

Figure 4

Write a program that, given two partitions of the same rectangle, finds the infimum and the supremum of these partitions.

Input

The input file contains one or more test cases. The first line of each test case gives the width w and height h of the rectangle

$$(0 < w, h \leq 20)$$

In the next $h + 1$ lines the two partitions are given, as in the sample. Each of these lines contains $4 * w + 3$ characters. The first $2 * w + 1$ of these belong to the first partition; the last $2 * w + 1$ of these belong to the second partition. A space separates the two partitions. Horizontal lines are created using underscores '_', vertical lines using '|'.

The input is terminated by a pair of zeroes.

Output

For every case in the input file the output contains a single line containing the case number (in the format shown in the sample), followed by the infimum and the supremum of the two partitions, using the same format as the input.

Place a blank line after the output of each test case.

Sample Input

```
4 3
```

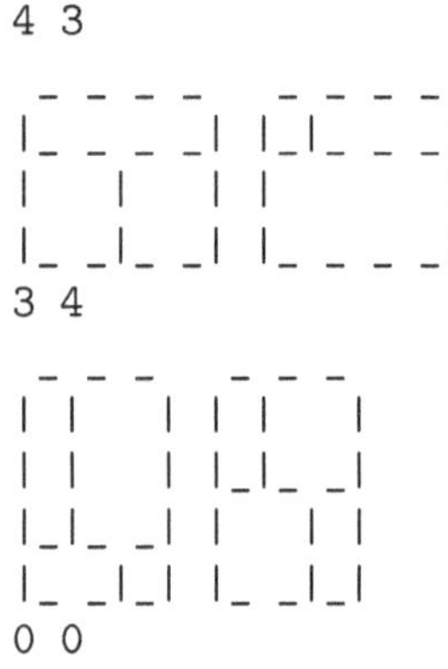

```
3 4
```

```
0 0
```

Sample Output

```
Case 1:
```

```
 _ _ _ _   _ _ _ _
|_|_ _ _ _| |_ _ _ _ _|
|   |   | |         |
|_ _|_ _| |_ _ _ _ _|
```

```
Case 2:
```

```
 _ _ _   _ _ _
| |   | |     |
|_|_ _| | |     |
|_|_|_| | |     |
|_ _|_| |_ _ _ _|
```

H   Silly Sort

Your younger brother has an assignment and needs some help. His teacher gave him a sequence of numbers to be sorted in ascending order. During the sorting process, the places of two numbers can be interchanged. Each interchange has a cost, which is the sum of the two numbers involved.

You must write a program that determines the minimal cost to sort the sequence of numbers.

Input

The input file contains several test cases. Each test case consists of two lines. The first line contains a single integer n $(n > 1)$, representing the number of items to be sorted. The second line contains n different integers (each positive and less than 1,000), which are the numbers to be sorted.

The input is terminated by a zero on a line by itself.

Output

For each test case, the output is a single line containing the test case number and the minimal cost of sorting the numbers in the test case.

Place a blank line after the output of each test case.

Sample Input

```
3
3 2 1
4
8 1 2 4
5
1 8 9 7 6
6
8 4 5 3 2 7
0
```

Sample Output

```
Case 1: 4

Case 2: 17

Case 3: 41

Case 4: 34
```

I Merrily, We Roll Along!

One method used to measure the length of a path is to roll a wheel (similar to a bicycle wheel) along the path. If we know the radius of the wheel and the number of revolutions it makes as it travels along the path, the length of the path can be computed.

This method works well if the path is smooth. But when there are curbs or other abrupt elevation changes in the path, the path distance may not be accurately determined, because the wheel may rotate around a point (like the edge of a curb), or the wheel may roll along a vertical surface. In this problem you are to determine the distance moved by the center of such a wheel as it travels along a path that includes only horizontal and vertical surfaces.

To measure a path, the wheel is placed with its center directly above the origin of the path. The wheel is then moved forward over the path as far as possible, always remaining in contact with the surface, ending with its center directly above the end of the path.

Consider the path shown in the illustration on the left below, and assume the wheel has a radius of 2. The path begins and ends with horizontal segments of length 2 at the same elevation. Between these there is a horizontal segment of length 2.828427 at 2 units below the elevation of the other two horizontal segments. To measure this path, the wheel is placed at position 1. It then moves horizontally to position 2, rotates 45 degrees to position 3, rotates another 45 degrees to position 4, and finally rolls horizontally to position 5. The center of the wheel moved a distance of 7.1416, not 6.8284.

In the illustration on the right below, the path begins and ends with horizontal segments of length 3, separated by a 7-unit wide region placed 7 units below the surface. If the wheel has a radius of 1, then it will move 26.142 units before reaching the end of the path.

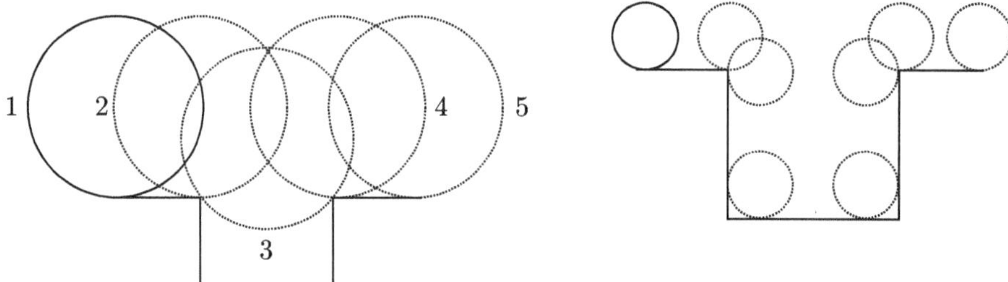

Input

For this problem there are multiple input cases. Each case begins with a positive real number specifying the radius of the wheel and an integer n, which is at least 1 but not greater than 50. There then follow n pairs of real numbers. The first number in each pair gives the horizontal distance along the path to the next vertical surface. The second number in each pair gives the signed change in the elevation of the path at the vertical surface, with positive numbers representing an increase in elevation. The vertical surfaces are always perpendicular to the horizontal surfaces. The elevation change in the nth pair will always be 0.

The input is terminated by a pair of zeroes.

Output

For each case, display the case number and the distance moved by the center of the wheel with 3 digits to the right of the decimal point.

Place a blank line after the output of each test case.

Sample Input

```
2.0 3
2.0 -2.0
2.828427 2.0
2.0 0.0
1.0 3
3.0 -7.0
7.0 7.0
3.0 0.0
1.0 3
1.0 4.0
2.0 4.0
1.0 0.0
0 0
```

Sample Output

```
Case 1: Distance = 7.142

Case 2: Distance = 26.142

Case 3: Distance = 5.142
```

WORLD FINALS 2003

BEVERLY HILLS, CALIFORNIA

World Champion

WARSAW UNIVERSITY

Tomasz Czajka
Krzysztof Onak
Andrzej Gasienica-Samek

Director of Judging

Dick Rinewalt   *Texas Christian University*

Chief Judge

Jo Perry   *North Carolina State University*

Judges

Osman Ay   *Zambak Publishing*
John Bonomo   *Westminster College*
Don Chamberlin   *IBM Almaden Research Center*
David Elizandro   *Tennessee Tech University*
Martin Kacer   *CTU Prague*
Peter Kluit   *Delft University of Technology*
Shahriar Manzoor   *Southeast University*
Miguel A. Revilla   *University of Valladolid*
Robert Roos   *Allegheny College*
Matthias Ruhl   *Google*
Stanley Wileman, Jr.   *University of Nebraska at Omaha*

CLI Live Archive problem numbers

2721   A   Building Bridges
2722   B   Light Bulbs
2723   C   Riding the Bus
2724   D   Eurodiffusion
2725   E   Covering Whole Holes
2726   F   Combining Images
2727   G   A Linking Loader
2728   H   A Spy in the Metro
2729   I   The Solar System
2730   J   Troll

A   Building Bridges

The City Council of New Altonville plans to build a system of bridges connecting all of its downtown buildings together so people can walk from one building to another without going outside. You must write a program to help determine an optimal bridge configuration.

New Altonville is laid out as a grid of squares. Each building occupies a connected set of one or more squares. Two occupied squares whose corners touch are considered to be a single building and do not need a bridge. Bridges may be built only on the grid lines that form the edges of the squares. Each bridge must be built in a straight line and must connect exactly two buildings.

For a given set of buildings, you must find the minimum number of bridges needed to connect all the buildings. If this is impossible, find a solution that minimizes the number of disconnected groups of buildings. Among possible solutions with the same number of bridges, choose the one that minimizes the sum of the lengths of the bridges, measured in multiples of the grid size. Two bridges may cross, but in this case they are considered to be on separate levels and do not provide a connection from one bridge to the other.

The figure below illustrates four possible city configurations. City 1 consists of five buildings that can be connected by four bridges with a total length of 4. In City 2, no bridges are possible, since no buildings share a common grid line. In City 3, no bridges are needed because there is only one building. In City 4, the best solution uses a single bridge of length 1 to connect two buildings, leaving two disconnected groups (one containing two buildings and one containing a single building).

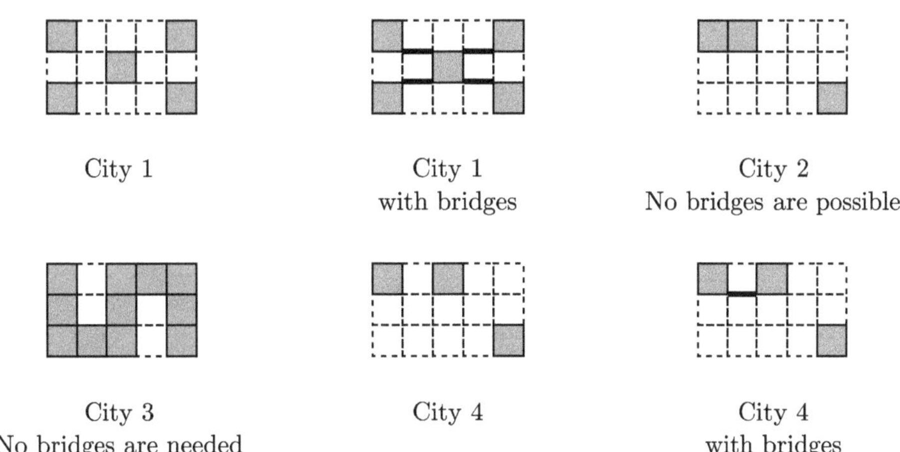

City 1   City 1 with bridges   City 2 No bridges are possible

City 3 No bridges are needed   City 4   City 4 with bridges

Input

The input data set describes several rectangular cities. Each city description begins with a line containing two integers r and c, representing the size of the city on the north-south and east-west axes measured in grid lengths ($1 \leq r \leq 100$ and $1 \leq c \leq 100$). These numbers are followed by exactly r lines, each consisting of c hash ('#') and dot ('.') characters. Each character corresponds to one square of the grid. A hash character corresponds to a square that is occupied by a building, and a dot character corresponds to a square that is not occupied by a building.

The input data for the last city will be followed by a line containing two zeros.

Output

For each city description, print two or three lines of output as shown below. The first line consists of the city number. If the city has fewer than two buildings, the second line is the sentence 'No bridges are needed.'. If the city has two or more buildings but none of them can be connected by bridges, the second line is the sentence 'No bridges are possible.'. Otherwise, the second line is 'N bridges of total length L' where N is the number of bridges and L is the sum of the lengths of the bridges of the best solution. (If N is 1, use the word 'bridge' rather than 'bridges.') If the solution leaves two or more disconnected groups of buildings, print a third line containing the number of disconnected groups.

Print a blank line between cases. Use the output format shown in the example.

Sample Input

```
3 5
#...#
..#..
#...#
3 5
##...
.....
....#
3 5
#.###
#.#.#
###.#
3 5
#.#..
.....
....#
0 0
```

Sample Output

```
City 1
4 bridges of total length 4

City 2
No bridges are possible.
2 disconnected groups

City 3
No bridges are needed.

City 4
1 bridge of total length 1
2 disconnected groups
```

B Light Bulbs

Hollywood's newest theater, the Atheneum of Culture and Movies, has a huge computer-operated marquee composed of thousands of light bulbs. Each row of bulbs is operated by a set of switches that are electronically controlled by a computer program. Unfortunately, the electrician installed the wrong kind of switches, and tonight is the ACM's opening night. You must write a program to make the switches perform correctly.

A row of the marquee contains n light bulbs controlled by n switches. Bulbs and switches are numbered from 1 to n, left to right. Each bulb can either be ON or OFF. Each input case will contain the initial state and the desired final state for a single row of bulbs.

The original lighting plan was to have each switch control a single bulb. However the electrician's error caused each switch to control two or three consecutive bulbs, as shown in Figure 1. The leftmost switch ($i = 1$) toggles the states of the two leftmost bulbs (1 and 2); the rightmost switch ($i = n$) toggles the states of the two rightmost bulbs ($n1$ and n). Each remaining switch ($1 < i < n$) toggles the states of the three bulbs with indices $i1$, i, and $i + 1$. (In the special case where there is a single bulb and a single switch, the switch simply toggles the state of that bulb.) Thus, if bulb 1 is ON and bulb 2 is OFF, flipping switch 1 will turn bulb 1 OFF and bulb 2 ON. The minimum cost of changing a row of bulbs from an initial configuration to a final configuration is the minimum number of switches that must be flipped to achieve the change.

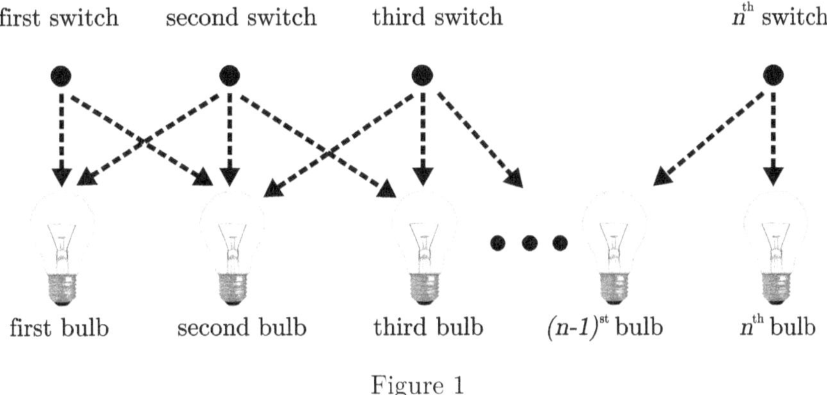

Figure 1

You can represent the state of a row of bulbs in binary, where 0 means the bulb is OFF and 1 means the bulb is ON. For instance, 01100 represents a row of five bulbs in which the second and third bulbs are both ON. You could transform this state into 10000 by flipping switches 1, 4, and 5, but it would be less costly to simply flip switch 2.

You must write a program that determines the switches that must be flipped to change a row of light bulbs from its initial state to its desired final state with minimal cost. Some combinations of initial and final states may not be feasible. For compactness of representation, decimal integers are used instead of binary for the bulb configurations. Thus, 01100 and 10000 are represented by the decimal integers 12 and 16.

Input

The input file contains several test cases. Each test case consists of one line. The line contains two non-negative decimal integers, at least one of which is positive and each of which contains at most

100 digits. The first integer represents the initial state of the row of bulbs and the second integer represents the final state of the row. The binary equivalent of these integers represents the initial and final states of the bulbs, where 1 means ON and 0 means OFF.

To avoid problems with leading zeros, assume that the first bulb in either the initial or the final configuration (or both) is ON. There are no leading or trailing blanks in the input lines, no leading zeros in the two decimal integers, and the initial and final states are separated by a single blank.

The last test case is followed by a line containing two zeros.

Output

For each test case, print a line containing the case number and a decimal integer representing a minimum-cost set of switches that need to be flipped to convert the row of bulbs from initial state to final state. In the binary equivalent of this integer, the rightmost (least significant) bit represents the n-th switch, 1 indicates that a switch has been flipped, and 0 indicates that the switch has not been flipped. If there is no solution, print 'impossible'. If there is more than one solution, print the one with the smallest decimal equivalent.

Print a blank line between cases. Use the output format shown in the example.

Sample Input

```
12 16
1 1
3 0
30 5
7038312 7427958190
4253404109 657546225
0 0
```

Sample Output

```
Case Number 1: 8

Case Number 2: 0

Case Number 3: 1

Case Number 4: 10

Case Number 5: 2805591535

Case Number 6: impossible
```

C   Riding the Bus

The latest research in reconfigurable multiprocessor chips focuses on the use of a single bus that winds around the chip. Processor components, which can be anywhere on the chip, are attached to *connecting points* on the bus so that they can communicate with each other.

Some research involves bus layout that uses recursively-defined "SZ" curves, also known as "S-shaped Peano curves." Two examples of these curves are shown below. Each curve is drawn on the unit square. The order-1 curve, shown on the left, approximates the letter "S" and consists of line segments connecting the points (0,0), (1,0), (1,0.5), (0,0.5), (0,1), and (1,1) in order. Each horizontal line in an "S" or "Z" curve is twice as long as each vertical line. For the order-1 curve, the length of a vertical line, *len*, is 0.5.

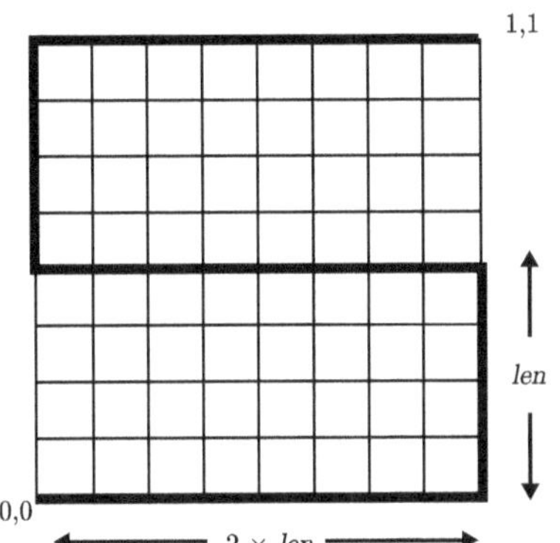

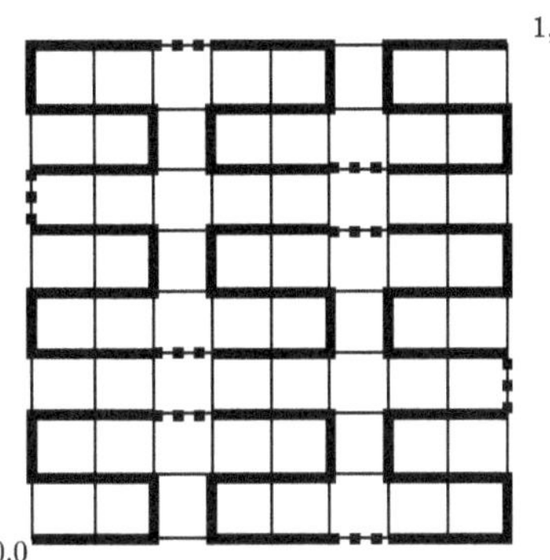

The order-2 curve, shown on the right, contains 9 smaller copies of the order-1 curve (4 of which are reversed left to right to yield "Z" curves). These copies are connected by line segments of length *len*, shown as dotted lines. Since the width and height of the order-2 curve is $8 \times len$, and the curve is drawn on the unit square, $len = 0.125$ for the order-2 curve.

The order-3 curve contains 9 smaller copies of the order-2 curve (with 4 reversed left to right), connected by line segments, as described for the order-2 curve. Higher order curves are drawn in a similar manner. The *connecting points* to which processor components attach are evenly spaced every *len* units along the bus. The first connecting point is at (0,0) and the last is at (1,1). There are 9^k connecting points along the order-k curve, and the total bus length is $(9^k - 1) \times len$ units.

You must write a program to determine the total distance that signals must travel between two processor components. Each component's coordinates are given as an x, y pair, $0 \le x \le 1$ and $0 \le y \le 1$, where x is the distance from the left side of the chip, and y is the distance from the lower edge of the chip. Each component is attached to the closest connecting point by a straight line. If multiple connecting points are equidistant from a component, the one with the smallest x coordinate and smallest y coordinate is used. The total distance a signal must travel between two components is the sum of the length of the lines connecting the components to the bus, and the length of the bus between the two connecting points. For example, the distance between components located at (0.5, 0.25) and (1.0, 0.875) on a chip using the order-1 curve is 3.8750 units.

Input

The input contains several cases. For each case, the input consists of an integer that gives the order of the SZ curve used as the bus (no larger than 8), and then four real numbers x_1, y_1, x_2, y_2

that give the coordinates of the processor components to be connected. While each processor component should actually be in a unique location not on the bus, your program must correctly handle all possible locations.

The last case in the input is followed by a single zero.

Output

For each case, display the case number (starting with 1 for the first case) and the distance between the processor components when they are connected as described. Display the distance with 4 digits to the right of the decimal point.

Use the same format as that shown in the sample output shown below. Leave a blank line between the output lines for consecutive cases.

Sample Input

```
1 0.5 .25 1 .875
1 0 0 1 1
2 .3 .3 .7 .7
2 0 0 1 1
0
```

Sample Output

```
Case 1.  Distance is 3.8750

Case 2.  Distance is 4.0000

Case 3.  Distance is 8.1414

Case 4.  Distance is 10.0000
```

D Eurodiffusion

On January 1, 2002, twelve European countries abandoned their national currency for a new currency, the euro. No more francs, marks, lires, guldens, kroner,..., only euros, all over the eurozone. The same banknotes are used in all countries. And the same coins? Well, not quite. Each country has limited freedom to create its own euro coins:

> "Every euro coin carries a common European face. On the obverse, member states decorate the coins with their own motif. No matter which motif is on the coin, it can be used anywhere in the 12 Member States. For example, a French citizen is able to buy a hot dog in Berlin using a euro coin with the imprint of the King of Spain." (source: http://europa.eu.int/euro/html/entry.html)

On January 1, 2002, the only euro coins available in Paris were French coins. Soon the first non-French coins appeared in Paris. Eventually, one may expect all types of coins to be evenly distributed over the twelve participating countries. (Actually this will not be true. All countries continue minting and distributing coins with their own motifs. So even in a stable situation, there should be an excess of German coins in Berlin.) So, how long will it be before the first Finnish or Irish coins are in circulation in the south of Italy? How long will it be before coins of each motif are available everywhere?

You must write a program to simulate the dissemination of euro coins throughout Europe, using a highly simplified model. Restrict your attention to a single euro denomination. Represent European cities as points in a rectangular grid. Each city may have up to 4 neighbors (one to the north, east, south and west). Each city belongs to a country, and a country is a rectangular part of the plane. The figure below shows a map with 3 countries and 28 cities. The graph of countries is connected, but countries may border holes that represent seas, or non-euro countries such as Switzerland or Denmark. Initially, each city has one million (1,000,000) coins in its country's motif. Every day a representative portion of coins, based on the city's beginning day balance, is transported to each neighbor of the city. A representative portion is defined as one coin for every full 1,000 coins of a motif.

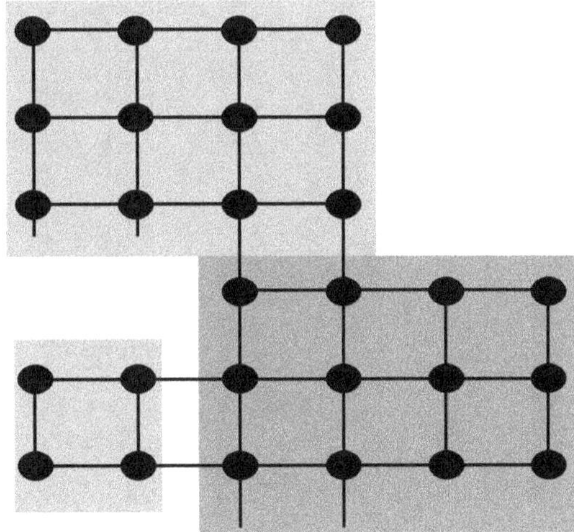

A city is *complete* when at least one coin of each motif is present in that city. A country is *complete* when all of its cities are complete. Your program must determine the time required for each country to become complete.

Input

The input consists of several test cases. The first line of each test case is the number of countries ($1 \leq c \leq 20$). The next c lines describe each country. The country description has the format: *name* $x_l\ y_l\ x_h\ y_h$, where *name* is a single word with at most 25 characters; x_l, y_l are the lower left city coordinates of that country (most southwestward city) and x_h, y_h are the upper right city coordinates of that country (most northeastward city). $1 \leq x_l \leq xh \leq 10$ and $1 \leq y_l \leq y_h \leq 10$.

The last case in the input is followed by a single zero.

Output

For each test case, print a line indicating the case number, followed by a line for each country with the country name and number of days for that country to become complete. Order the countries by days to completion. If two countries have identical days to completion, order them alphabetically by name.

Use the output format shown in the example.

Sample Input

```
3
France   1 4 4 6
Spain        3 1 6 3
Portugal    1 1 2 2
1
Luxembourg  1 1 1 1
2
Netherlands 1 3 2 4
Belgium     1 1 2 2
0
```

Sample Output

```
Case Number 1
    Spain    382
    Portugal    416
    France    1325
Case Number 2
    Luxembourg    0
Case Number 3
    Belgium    2
    Netherlands    2
```

E   Covering Whole Holes

Can you cover a round hole with a square cover? You can, as long as the square cover is big enough. It obviously will not be an exact fit, but it is still possible to cover the hole completely.

The Association of Cover Manufacturers (ACM) is a group of companies that produce covers for all kinds of holes – manholes, holes on streets, wells, ditches, cave entrances, holes in backyards dug by dogs to bury bones, to name only a few. ACM wants a program that determines whether a given cover can be used to completely cover a specified hole. At this time, they are interested only in covers and holes that are rectangular polygons (that is, polygons with interior angles of only 90 or 270 degrees). Moreover, both cover and hole are aligned along the same coordinate axes, and are not supposed to be rotated against each other – just translated relative to each other.

Input

The input consists of several descriptions of covers and holes. The first line of each description contains two integers h and c ($4 \leq h \leq 50$ and $4 \leq c \leq 50$), the number of points of the polygon describing the hole and the cover respectively. Each of the following h lines contains two integers x and y, which are the vertices of the hole's polygon in the order they would be visited in a trip around the polygon. The next c lines give a corresponding description of the cover. Both polygons are rectangular, and the sides of the polygons are aligned with the coordinate axes. The polygons have positive area and do not intersect themselves.

The last description is followed by a line containing two zeros.

Output

For each problem description, print its number in the sequence of descriptions. If the hole can be completely covered by moving the cover (without rotating it), print 'Yes' otherwise print 'No'. Recall that the cover may extend beyond the boundaries of the hole as long as no part of the hole is uncovered. Follow the output format in the example given below.

Sample Input

```
4 4
0 0
0 10
10 10
10 0
0 0
0 20
20 20
20 0
4 6
0 0
0 10
10 10
10 0
0 0
0 10
```

```
10 10
10 1
9 1
9 0
0 0
```

Sample Output

```
Hole 1: Yes
Hole 2: No
```

F   Combining Images

As the exchange of images over computer networks becomes more common, the problem of image compression takes on increasing importance. Image compression algorithms are used to represent images using a relatively small number of bits.

One image compression algorithm is based on an encoding called a "Quad Tree." An image has a Quad Tree encoding if it is a square array of binary pixels (the value of each pixel is 0 or 1, called the "color" of the pixel), and the number of pixels on the side of the square is a power of two.

If an image is homogeneous (all its pixels are of the same color), the Quad Tree encoding of the image is 1 followed by the color of the pixels. For example, the Quad Tree encoding of an image that contains pixels of color 1 only is 11, regardless of the size of the image.

If an image is heterogeneous (it contains pixels of both colors), the Quad Tree encoding of the image is 0 followed by the Quad Tree encodings of its upper-left quadrant, its upper-right quadrant, its lower-left quadrant, and its lower-right quadrant, in order.

The Quad Tree encoding of an image is a string of binary digits. For easier printing, a Quad Tree encoding can be converted to a Hex Quad Tree encoding by the following steps:

a. Prepend a 1 digit as a delimiter on the left of the Quad Tree encoding.

b. Prepend 0 digits on the left as necessary until the number of digits is a multiple of four.

c. Convert each sequence of four binary digits into a hexadecimal digit, using the digits 0 to 9 and capital A through F to represent binary patterns from 0000 to 1111.

For example, the Hex Quad Tree encoding of an image that contains pixels of color 1 only is 7, which corresponds to the binary string 0111.

You must write a program that reads the Hex Quad Tree encoding of two images, computes a new image that is the intersection of those two images, and prints its Hex Quad Tree encoding. Assume that both input images are square and contain the same number of pixels (although the lengths of their encodings may differ). If two images A and B have the same size and shape, their intersection (written as A & B) also has the same size and shape. By definition, a pixel of A & B is equal to 1 if and only if the corresponding pixels of image A and image B are both equal to 1.

The following figure illustrates two input images and their intersection, together with the Hex Quad Tree encodings of each image. In the illustration, shaded squares represent pixels of color 1.

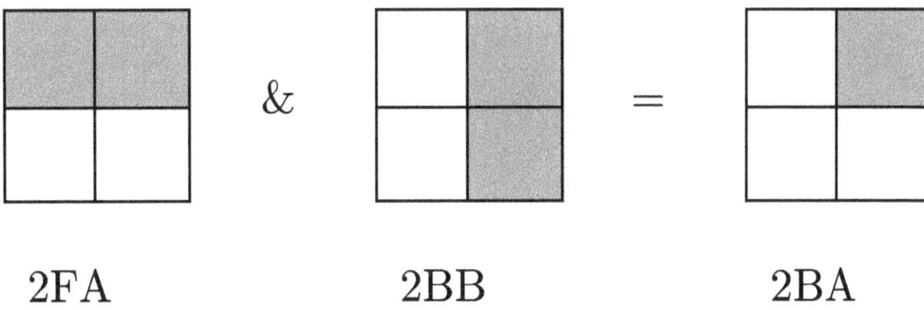

2FA   2BB   2BA

Input

The input data set contains a sequence of test cases, each of which is represented by two lines of input. In each test case, the first input line contains the Hex Quad Tree encoding of the first image and the second line contains the Hex Quad Tree encoding of the second image. For each input image, the number of hexadecimal digits in its Hex Quad Tree encoding will not exceed 100.

The last test case is followed by two input lines, each containing a single zero.

Output

For each test case, print 'Image' followed by its sequence number. On the next line, print the Hex Quad Tree encoding of the intersection of the two images for that test case. Separate the output for consecutive test cases with a blank line.

Sample Input

```
2FA
2BB
2FB
2EF
7
2FA
0
0
```

Sample Output

```
Image 1:
2BA

Image 2:
2EB

Image 3:
2FA
```

G   A Linking Loader

An *object module* is produced by a compiler as a result of processing a source program. A *linking loader* (or just a *linker*) is used to combine the multiple object modules used when a program contains several separately compiled modules. Two of its primary tasks are to relocate the code and data in each object module (since the compiler does not know where in memory a module will be placed), and to resolve symbolic references from one module to another. For example, a main program may reference a square root function called `sqrt`, and that function may be defined in a separate source module. The linker will then minimally have to assign addresses to the code and data in each module, and put the address of the `sqrt` function in the appropriate location(s) in the main module's code.

An object module contains (in order) zero or more *external symbol definitions*, zero or more *external symbol references*, zero or more bytes of code and data (that may include references to the values of external symbols), and an end of module marker. In this problem, an object module is represented as a sequence of text lines, each beginning with a single uppercase character that characterizes the remainder of the line. The format of each of these lines is as follows. Whitespace (one or more blanks and/or tab characters) will appear between the fields in these lines. Additional whitespace may follow the last field in each line.

- A line of the form 'D *symbol offset*' is an external symbol definition. It defines *symbol* as having the address *offset* bytes greater than the address where the first byte of code and data for the current object module is located by the linker. A *symbol* is a string of no more than eight upper case alphabetic characters. The *offset* is a hexadecimal number with no more than four digits (using only upper case alphabetic characters for the digits A through F). For example, in a module that is loaded starting at the address 100_{16}, the line 'D `START` 5C' indicates that the symbol `START` is defined as being associated with the address $15C_{16}$. The number of "D" lines in a test case is at most 100.

- A line of the form 'E *symbol*' is an external symbol reference, and indicates that the value of *symbol* (presumably defined in another object module) may be referenced as part of the code and data for the current module. For example, the line 'E `START`' indicates that the value of the symbol `START` (that is, the address defined for it) may be used as part of the code and data for the module. Each of the "E" lines for each module is numbered sequentially, starting with 0, so they can be referenced in the "C" lines.

- A line of the form 'C *n* $byte_1$ $byte_2$ ...$byte_n$' specifies the first or next *n* bytes of code and data for the current module. The value *n* is specified as a one or two digit hexadecimal number, and will be no larger than 10 hexadecimal. Each *byte* is either a one or two digit hexadecimal number, or a dollar sign. The first byte following a dollar sign (always on the same line) gives the 0-origin index of an external symbol reference for this module, and identifies the symbol which is to have its 16-bit value inserted at the current point in the linked program (that is, in the location indicated by the dollar sign and the following byte). The high-order byte is placed in the location indicated by the dollar sign. The values specified for the other bytes (those not following a dollar sign) are loaded into sequential memory locations, starting with the first (lowest) unused memory location. For example, the line 'C 4 25 $ 0 37' would cause the values 25_{16} 01_{16} $5C_{16}$ and 37_{16} to be placed in the next four unused memory locations, assuming the first "E" line for the current module specified a symbol defined as having the address $15C_{16}$. If the 0-origin index of the external symbol reference is an undefined symbol, the 16-bit value inserted at the current point in the linked program is 0000_{16}.

- A line of the form 'Z' marks the end of an object module.

You may assume that no address requires more than four hexadecimal digits. Lines are always given in the order shown above. There are no syntax errors in the input.

Input

This problem has multiple input cases. The input for each case is one or more object modules, in sequence, that are to be linked, followed by a line beginning with a dollar sign. The first address at which code is to be loaded in each case is 100_{16}.

The last case will be followed by a line containing only a dollar sign.

Output

For each case, print the case number (starting with 1), the 16-bit checksum of the loaded bytes (as described below), and the load map showing the address of each externally defined or referenced symbol, in ascending order of symbol name. For undefined symbols, print the value as four question marks, but use zero as the symbol's value when it is referenced in "C" lines. If a symbol is defined more than once, print 'M' following the address shown in the load map, and use the value from the first definition encountered in any object module to satisfy external references. Format the output exactly as shown in the samples.

The 16-bit checksum is computed by first setting it to zero. Then, for each byte assigned to a memory location by the loader, in increasing address order, circularly left shift the checksum by one bit, and add the byte from the memory location, discarding any carry out of the low-order 16 bits.

Sample Input

```
D MAIN 0
D END 5
C 03 01 02 03
C 03 04 05 06
Z
$
D ENTRY 4
E SUBX
E SUBY
C 10 1 2 3 4 5 $ 0 6 7 8 9 A B C D E
C 8 10 20 30 40 50 60 70 80
C 8 90 A0 B0 C0 D0 E0 $ 1
C 5 $ 0 FF EE DD
Z
D SUBX 01
C 06 A B C D E F
Z
D SUBX 05
C 06 51 52 53 54 55 56
Z
$
$
```

Sample Output

```
Case 1: checksum = 0078
   SYMBOL    ADDR
  --------   ----
   END       0105
   MAIN      0100

Case 2: checksum = 548C
   SYMBOL    ADDR
  --------   ----
   ENTRY     0104
   SUBX      0126 M
   SUBY      ????
```

H A Spy in the Metro

Secret agent Maria was sent to Algorithms City to carry out an especially dangerous mission. After several thrilling events we find her in the first station of Algorithms City Metro, examining the time table. The Algorithms City Metro consists of a single line with trains running both ways, so its time table is not complicated.

Maria has an appointment with a local spy at the last station of Algorithms City Metro. Maria knows that a powerful organization is after her. She also knows that while waiting at a station, she is at great risk of being caught. To hide in a running train is much safer, so she decides to stay in running trains as much as possible, even if this means traveling backward and forward. Maria needs to know a schedule with minimal waiting time at the stations that gets her to the last station in time for her appointment. You must write a program that finds the total waiting time in a best schedule for Maria.

The Algorithms City Metro system has N stations, consecutively numbered from 1 to N. Trains move in both directions: from the first station to the last station and from the last station back to the first station. The time required for a train to travel between two consecutive stations is fixed since all trains move at the same speed. Trains make a very short stop at each station, which you can ignore for simplicity. Since she is a very fast agent, Maria can always change trains at a station even if the trains involved stop in that station at the same time.

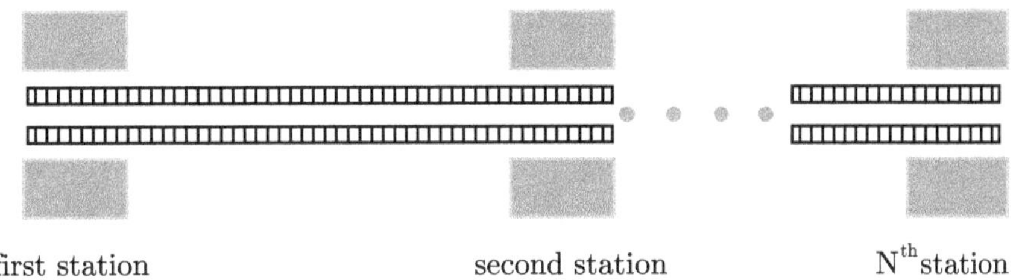

Input

The input file contains several test cases. Each test case consists of seven lines with information as follows.

Line 1. The integer N $(2 \leq N \leq 50)$, which is the number of stations.

Line 2. The integer T $(0 \leq T \leq 200)$, which is the time of the appointment.

Line 3. $N - 1$ integers: $t_1, t_2, \ldots, t_{N-1}$ $(1 \leq t_i \leq 20)$, representing the travel times for the trains between two consecutive stations: t_1 represents the travel time between the first two stations, t_2 the time between the second and the third station, and so on.

Line 4. The integer $M1$ $(1 \leq M1 \leq 50)$, representing the number of trains departing from the first station.

Line 5. $M1$ integers: $d_1, d_2, \ldots, d_{M1}$ $(0 \leq d_i \leq 250$ and $d_i < d_{i+1})$, representing the times at which trains depart from the first station.

Line 6. The integer $M2$ ($1 \leq M2 \leq 50$), representing the number of trains departing from the N-th station.

Line 7. $M2$ integers: $e_1, e_2, \ldots, e_{M2}$ ($0 \leq e_i \leq 250$ and $e_i < e_{i+1}$) representing the times at which trains depart from the N-th station.

The last case is followed by a line containing a single zero.

Output

For each test case, print a line containing the case number (starting with 1) and an integer representing the total waiting time in the stations for a best schedule, or the word 'impossible' in case Maria is unable to make the appointment. Use the format of the sample output.

Sample Input

```
4
55
5 10 15
4
0 5 10 20
4
0 5 10 15
4
18
1 2 3
5
0 3 6 10 12
6
0 3 5 7 12 15
2
30
20
1
20
7
1 3 5 7 11 13 17
0
```

Sample Output

```
Case Number 1: 5
Case Number 2: 0
Case Number 3: impossible
```

I The Solar System

It is common knowledge that the Solar System consists of the sun at its center and nine planets moving around the sun on elliptical orbits. Less well known is the fact that the planets' orbits are not at all arbitrary. In fact, the orbits obey three laws discovered by Johannes Kepler. These laws, also called "The Laws of Planetary Motion," are the following.

1. The orbits of the planets are ellipses, with the sun at one focus of the ellipse. (Recall that the two foci of an ellipse are such that the sum of the distances to them is the same for all points on the ellipse.)

2. The line joining a planet to the sun sweeps over equal areas during equal time intervals as the planet travels around the ellipse.

3. The ratio of the squares of the revolutionary periods of two planets is equal to the ratio of the cubes of their semi major axes.

By Kepler's first law, the path of the planet shown in the figure on the left is an ellipse. According to Kepler's second law, if the planet goes from M to N in time t_A and from P to Q in time t_B and if $t_A = t_B$, then area A equals area B. Kepler's third law is illustrated next.

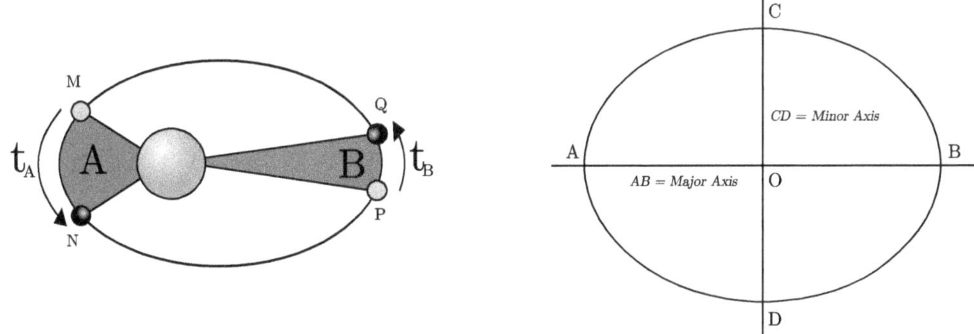

Consider an ellipse whose center is at the origin 0 and that is symmetric with respect to the two coordinate axes. The x-axis intersects the ellipse at points A and B and the y-axis intersects the ellipse at points C and D. Set $a = \frac{1}{2}|AB|$ and $b = \frac{1}{2}|CD|$. Then the ellipse is defined by the equation $\frac{x^2}{a^2} + \frac{y^2}{b^2} = 1$. If $a \geq b$, AB is called the major axis, CD the minor axis, and OA (with length a) is called the semi major axis. When two planets are revolving around the sun in times t_1 and t_2 respectively, and the semi major axes of their orbits have lengths a_1 and a_2, then according to Kepler's third law $\left(\frac{t_1}{t_2}\right)^2 = \left(\frac{a_1}{a_2}\right)^3$.

In this problem, you are to compute the location of a planet using Kepler's laws. You are given the description of one planet in the Solar System (i.e., the length of its semi-major axis, semi-minor axis, and its revolution time) and the description of a second planet (its semi-major axis and semi-minor axis). Assume that the second planet's orbit is aligned with the coordinate axes (as in the above figure), that it moves in counter clockwise direction, and that the sun is located at the focal point with non-negative x-coordinate. You are to compute the position of the second planet a specified amount of time after it starts at the point with maximal x-coordinate on its orbit (point B in the above figure).

Input

The input file contains several descriptions of pairs of planets. Each line contains six integers $a_1, b_1, t_1, a_2, b_2, t$. The first five integers are positive, and describe two planets as follows:

a_1 = semi major axis of the first planet's orbit
b_1 = semi minor axis of the first planet's orbit
t_1 = period of revolution of the first planet (in days)
a_2 = semi major axis of the second planet's orbit
b_2 = semi minor axis of the second planet's orbit

The non-negative integer t is the time (in days) at which you have to determine the position of the second planet, assuming that the planet starts in position $(a_2, 0)$.

The last description is followed by a line containing six zeros.

Output

For each pair of planets described in the input, produce one line of output. For each line, print the number of the test case. Then print the x- and y-coordinates of the position of the second planet after t days. These values must be exact to three digits to the right of the decimal point. Follow the format of the sample output provided below.

Sample Input

```
10 5 10 10 5 10
10 5 10 20 10 10
0 0 0 0 0 0
```

Sample Output

```
Solar System 1: 10.000 0.000
Solar System 2: -17.525 4.819
```

J Toll

Sindbad the Sailor sold 66 silver spoons to the Sultan of Samarkand. The selling was quite easy; but delivering was complicated. The items were transported over land, passing through several towns and villages. Each town and village demanded an entry toll. There were no tolls for leaving. The toll for entering a *village* was simply one item. The toll for entering a *town* was one piece per 20 items carried. For example, to enter a town carrying 70 items, you had to pay 4 items as toll. The towns and villages were situated strategically between rocks, swamps and rivers, so you could not avoid them.

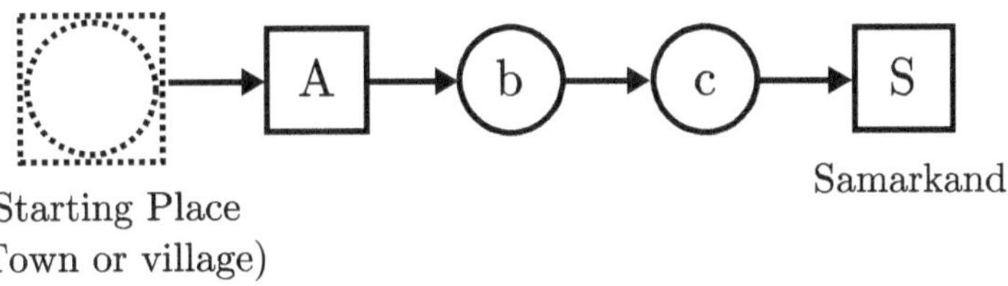

Figure 1: To reach Samarkand with 66 spoons, traveling through a town followed by two villages, you must start with 76 spoons.

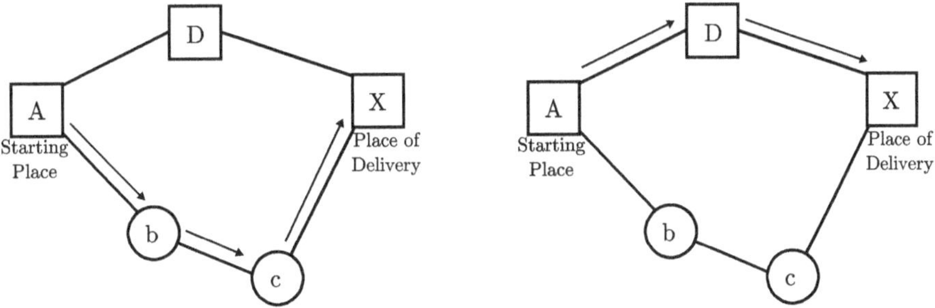

Figure 2: The best route to reach X with 39 spoons, starting from A, is A→b→c→X, shown with arrows in the figure on the left. The best route to reach X with 10 spoons is A→D→X, shown in the figure on the right. The figures display towns as squares and villages as circles.

Predicting the tolls charged in each village or town is quite simple, but finding the best route (the cheapest route) is a real challenge. The best route depends upon the number of items carried. For numbers up to 20, villages and towns charge the same. For large numbers of items, it makes sense to avoid towns and travel through more villages, as illustrated in Figure 2.

You must write a program to solve Sindbad's problem. Given the number of items to be delivered to a certain town or village and a road map, your program must determine the total number of items required at the beginning of the journey that uses a cheapest route.

Input

The input consists of several test cases. Each test case consists of two parts: the roadmap followed by the delivery details.

The first line of the roadmap contains an integer n, which is the number of roads in the map $(0 \leq n)$. Each of the next n lines contains exactly two letters representing the two endpoints of a road. A capital letter represents a town; a lower case letter represents a village. Roads can be traveled in either direction.

Following the roadmap is a single line for the delivery details. This line consists of three things: an integer p $(0 < p \leq 1000)$ for the number of items that must be delivered, a letter for the starting place, and a letter for the place of delivery. The roadmap is always such that the items can be delivered.

The last test case is followed by a line containing the number -1.

Output

The output consists of a single line for each test case. Each line displays the case number and the number of items required at the beginning of the journey. Follow the output format in the example given below.

Sample Input

```
1
a Z
19 a Z
5
A D
D X
A b
b c
c X
39 A X
-1
```

Sample Output

```
Case 1: 20
Case 2: 44
```

WORLD FINALS 2004

PRAGUE, CZECH REPUBLIC

World Champion

ST. PETERSBURG INSTITUTE OF FINE MECHANICS AND OPTICS

Dmitri Pavlov

Pavel Mavrin

Sergey Orshanskiy

Director of Judging

Dick Rinewalt *Texas Christian University*

Chief Judge

Jo Perry *North Carolina State University*

Judges

Osman Ay	*Zambak Publishing*
John Bonomo	*Westminster College*
Don Chamberlin	*IBM Almaden Research Center*
David Elizandro	*Tennessee Tech University*
Derek Kisman	*Google*
Peter Kluit	*Delft University of Technology*
Shahriar Manzoor	*Southeast University*
Miguel A. Revilla	*University of Valladolid*
Robert Roos	*Allegheny College*
Matthias Ruhl	*Google*
Stanley Wileman, Jr.	*University of Nebraska at Omaha*

CLI Live Archive problem numbers

2993	A	Carl the Ant
2994	B	Heliport
2995	C	Image Is Everything
2996	D	Insecure in Prague
2997	E	Intersecting Dates
2998	F	Merging Maps
2999	G	Navigation
3000	H	Tree-Lined Streets
3001	I	Suspense!
3002	J	Air Traffic Control

A Carl the Ant

Ants leave small chemical trails on the ground in order to mark paths for other ants to follow. Ordinarily these trails follow rather straight lines. But in one ant colony there is an ant named Carl, and Carl is not an ordinary ant. Carl will often zigzag for no apparent reason, sometimes crossing his own path numerous times in the process. When other ants come to an intersection, they always follow the path with the strongest scent, which is the most recent path t hat leads away from the intersection point.

Ants are 1 centimeter long, move and burrow at 1 centimeter per second, and follow their paths exactly (bending at right angles when moving around corners). Ants cannot cross or overlap each other. If two ants meet at the exact same instant at an intersection point, the one that has been on Carl's path the longest has the right of way; otherwise, the ant that has been waiting the longest at an intersection will move first.

Carl burrows up from the ground to start at the origin at time 0. He then walks his path and burrows back down into the ground at the endpoint. The rest of the ants follow at regular intervals. Given the description of Carl's path and when the other ants start the path, you are to determine how long it takes the entire set of ants to finish burrowing back into the ground. All the ants are guaranteed to finish.

Input

Input consists of several test cases. The first line of the input file contains a single integer indicating the number of test cases .

The input for each test case starts with a single line containing three positive integers n ($1 \le n \le 50$), m ($1 \le m \le 100$), and d ($1 \le d \le 100$). Here, n is the number of line segments in Carl's path, m is the number of ants traveling the path (including Carl), and d is the time delay before each successive ant's emergence. Carl (who is numbered 0) starts at time 0. The next ant (ant number 1) will emerge at time d, the next at time $2d$, and so on. If the burrow is blocked, the ants will emerge as soon as possible in the correct order.

Each of the next n lines for the test case consists of a unique integer pair x y ($-100 \le x, y \le 100$), which is the endpoint of a line segment of Carl's path, in the order that Carl travels. The first line starts at the origin (0,0) and the starting point of every subsequent line is the endpoint of the previous line.

For simplicity, Carl always travels on line segments parallel to the axes, and no endpoints lie on any segment other than the ones which they serve as an endpoint.

Output

The output for each case is described as follows:

```
Case C:
Carl finished the path at time t1
The ants finished in the following order:
a1a2a3...am
The last ant finished the path at time t2
```

Here, C is the case number (starting at 1), $a_1, a_2, a_3, \ldots, a_m$ are the ant numbers in the order that they go back underground, and t_1 and t_2 are the times (in seconds) at which Carl and the last ant finish going underground. You should separate consecutive cases with a single blank line.

Sample Input

```
2
4 7 4
0 4
2 4
2 2
-2 2
4 7 2
0 4
2 4
2 2
-2 2
```

Sample Output

```
Case 1:
Carl finished the path at time 13
The ants finished in the following order:
0 2 1 3 4 5 6
The last ant finished the path at time 29

Case 2:
Carl finished the path at time 13
The ants finished in the following order:
0 4 1 5 2 6 3
The last ant finished the path at time 19
```

B Heliport

In these fast-paced times, companies are investing in heliports to reduce travel time for their busy executives. The heliports are typically circular landing pads, constructed on the roofs of the companies' headquarters.

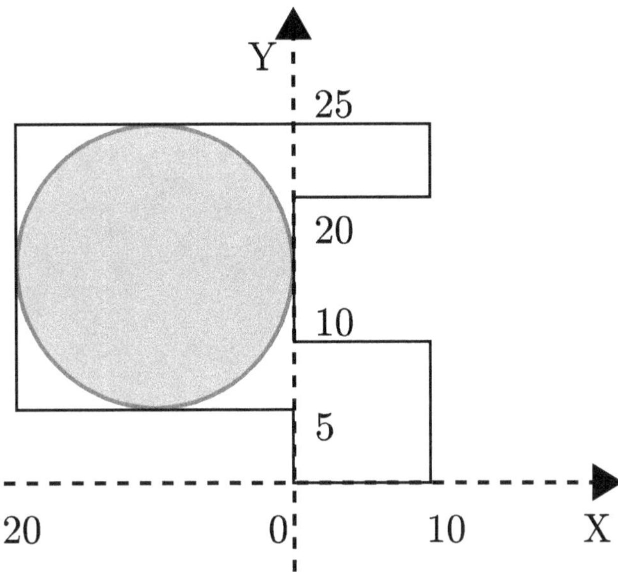

You must write a program that finds the largest radius for a circular heliport that can be constructed on the flat roof of a building that is in the form of a simple polygon. Since this is merely the design phase of the construction effort, your program must find only the radius of the heliport. The maximum radius for a heliport in the diagram shown is 10.

Input

The input file contains several test cases. Each test case consists of two lines. The first line consists of an even integer n ($4 \le n \le 20$), which is the number of the sides of the building. The second line consists of n pairs of the form (m, d), where m is an integer ($1 \le m \le 50$) and d is a letter (U, R, D, L). Assuming the roof is drawn on the Cartesian plane, m is the length of a roof boundary segment and d is the direction of that segment as you travel counterclockwise around the roof. U, R, D, and L mean "Up," "Right," "Down," and "Left" respectively. The boundary segments of the roof, which are parallel to the x and y axes, are given in counterclockwise order. The starting position is the origin $(0, 0)$.

Input for the last test case is followed by a line consisting of the number 0.

Output

For each test case, the output consists of a separate line containing the case number (starting with 1) and a real number (rounded to two digits after the decimal point) representing the radius of the heliport. Print a blank line between cases as shown in the sample output.

Sample Input

```
4
2 R 2 U 2 L 2 D
10
10 R 10 U 10 L 10 U 10 R 5 U 30 L 20 D 20 R 5 D
0
```

Sample Output

```
Case Number 1 radius is: 1.00

Case Number 2 radius is: 10.00
```

C   Image Is Everything

Your new company is building a robot that can hold small lightweight objects. The robot will have the intelligence to determine if an object is light enough to hold. It does this by taking pictures of the object from the 6 cardinal directions, and then inferring an upper limit on the object's weight based on those images. You must write a program to do that for the robot.

You can assume that each object is formed from an $N \times N \times N$ lattice of cubes, some of which may be missing. Each $1 \times 1 \times 1$ cube weighs 1 gram, and each cube is painted a single solid color. The object is not necessarily connected.

Input

The input for this problem consists of several test cases representing different objects. Every case begins with a line containing N, which is the size of the object ($1 \le N \le 10$). The next N lines are the different $N \times N$ views of the object, in the order front, left, back, right, top, bottom. Each view will be separated by a single space from the view that follows it. The bottom edge of the top view corresponds to the top edge of the front view. Similarly, the top edge of the bottom view corresponds to the bottom edge of the front view. In each view, colors are represented by single, unique capital letters, while a period (.) indicates that the object can be seen through at that location.

Input for the last test case is followed by a line consisting of the number 0.

Output

For each test case, print a line containing the maximum possible weight of the object, using the format shown below.

Sample Input

```
3
.R. YYR .Y. RYY .Y. .R.
GRB YGR BYG RBY GYB GRB
.R. YRR .Y. RRY .R. .Y.
2
ZZ ZZ ZZ ZZ ZZ ZZ
ZZ ZZ ZZ ZZ ZZ ZZ
0
```

Sample Output

```
Maximum weight: 11 gram(s)
Maximum weight: 8 gram(s)
```

D   Insecure in Prague

Prague is a dangerous city for developers of cryptographic schemes. In 2001, a pair of researchers in Prague announced a security flaw in the famous PGP encryption protocol. In Prague in 2003 , a flaw was discovered in the SSL/TLS (Secure Sockets Layer and Transport Layer Security) protocols. However, Prague's reputation for being tough on cryptographic protocols hasn't stopped the part-time amateur cryptographer and full-time nutcase, Immanuel Kant-DeWitt (known to his friends as "I. Kant-DeWitt"), from bringing his latest encryption scheme to Prague. Here's how it works:

A plain text message p of length n is to be transmitted. The sender chooses an integer $m \geq 2n$, and integers s, t, i, and j, where $0 \leq s, t, i, j < m$ and $i < j$. The scheme works as follows: m is the length of the transmitted ciphertext string, c. Initially, c contains m empty slots. The first letter of p is placed in position s of c. The k-th letter, $k \geq 2$, is placed by skipping over i empty slots in c after the $(k-1)$-st letter, wrapping around to the beginning of c if necessary. Slots already containing letters are not counted as empty. For instance, if the message is PRAGUE, if $s = 1$, $i = 6$, and $m = 15$, then the letters are placed in c as follows:

A	P		U					R	G			E		
0	1	2	3	4	5	6	7	8	9	10	11	12	13	14

Starting with the first empty slot in or after position t in string c, the plain text message is entered again, but this time skipping j empty slots between letters. For instance, if $t = 0$ and $j = 8$, the second copy of p is entered as follows (beginning in position 2, the first empty slot starting from $t = 0$):

A	**P**	**P**	U	**R**		**A**	**U**	R	G	**E**	**G**	E		
0	1	2	3	4	5	6	7	8	9	10	11	12	13	14

Finally, any remaining unfilled slots in c are filled in with randomly chosen letters:

A	P	P	U	R	**A**	A	U	R	G	E	G	E	**W**	**E**
0	1	2	3	4	5	6	7	8	9	10	11	12	13	14

Kant-DeWitt believes that the duplication of the message, combined with the use of random letters, will confuse decryption schemes based upon letter frequencies and that, without knowledge of s and i, no one can figure out what the original message is. Your job is to try to prove him wrong. Given a number of ciphertext strings (and no additional information), you will determine the longest possible message that could have been encoded using the Kant-DeWitt method.

Input

A number of ciphertext strings, one per line. Each string will consist only of upper case alphabetic letters, with no leading or trailing blanks; each will have length between 2 and 40.

Input for the last test case is followed by a line consisting of the letter X.

Output

For each input ciphertext string, print the longest string that could be encrypted in the ciphertext. If more than one string has the longest length, then print 'Codeword not unique'. Follow the format of the sample output given below.

Sample Input

```
APPURAAURGEGEWE
ABABABAB
THEACMPROGRAMMINGCONTEST
X
```

Sample Output

```
Code 1: PRAGUE
Code 2: Codeword not unique
Code 3: Codeword not unique
```

E Intersecting Dates

A research group is developing a computer program that will fetch historical stock market quotes
from a service that charges a fixed fee for each day's quotes that it delivers. The group has examined
the collection of previously-requested quotes and discovered a lot of duplication, resulting in wasted
money. So the new program will maintain a list of all past quotes requested by members of the
group. When additional quotes are required, only quotes for those dates not previously obtained
will be fetched from the service, thus minimizing the cost. You are to write a program that d
etermines when new quotes are required. Input for the program consists of the date ranges for
which quotes have been requested in the past and the date ranges for which quotes are required.
The program will then determine the date ranges for which quotes must be fetched from the service.

Input

There will be multiple input cases. The input for each case begins with two non-negative integers
NX and NR, $(0 \leq NX, NR \leq 100)$. NX is the number of existing date ranges for quotes requested
in the past. NR is the number of date ranges in the incoming requests for quotes. Following these
are $NX + NR$ pairs of dates. The first date in each pair will be less than or equal to the second
date in the pair. The first NX pairs specify the date ranges of quotes which have been requested
and obtained in the past, and the next NR pairs specify the date ranges for which quotes are
required. Two zeroes will follow the input data for the last case. Each input date will be given in
the form $YYYYMMDD$. $YYYY$ is the year (1700 to 2100), MM is the month (01 to 12), and
DD is the day (in the allowed range for the given month and year).

Recall that months 04, 06, 09, and 11 have 30 days, months 01, 03, 05, 07, 08, 10, and 12 have
31 days, and month 02 has 28 days except in leap years, when it has 29 days. A year is a leap year
if it is evenly divisible by 4 and is not a century year (a multiple of 100), or if it is divisible by 400.

Output

For each input case, display the case number (1, 2, ...) followed by a list of any date ranges for
which quotes must be fetched from the service, one date range per output line. Use the American
date format shown in the sample output below. Explicitly indicate (as shown) if no additional
quotes must be fetched. If two date ranges are contiguous or overlap, then merge them into a
single date range. If a date range consists of a single date, print it as a single date, not as a range
consisting of two identical dates. Display the date ranges in chronological order, starting with the
earliest date range.

Sample Input

```
1 1
19900101 19901231
19901201 20000131
0 3
19720101 19720131
19720201 19720228
19720301 19720301
1 1
20010101 20011231
20010515 20010901
0 0
```

Sample Output

```
Case 1:
    1/1/1991 to 1/31/2000

Case 2:
    1/1/1972 to 2/28/1972
    3/1/1972

Case 3:
    No additional quotes are required.
```

F Merging Maps

Pictures taken from an airplane or satellite of an ar ea to be mapped are often of sufficiently high resolution to uniquely identify major features. Since a single picture can cover only a small portion of the earth, mapping larger areas requires taking pictures of smaller overlapping areas, and then merging these to produce a map of a larger area.

For this problem you are given several maps of rectangular areas, each represented as an array of single-character cells. A cell contains an uppercase alphabetic character ('A' to 'Z') if its corresponding area contains an identifiable major feature. Different letters correspond to different features, but the same major feature (such as a road) may be identified in multiple cells. A cell contains a hyphen ('-') if no identifiable feature is located in the cell area. Merging two maps means overlaying them so that one or more common major features are aligned. A cell containing a major feature in one map can be overlaid with a cell not containing a major feature in the other. However, different major features (with diff erent letters) cannot be overlaid in the same cell.

```
        --A-C      C----      C----      ----D      -D--C
        ----D      D---F      -----      -E--B      ----G
        ----B      B----      B-A-C      -----      ----B
 Map #    1          2          3          4          5
```

Consider the five 3-row, 5-column maps shown above. The rightmost column of map 1 perfectly matches the leftmost column of map 2, so those maps could be overlaid to yield a 3-row, 9-column map. But map 1 could also overlay map 3 as well, since the C and B features in the rightmost column of map 1 match those in the leftmost column of map 3; the D does not perfectly match the '-' in the center of the column, but there is no conflict. In a similar manner, the top row of map 1 could also overlay the bottom row of map 3.

The "score" of a pair of maps indicates the extent to which the two maps match. The score of an overlay of a pair of maps is the number of cells containing major features that coincide in the overlay that gives the best match. The score for the map pair is the maximum score for the possible overlays of the maps. Thus, the score for a pair of maps each having 3 rows and 5 columns must be in the range 0 to 15.

An "offset" is a pair of integers (r, c) that specifies how two maps, a and b, are overlaid. The value of r gives the offset of rows in b relative to rows in a; similarly, c gives the offset of columns in b relative to columns in a. For example, the overlay of map 1 and map 2 shown above has the offset (0,4) and a score of 3. The two overlays of map 1 and map 3 yielding scores of 2 have offsets of (0,4) and (-2,0).

The following steps describe how to merge a sequence of maps:

1. Merge the pair of maps in the sequence that yield the highest positive score (resolving ties by choos ing pair that has the map with the lowest sequence number).

2. Remove the maps that were merged from the sequence.

3. Add the resulting merged map to the sequence, giving it the next larger sequence number.

In the example above, maps 1 and 2 would be merged to produce map 6, and maps 1 and 2 would be removed from the sequence. Steps 1, 2 and 3 are repeated until only a single map remains in the sequence, or until none of the maps in the sequence can be merged (that is, until the overlay score for each possible map pair is zero).

If two maps can be merged in several ways to yield the same score, then merge them using the smallest row offset. If the result is still ambiguous, use the smallest row offset and the smallest column offset.

Input

The input will contain one or more sets of data, each containing between 2 and 10 maps. Each set of data begins with an integer specifying the number of maps in the sequence. The maps follow, each beginning with a line containing two integers NR and NC ($1 \le NR, NC \le 10$) that specify the number of rows and columns in the map that immediately follows on the next NR lines. The first NC characters on each of these NR lines are the map data, and any trailing characters on such lines are to be ignored.

Input for the last test case is followed by a line consisting of the number 0.

Output

For each set of data, display the input case number (1, 2, ...) and the merged maps, each identified with its sequence number and enclosed by a border. The output should be formatted as shown in the samples below. No merged map will have more than 70 columns.

Sample Input

```
5
3 5
--A-C
----D
----B
3 5
C----
D---F
B----
3 5
C----
-----
B-A-C
3 5
----D
-E--B
-----
3 5
-D--C
----G
----B
2
3 5
----A
----B
----C
3 5
A----
B----
D----
0
```

Sample Output

```
Case 1
    MAP 9:
    +-------------+
    |-D--C--------|
    |----G--------|
    |----B-A-C----|
    |--------D---F|
    |-----E--B----|
    |-------------|
    +-------------+

Case 2
    MAP 1:
    +-----+
    |----A|
    |----B|
    |----C|
    +-----+

    MAP 2:
    +-----+
    |A----|
    |B----|
    |D----|
    +-----+
```

G Navigation

Global Positioning System (GPS) is a navigation system based on a set of satellites orbiting approximately 20,000 kilometers above the earth. Each satellite follows a known orbit and transmits a radio signal that encodes the current time. If a GPS-equipped vehicle has a very accurate clock, it can compare its own local time with the time encoded in the signals received from the satellites. Since radio signals propagate at a known rate, the vehicle can compute the distance between its current location and the location of the satellite when the signal was broadcast. By measuring its distance from several satellites in known orbits, a vehicle can compute its position very accurately.

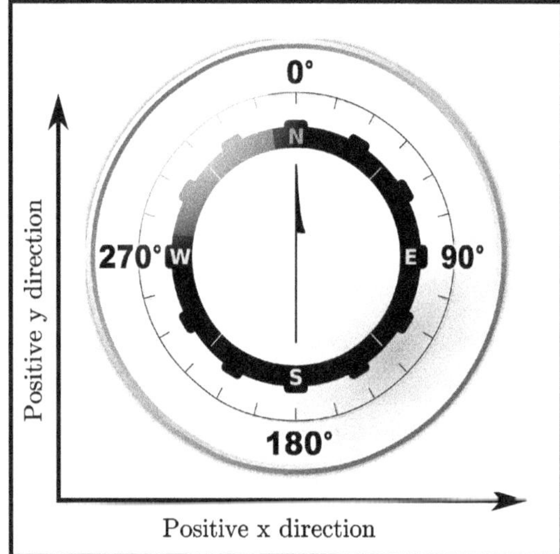

Figure 1: The Compass
Figure 2: 1st Sample Input

You must write a simple "autopilot" program based on GPS navigation. To make the problem easier, we state it as a two-dimen sional problem. In other words, you do not need to take into account the curvature of the earth or the altitude of the satellites. Furthermore, the problem uses speeds that are more appropriate for airplanes and sound waves than for satellites and radio waves.

Given a set of signals from moving sources, your program must compute the receiving position on the Cartesian plane. Then, given a destination point on the plane, your program must compute the compass heading required to go from the receiving position to the destination. All compass headings are stated in degrees. Compass heading 0 (North) corresponds to the positive y direction, and compass heading 90 (East) corresponds to the positive x direction, as shown in Figure 1.

Input

The input consists of multiple data sets.

The first line of input in each data set contains an integer N ($1 \le N \le 10$), which is the number of signal sources in the set. This is followed by three floating point numbers: t, x, and y. Here, t denotes the exact local time when all the signals are received, represented in seconds after the reference time (time 0), and x and y represent the coordinates of the destination point on the Cartesian plane. Each of the next N lines contains four floating-point numbers that carry information about one signal source. The first two numbers represent the known position of the signal source on the Cartesian plane at the reference time. The third number represents the direction of travel of the signal source in the form of a compass heading D ($0 \leq D < 360$). The fourth number is the time that is encoded in the signal-that is, the time when the signal was transmitted, represented in seconds after the reference time. The magnitudes of all numbers in the input file are less than 10,000 and no floating-point number has more than 5 digits after the decimal point.

The last data set is followed by a line containing four zeros.

The unit distance in the coordinate space is one meter. Assume that each signal source is moving over the Cartesian plane at a speed of 100 meters per second and that the broadcast signal propagates at a speed of 350 meters per second. Due to inaccuracies in synchronizing clocks, assume that your distance calculations are accurate only to 0.1 meter. That is, if two points are computed to be within 0.1 meter of each other, you should treat them as the same point. There is also the possibility that a signal may have been corrupted in transmission, so the data received from multiple signals may be inconsistent.

Output

For each trial, print the trial number followed by the compass heading from the receiving location to the destination, in degrees rounded to the nearest integer. Use the labeling as shown in the example output. If the signals do not contain enough information to compute the receiving location (that is, more than one position is consistent with the signals), print 'Inconclusive'. If the signals are inconsistent (that is, no position is consistent with the signals), print 'Inconsistent'. If the receiving location is within 0.1 meter of the destination, print 'Arrived'. If the situation is Inconclusive or Inconsistent, then you do not need to consider the case Arrived.

Figure 2 above corresponds to the first sample input. The locations of the three satellites at time $t = 0$ are A (-100,350), B (350,-100) and C (350,800). The signals received by the GPS unit were transmitted at time $t = 1.75$, when the satellites were at locations A', B', and C' (however, in general the signals received by the GPS unit might have been transmitted at different times). The signals from the three satellites converge at D at time $t = 2.53571$, which means D is the location of the receiving GPS unit. From point D, a compass course of 45 degrees leads toward the destination point of (1050, 1050).

Sample Input

```
3  2.53571  1050.0  1050.0
-100.0    350.0    90.0  1.75
 350.0  -100.0     0.0  1.75
 350.0   800.0  180.0  1.75
2  2.0  1050.0  1050.0
-100.0    350.0    90.0  1.0
 350.0  -100.0     0.0  1.0
0  0  0  0
```

Sample Output

```
Trial 1: 45 degrees
Trial 2: Inconclusive
```

H Tree-Lined Streets

The city council of Greenville recently voted to improve the appearance of inner city streets. To provide more greenery in the scenery, the city council has decided to plant trees along all major streets and avenues. To get an idea of how expensive this urban improvement project will be, the city council wants to determine how many trees will be planted. The planting of trees is limited in two ways:

- Along a street, trees have to be planted at least 50 meters apart. This is to provide adequate grow ing space, and to keep the cost of the project within reasonable limits.

- Due to safety concerns, no tree should be planted closer than 25 meters along a street to the nearest int ersection. This is to ensure that traffic participants can easily see each other approaching an intersection. Traffic safety should not be compromised by reducing visibility.

All streets considered in this project are straight . They have no turns or bends.

The city council needs to know the maximum number of trees that can be planted under these two restrictions.

Input

The input consists of descriptions of several street maps. The first line of each description contains an integer n ($1 \leq n \leq 100$), which is the number of streets in the map. Each of the following n lines describes a street as a line segment in the Cartesian plane. An input line describing a street contains four integers x_1, y_1, x_2, and y_2. This means that this street goes from point (x_1, y_1) to point (x_2, y_2). The coordinates x_1, y_1, x_2, and y_2 are given in meters, ($0 \leq x1, y1, x2, y2 \leq 100000$). Every street has a positive length. Each end point lies on exactly one street.

For each street, the distances between neighboring intersections and/or the end points of the street are not exact multiples of 25 meters. More precisely, the difference of such a distance to the nearest multiple of 25 meters will be at least 0.001 meters. At each intersection, exactly two streets meet.

Input for the last street map description is followed by a line consisting of the number 0.

Output

For each street map described in the input, first print its number in the sequence. Then print the maximum number of trees that can be planted under the restrictions specified above. Follow the format in the sample output given below.

Sample Input

```
3
0  40  200  40
40  0  40  200
0  200  200  0
4
0  30  230  30
0  200  230  200
```

```
30 0 30 230
200 0 200 230
3
0 1 121 1
0 0 121 4
0 4 121 0
0
```

Sample Output

```
Map 1
Trees = 13
Map 2
Trees = 20
Map 3
Trees = 7
```

I Suspense!

Jan and Tereza live in adjoining buildings and their apartments face one another. For their school science project, they want to construct a miniature suspension bridge made of rope, string, and cardboard connecting their two buildings. Two pieces of identical-length rope form the main suspension cables, which are attached to the bottoms of their windows. The cardboard "roadbed" of the bridge is held up by numerous strings tied to the main cables. The horizontal bridge roadbed lies exactly one meter below the lowest point of the ropes. For aesthetic reasons, the roadbed should be at least two meters below the lower edge of the lower of the two students' windows. The laws of physics dictate that each suspension rope forms a parabola.

While Jan and Tereza don't plan to walk on this model bridge, there is a serious problem: some of the occupants of the apartment buildings own pet cats, and others own pet birds. Jan and Tereza want to be sure that their bridge doesn't provide a way for a cat to reach a bird. Jan and Tereza have observed that a cat cannot jump as high as 0.5 meters, and will not jump down as far as 3 meters. So as long as the bridge roadbed lies at least 0.5 meters above the bottom of a cat's window, or at least 3 meters below the bottom of a cat's window, the cat will not jump onto it. Likewise, a cat that successfully jumps onto the roadbed will not be able to reach a bird's window if the roadbed lies at least 0.5 meters below the bottom of the bird's window, or at least 3 meters above the bottom of the bird's window. Cats are concerned only with reaching birds, and they do not worry about returning home.

The figure below shows Jan's apartment ("**J**") and Tereza's apartment ("**T**") with a rope joining the bottoms of their windows and the cardboard roadbed one meter below the lowest point of the rope. The cat on the second floor can reach the bird on the second floor using the bridge.

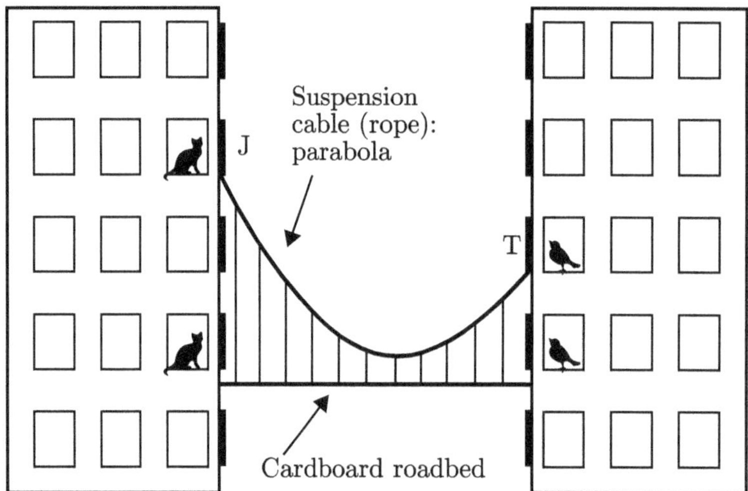

You must write a program to determine how much rope Jan and Tereza need to construct each cable for a bridge that won't endanger any of the birds in their two buildings.

Input for your program will be: the distance between the two buildings, in meters; the floor numbers for Jan and Tereza (with the lowest, or ground floor in each building numbered 1), the kinds of pets living in all the floors up through Jan's floor, and the kinds of pets living in all the floors up through Tereza's floor. Your program must determine the length of the longest cable that can be used to suspend a bridge between the two buildings that does not permit any cat to reach a bird by means of the bridge. The roadbed of the bridge must lie at least 1 meter above the ground and must lie exactly one meter below the lowest point of the suspension cables. It must also lie at least two meters below the lower of the two windows of Jan and Tereza. All rooms in the buildings are exactly 3 meters tall; all windows are exactly 1.5 meters tall and the bottom of each window lies exactly 1 meter above the floor of each room.

Input

The input will describe several cases, each of which has three lines. The first line will contain two positive integers j and t $(2 \leq j, t \leq 25)$ representing Jan's floor and Tereza's floor, and a real value d $(1 \leq d \leq 25)$ representing the distance, in meters, between the buildings. The second line will contain j uppercase letters $l_1, l_2, \ldots, l_j$ separated by whitespace. Letter l_k is 'B' if a bird lives on floor number k of Jan's building, 'C' if a cat lives on floor number k, and 'N' if neither kind of pet lives on floor number k. The third line similarly contains t uppercase letters representing the same kind of information for the floor s in Tereza's building. The last case is followed by a line containing three zeroes.

Output

For each case, print the case number (1, 2, ...) and the largest value c such that two cables, each of length c, can be used to suspend a bridge from the lower edges of Jan's and Tereza's windows so that the bridge floor lies one meter below the lowest point in the cable, lies at least 1 meter above the ground, lies at least two meters below Jan and Tereza's windows, and does not allow a cat to reach a bird. The lengt h should be rounded to three places following the decimal point. If no such bridge can be constructed, print 'impossible'. Print a blank line between the output for consecutive cases. Your output format should imitate the sample output.

Sample Input

```
4 3 5.0
N C N C
N B B
4 3 5.0
C B C C
B C B
0 0 0
```

Sample Output

```
Case 1: 14.377

Case 2: impossible
```

J Air Traffic Control

In order to avoid midair collisions, most commercial flights are monitored by ground-based air traffic control centers that track their position using radar. For this problem, you will be given information on a set of airplanes and a set of control centers, and you must compute how monitoring of the airplanes is distributed among the control centers. The position of each airplane is represented by a unique (x, y) coordinate pair. For the purpose of this problem, the height (altitude) of the airplanes can be ignored.

The number of airplanes that can be monitored by a given control center varies from time to time due to changes in staff and equipment. At any given time, each control center monitors as many planes as it can, choosing the airplanes to be monitored according to the following priorities:

(1) it will prefer to monitor planes that are closer to the control center rather than ones that are farther away;

(2) if two airplanes are equally distant from the center and the center can monitor only one of them, it will choose the one that is farther to the north (positive y-axis);

(3) if two airplanes are equally distant and have the same y-coordinate, the center will give preference to the airplane that is farther to the east (positive x-axis).

At any given moment, each control center has a circular "span of control" whose radius is the distance to the farthest airplane being monitored by the control center. All airplanes inside the span of control are monitored by the control center. Airplanes on the boundary of the span of control may or may not be monitored by the control center, depending on its capacity and on the priorities listed above.

You will not be given the positions of the control centers. Instead, for each control center, you will be given the number of airplanes that it is currently monitoring, and two points that are on the boundary of its current span of control. With this information, you can compute the position of the control center and decide which airplanes it is monitoring. If the data is consistent with more than one possible span of control, you should choose the span that includes the airplane that is farthest to the north, breaking ties by choosing the airplane that is farthest to the north then to the east.

The figure below, which shows four airplanes and two control centers, illustrates the problem. Each control center is represented by a circular span of control and by two points on the boundary of this span, labeled A and B. P1, P2, P3, and P4 label the four airplanes. In this example, airplanes P1 and P4 are each being monitored by a single control center, airplane P3 is being monitored by two control centers, and airplane P2 is not being monitored by either control center.

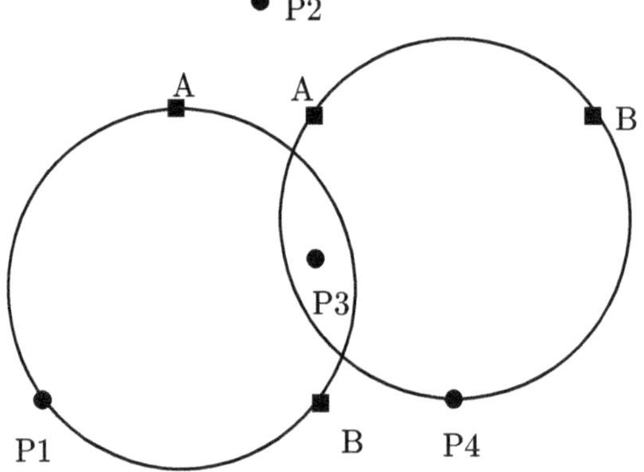

Input

The input consists of several trial data sets. The first line of input in each trial data set contains two integers NP $(0 < NP < 100)$ and NC $(0 < NC < 10)$, which represent the number of airplanes and the number of control centers, respectively. Each of the next NP lines contains two floating-point numbers that represent the (x, y) coordinates of one airplane. Each of the next NC lines describes one control center. Each contains an integer between 0 and NP (inclusive) indicating the number of airplanes monitored by the control center, followed by two pairs of floating point numbers that represent the (x, y) coordinates of two points on the boundary of its span of control (neither of which is the position of an airplane). If two distances differ by less than 0.00001, you should treat them as the same distance.

The last data set is followed by a line containing two zeros.

Output

For each trial, compute the number of airplanes that are monitored by zero control centers, the number of airplanes that are monitored by one control center, and so on up to the number of airplanes that are monitored by NC control centers. Print the trial number followed by a sequence of $NC + 1$ integers, where the i-th integer in the sequence represents the number of airplanes that are monitored by $i - 1$ control centers. If data for one of the control centers is inconsistent, print 'Impossible' instead of the sequence of integers for that trial. Use the format shown in the example output, and print a blank line after each trial.

Sample Input

```
4   2
3.0   0.0
0.0   0.0
1.6   2.8
2.0   1.0
2   1.0   2.0   2.0   0.0
2   2.0   2.0   4.0   2.0
2   1
0.0   0.5
0.0   -0.5
0   -1.0   0.0   1.0   0.0
0   0
```

Sample Output

```
Trial 1:  1   2   1

Trial 2:  Impossible
```

WORLD FINALS 2005

SHANGHAI, CHINA

World Champion

SHANGHAI JIAOTONG UNIVERSITY

Wenyuan Dai

Shuang Zhao

Bohai Yang

Director of Judging
Dick Rinewalt *Texas Christian University*

Chief Judge
Jo Perry *North Carolina State University*

Judges
Osman Ay *Zambak Publishing*
John Bonomo *Westminster College*
Don Chamberlin *IBM Almaden Research Center*
David Elizandro *Tennessee Tech University*
Derek Kisman *Google*
Peter Kluit *Delft University of Technology*
Shahriar Manzoor *Southeast University*
Robert Roos *Allegheny College*
Matthias Ruhl *Google*
Stanley Wileman, Jr. *University of Nebraska at Omaha*

CLI Live Archive problem numbers
3269 A Eyeball Benders
3270 B Simplified GSM Network
3271 C The Traveling Judges Problem
3272 D cNteSahruPfefrlefe
3273 E Lots of Sunlight
3274 F Crossing Streets
3275 G Tiling the Plane
3276 H The Great Wall Game
3277 I Workshops
3278 J Zones

A Eyeball Benders

"Eyeball benders" are a popular kind of puzzle in which the reader must identify a common object based on a close-up view of a part of that object. For instance, an image that looks like a regular array of colored cones might be a view of an open box of new crayons. Figure 1 shows an example where the puzzle is on the left and the solution is on the right.

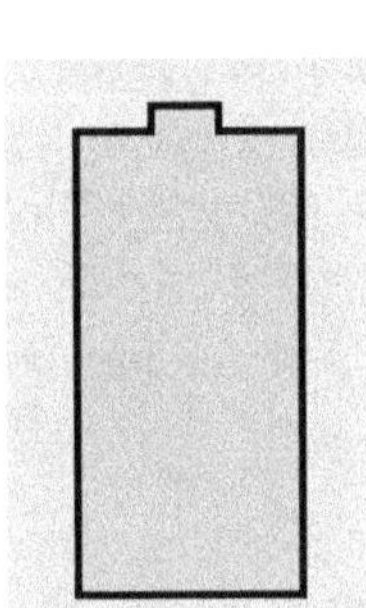
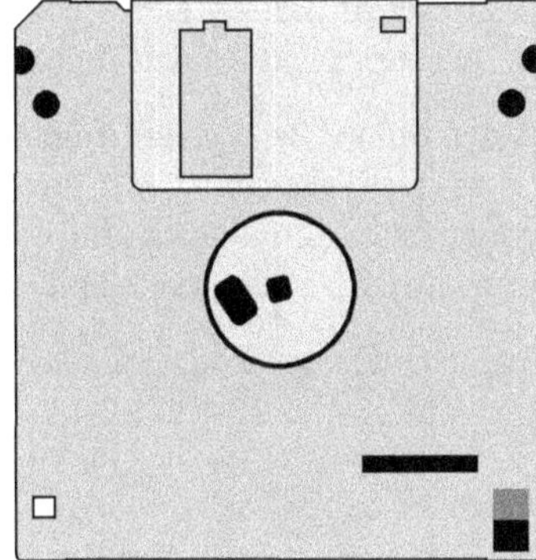

Figure 1. A sample eyeball-bender puzzle and solution image (a floppy disk)

You must verify solutions to a simplified version of the "eyeball bender" puzzle. You will be given a number of pairs of images, each one a collection of line segments. All line segments will be either horizontal or vertical, and they include their endpoints. Figure 2 shows an example.

You must determine whether the images form a valid pair in which the first image is a magnified view of some portion of the second image. Lines are assumed to have zero thickness in both images. At least one endpoint in the puzzle image of a valid pair must be an endpoint of a line segment in the solution image.

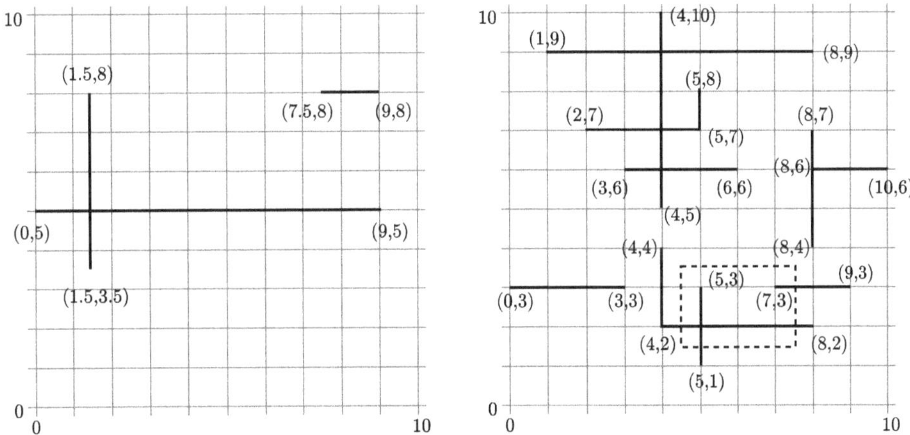

Figure 2. The left image is the portion of the right image inside the dotted rectangle, magnified 3 times.

Coordinates describe *relative* positions and scale within a single image. The coordinates in one image do not necessarily use the same origin or scale as those in the other image. The magnification of the puzzle image relative to the solution image is required to be greater than or equal to 1. For Figure 2, your program should determine that this is a valid puzzle/solution image pair.

Input

The input consists of multiple cases. The input for each case begins with two positive integers M and N, $(1 \leq M, N \leq 50)$. M is the number of line segments in the puzzle image. N is the number of line segments in the proposed solution image. The following lines contain $M + N$ pairs of points. The first M pairs of points are the endpoints of the line segments in the puzzle image; the remaining N pairs are the endpoints of the line segments in the proposed solution image. The x and y coordinates for each pair satisfy $-100 \leq x, y \leq 100$ and are given to at most three decimal places of precision. All input values are separated by white space (blanks or new line characters).

No pair of distinct points in a given image will be closer than .005 to another (relative to the scale of the image) and all segments will have length at least .005. No two horizontal segments overlap and no two vertical segments overlap. However, horizontal segments may intersect vertical segments either internally or at segment endpoints.

The input data for the last case is followed by a line consisting of the integers '0 0'.

Output

For each input case, display the case number (1, 2, ...) followed by the words 'valid puzzle' if the proposed solution image matches a closed rectangular sub-region of the puzzle image (including at least one endpoint), magnified by a factor of one or greater, and possibly translated by some amount. Line segments that are not included in the puzzle image will be at least 0.005 distant from the rectangle.

If the match condition fails to hold, print 'impossible'. Follow the format of the sample output.

Sample Input

```
3 12
9 8 7.5 8 1.5 8 1.5 3.5
0 5 9 5
4 2 8 2 5 7 2 7 10 6 8 6 8 7 8 4
1 9 8 9
9 3 7 3 4 10 4 5
4 2 4 4 5 8 5 7 3 6 6 6 0 3 3 3 5 1 5 3
4 12
-50 -5 50 -5 0 10 0 -10 50 5 -50 5 -50 0 50 0
4 2 8 2 5 7 2 7 10 6 8 6 8 7 8 4
1 9 8 9
9 3 7 3 4 10 4 5
4 2 4 4 5 8 5 7 3 6 6 6 0 3 3 3 5 1 5 3
0 0
```

Sample Output

```
Case 1: valid puzzle

Case 2: impossible
```

B Simplified GSM Network

Mobile phones have changed our lifestyle dramatically in the last decade. Mobile phones have a variety of protocols to connect with one another. One of the most popular networks for mobile phones is the GSM (Global System for Mobile Communication) network.

In a typical GSM network, a mobile phone connects with the nearest BTS (Base Transceiver Station). A BSC (Base Station Center) controls several BTSs. Several BSCs are controlled by one MSC (Mobile Services Switching Center), and this MSC maintains a connection with several other MSCs, a PSTN (Public Switched Telecom Network) and an ISDN (Integrated Services Digital Network).

This problem uses a simplified model of the conventional GSM network. Our simplified network is composed of up to fifty BTS towers. When in use, a mobile phone always connects to its nearest BTS tower. The area covered by a single BTS tower is called a cell. When an active mobile phone is in motion, as it crosses cell boundaries it must seamlessly switch from one BTS to another. Given the description of a map consisting of cities, roads and BTS towers, you must determine the minimum number of BTS switches required to go from one city to another.

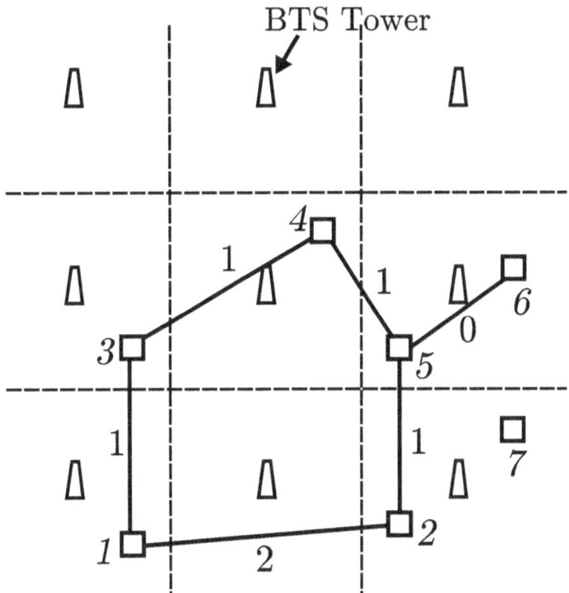

Figure: Cities here are represented by squares and BTS towers by trapezoids. Solid lines are roads. The dotted lines show 9 different cells. The minimum number of switches required to go from city 1 to city 6 is (2+1+0)=3. Note that city 7 is isolated and cannot be reached.

Each tower and each city location is to be considered as a single point in a two-dimensional Cartesian coordinate system. If there is a road between two cities, assume that the road is a straight line segment connecting these two cities. For example, in the figure, traveling on the road from city 1 to city 2 will cross two cell boundaries and thus requires two switches. Traveling from city 2 to city 5 crosses one cell boundary and traveling from city 5 to city 6 requires no switch. Traveling this route from city 1 to city 6 requires three total switches. Note than any other path from city 1 to city 6 requires more than three switches. If there is more than one possible way to get from one city to another, your program must find the optimal route.

Input

The input file contains several test cases. The first line of each test case contains four integers: $B(1 \le B \le 50)$, the number of BTS towers; $C(1 \le C \le 50)$, the number of cities; $R(0 \le R \le 250)$, the number of roads; and $Q(1 \le Q \le 10)$, the number of queries. Each of the next B lines contains two floating-point numbers x and y, the Cartesian coordinates of a BTS tower. Each of the next C lines contains two floating-point numbers x_i, y_i that indicate the Cartesian coordinates of the ith city $(1 \le i \le C)$. Each of the next R lines contains two integers m and n $(1 \le m, n \le C)$, which indicate that there is a road between the m-th and the n-th city. Each of the next Q lines contains two integers s and d $(1 \le s, d \le C)$, the source and destination cities.

No coordinate will have an absolute value greater than 1000. No two towers will be at the same location. No two cities will be at the same location, and no city will lie on a cell boundary. No road will be coincident with a cell boundary, nor contain a point lying on the boundary of three or more cells. The input will end with a line containing four zeros.

Output

For each input set, you should produce $Q+1$ lines of output, as shown below. The first line should contain the number of the test case. Q lines should follow, one for each query, each containing an integer indicating the minimum number of switches required to go from city s to city d. If it is not possible to go from city s to city d, print the line 'Impossible' instead.

Sample Input	Sample Output
9 7 6 2	Case 1:
5 5	3
15 5	Impossible
25 5	
5 15	
15 15	
25 15	
5 25	
15 25	
25 25	
8 2	
22 3	
8 12	
18 18	
22 12	
28 16	
28 8	
1 2	
1 3	
2 5	
3 4	
4 5	
5 6	
1 6	
1 7	
0 0 0 0	

C The Traveling Judges Problem

A group of judges must get together to judge a contest held in a particular city, and they need to figure out the cheapest way of renting cars in order to get everyone to the contest. They observed that it might be cheaper if several judges share a rental car during all or part of the trip, thus reducing the overall cost. Your task is to identify the routes the judges should take in order to minimize the total cost of their car rentals.

We will make the following assumptions:

- The cost of a rental car is proportional to the distance it is driven. There are no charges for more than one occupant in the car, fuel, insurance, or leaving the car in a city other than that in which it was rented.

- All rental cars are billed at the same rate per mile.

- A rental car can accommodate any number of passengers.

- At most one road directly connects any pair of cities. Each road is two-way and has an integer length greater than zero.

- There is at least one route from every judge's starting city to the city in which the contest is held.

- All judges whose routes to the contest take them from or through the same city travel from that city to the contest together. (A judge might arrive at a city in one car and leave that city in a different car.)

Input

The input contains several test cases. Each test case includes a route map, the destination city where the contest is being held, and the cities where the judges are initially located.

Each case appears in the input as a list of integers separated by blanks and/or ends of lines. The order and interpretation of the integers in each case is as follows:

- NC-the number of cities that appear in the route map; this will be no larger than 20.

- DC-the number of the destination city, assuming the cities are numbered 1 to NC.

- NR-the number of roads in the route map. Each road connects a distinct pair of cities.

- For each of the NR roads, three integers $C1$, $C2$, and $DIST$. $C1$ and $C2$ identify two cities connected by a road, and $DIST$ gives the distance between these cities along that road.

- NJ-the number of judges. This number will be no larger than 10.

- NJ-integers, one for each judge each of these is a city number identifying the initial location of that judge.

The data for the last case will be followed by a line consisting of the integer '-1'.

Output

For each test case, display the case number $(1, 2, \ldots)$ and the shortest total distance traveled by the rental cars conveying the judges to the contest. Then display the list of routes used by the judges, each route on a separate line, in the same order as the ordering of starting cities given in the input. Each route consists of the cities that the corresponding judge must visit, listed in the order in which they are visited, starting with the judge's starting city and ending with the contest city. Any other cities along the route are listed in the order in which they are visited during the judge's travels. Separate the numbers in the route with '-', and precede each route by three spaces.

If multiple sets of routes have the same minimum distance, choose a set that requires the fewest number of cities. If several sets of cities of the same cardinality may be used, choose the set that comes lexicographically first when ordered by city number (e.g., {2, 3, 6} rather than {2, 10, 5}). If multiple routes are still available, output any set of routes that meets the requirements.

Follow the format of the sample output.

Sample Input

```
5
3
5
1 2 1
2 3 2
3 4 3
4 5 1
2 4 2
2
5 1

4
4
3
1 3 1
2 3 2
3 4 2
2
1 2

3 3 3
1 2 2
1 3 3
2 3 1
2 2 1

-1
```

Sample Output

```
Case 1: distance = 6
   5-4-2-3
   1-2-3

Case 2: distance = 5
   1-3-4
   2-3-4

Case 3: distance = 3
   2-3
   1-2-3
```

D cNteSahruPfefrlefe

Preston Digitation is a magician who specializes in card tricks. One thing Preston cannot get just right is perfect in-shuffles. A perfect in-shuffle is one where a deck of 52 cards is divided in half and then the two halves are perfectly interleaved so that the top card of the lower half of the deck becomes the top card of the shuffled deck. If we number the cards 0 (top) to 51 (bottom), the resulting deck after a perfect in-shuffle will look like the following:

$$26\ 0\ 27\ 1\ 28\ 2\ 29\ 3\ 30\ 4\ 31\ 5\ 32\ 6\ \ldots\ 51\ 25$$

Preston finds that he makes at most one mistake per shuffle. For example, cards 2 and 28 might end up interchanged, resulting in a shuffled deck that looks like this:

$$26\ 0\ 27\ 1\ 2\ 28\ 29\ 3\ 30\ 4\ 31\ 5\ 32\ 6\ \ldots\ 51\ 25$$

These exchanges of two adjacent cards are the only mistakes Preston makes. After one shuffle, it is easy for him to see if and where he has made a mistake, but after several shuffles this becomes increasingly difficult. He would like you to write a program that can determine his mistakes (if any).

Input

Input will consist of multiple problem instances. The first line will be a single integer indicating the number of problem instances. Each problem instance will consist of a single line containing the cards of a deck which has been shuffled between 1 and 10 times. All decks will be of size 52.

Note: The sample input below shows multiple lines for a problem instance. The actual input data for a problem instance is contained on a single line.

Output

For each problem instance, output the case number (starting at 1), followed by the number of shuffles that were used for that instance. If there were no mistakes made during the shuffling, output the line

```
No error in any shuffle
```

Otherwise, output a set of lines of the form

```
Error in shuffle n at location m
```

where n is a shuffle where an error occurred and m is the location of the error. Shuffles are numbered starting with 1 and the location value should indicate the first location of the two cards that were swapped in that shuffle (where the top of the deck is position 0). In the example described above, the cards in positions 4 and 5 (the cards numbered 2 and 28) are incorrect, so m would be 4 in this case. List all errors in order of increasing n. If one or more shuffles have no errors, do not print any line for them. If there are multiple solutions, pick the solution with the fewest number of errors (all test cases will have a unique solution of minimum size).

Sample Input

```
3
26 0 27 1 2 28 29 3 30 4 31 5 32 6 33 7 34
8 35 9 36 10 37 11 38 12 39 13 40 14 41 15
42 16 43 17 44 18 45 19 46 20 47 21 48 22
49 23 50 24 51 25
26 0 27 1 28 2 29 3 30 4 31 5 32 6 33 7 34
8 35 9 36 10 37 11 38 12 39 13 40 14 41 15
42 16 43 17 44 18 45 19 46 20 47 21 48 22
49 23 50 24 51 25
49 26 43 40 37 34 31 28 25 22 19 16 13 10
7 4 1 51 48 45 42 39 36 33 24 27 30 21 18
15 12 9 6 3 0 50 47 44 41 38 35 32 29 46
23 20 17 2 11 8 5 14
```

Sample Output

```
Case 1
Number of shuffles = 1
Error in shuffle 1 at location 4

Case 2
Number of shuffles = 1
No error in any shuffle

Case 3
Number of shuffles = 9
Error in shuffle 3 at location 3
Error in shuffle 7 at location 11
Error in shuffle 8 at location 38
```

E Lots of Sunlight

The Apartment Construction Management (ACM) has several new high-rise apartment buildings in suburban Shanghai. With the booming economy, ACM expects a considerable profit on apartment leases. Because their apartments receive more direct sunlight, the company claims that these are nicer than others in the area. No other buildings obstruct the sunlight path to apartments in ACM's tall buildings.

ACM wants to verify this claim by telling potential residents exactly how much sunlight a given apartment receives. To offer customers a representative sample of sunlight hours, the company wants to advertise the sunlight hours for April 6, 2005. On that day in Shanghai, the sun rises at 5:37 am, and sets at 6:17 pm.

As shown above, apartments are in a series of buildings aligned east to west. The last two digits of the apartment number identify the building, starting with 01 for the east-most building. The other digits encode the apartment floor, with 1 as the ground floor.

The sun rises in the east and travels at a constant radial speed across the sky, until setting in the west. The only shadows are created by buildings (i.e. each building can cast a shadow on one or more other buildings). An apartment is considered to receive sunlight when either its eastern or western exterior wall is fully covered in sunlight or when the sun is directly overhead.

Input

The input file contains a series of descriptions of apartment complexes. Each description starts with a line containing a single integer n ($1 \le n < 100$) that is the number of apartment buildings in the complex. The next line has two integers w, the width (in east-west direction), and h, each apartment's height in meters. Next is a list of integers $m(1)$, $d(1)$, $m(2)$, $d(2)$, ..., $d(n-1)$, $m(n)$, where $m(i)$ is the number of apartments in apartment building i, and $d(i)$ is the distance, in meters, between the apartment building i and apartment building $i+1$.

The apartment complex description is followed by an integer list of apartments to query for sunlight hours and is terminated by a zero. The input file is terminated by a line consisting of the integer zero.

Output

For each apartment complex description, output its number in the sequence of descriptions. Then for each query, output the corresponding sunlight hours, using the 24-hour time format. Truncate all times down to the nearest second. If the query refers to an apartment that does not exist, indicate that the apartment does not exist. Follow the format shown in the sample output.

Sample Input

```
3
6 4
5 6 3 3 4
302 401 601 303 0
4
5 3
4 5 7 8 5 4 3
101 302 503 0
0
```

Sample Output

```
Apartment Complex: 1

Apartment 302: 10:04:50 - 13:23:47

Apartment 401: 05:37:00 - 17:13:57

Apartment 601: Does not exist

Apartment 303: 09:21:19 - 18:17:00

Apartment Complex: 2

Apartment 101: 05:37:00 - 12:53:32

Apartment 302: 09:08:55 - 14:52:47

Apartment 503: 09:01:12 - 18:17:00
```

F   Crossing Streets

Peter Longfoot is a student at the university of Suburbia. Every morning, Peter leaves home to walk to the university. Many other students are driving their cars or riding their bicycles to campus, but Peter prefers to walk, avoiding the chaotic traffic of the city as much as possible.

Unfortunately, Peter cannot avoid the traffic entirely, since he has to cross streets in order to reach the university. Recently, Peter has wondered how to minimize the number of streets he has to cross. For example, in the following map, streets are drawn as horizontal and vertical lines. To reach the university starting at his home, Peter has to cross at least two streets. Peter cannot cross a street pair at an intersection and Peter cannot walk along a street.

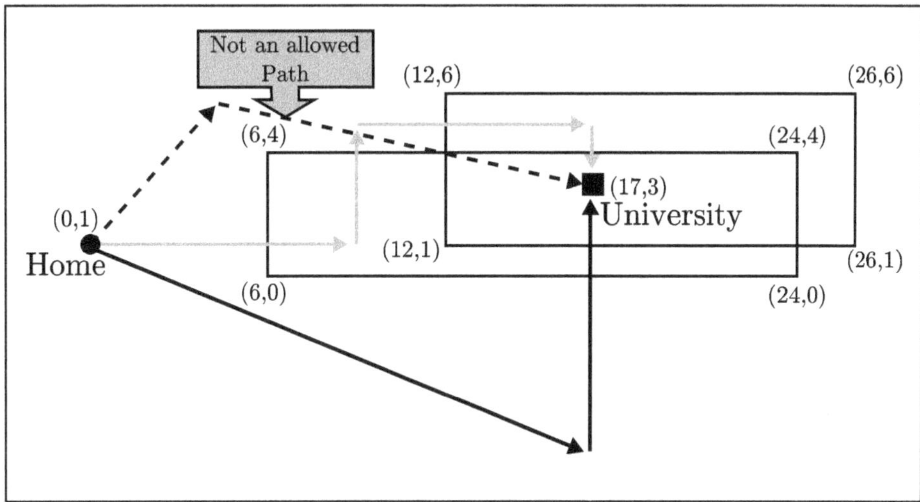

Figure: Streets are shown as straight lines and the arrows show possible walking paths for Peter. The black arrows show one possible path for Peter where he only has to cross two streets. The gray arrows show a path for Peter where he needs to cross four streets. The path shown by the dotted arrows is not legal because it crosses two streets at an intersection. The figure above corresponds to the first sample input.

Peter knows the locations of all streets in the city, but he has trouble figuring out the best way to the university. So you must write a program to help him.

Input

The input consists of several descriptions of cities. Each description starts with a line containing a single integer n ($1 \leq n \leq 500$), the number of streets in the city. This is followed by n lines, each containing four integers x_1, y_1, x_2, y_2, indicating that there is a street from coordinates (x_1, y_1) to (x_2, y_2). All streets are parallel to either the x- or y-axis, since the city is built on a square grid. Streets can overlap, in which case they are counted as only one street. The city description is concluded by a line containing four integers x_h, y_h, x_u, y_u, the coordinates (x_h, y_h) of Peter's home, and the coordinates (x_u, y_u) of the university, respectively. Neither Peter's home nor the university will be located on a street. You should consider the streets as straight-line segments, so the streets have no width. Although the endpoints of the streets are integers, Peter doesn't need to walk along the grids. He can walk in any direction he likes. The magnitudes of all integers in the input file are less than 2×10^9.

The input is terminated by a line consisting of the integer zero.

Output

For each city description, first output its number in the sequence of descriptions. Then output the minimum number of streets that Peter has to cross to go from his home to the university.

Follow the format of the sample output.

Sample Input

```
8
6 0 24 0
24 0 24 4
24 4 6 4
6 4 6 0
12 1 26 1
26 1 26 6
26 6 12 6
12 6 12 1
0 1 17 3
1
10 10 20 10
1 1 30 30
0
```

Sample Output

```
City 1
Peter has to cross 2 streets
City 2
Peter has to cross 0 streets
```

G Tiling the Plane

A polygon is said to "tile the plane" if a collection of identical copies of the polygon can be assembled to fill an unbounded two-dimensional plane without any gaps or overlap. For example, Figure 1 shows an L-shaped polygon, and Figure 2 shows how a portion of the plane can be tiled with copies of the polygon. You must write a program to determine whether a given polygon can tile the plane.

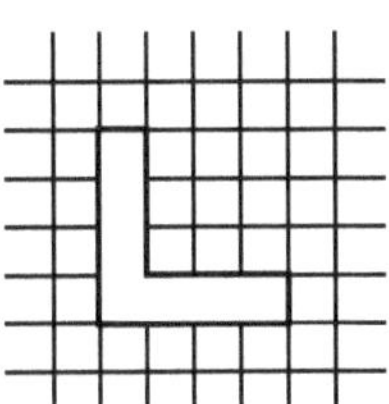

Figure 1: A test polygon shown
against a grid of unit squares

Figure 2: A portion of the plane
tiled with the test polygon

Each test case consists of a closed polygon in which every vertex is at a right angle and the length of every side is an integer multiple of a unit length. You may make as many copies of the polygon as you like, and you may move them over the plane, but you may not rotate or reflect any polygon.

You might find the following information useful: It is known that there are only two fundamentally different tilings of the plane, the regular tiling by squares (chessboard tiling) and the tiling by regular hexagons (honeycomb tiling). A polygon can therefore tile the plane if and only if it satisfies one of the following two conditions:

1. There are points A, B, C, D in order on the polygon boundary (the points are not necessarily vertices of the polygon) such that the polygon boundaries from A to B and from D to C are congruent and the boundaries from B to C and from A to D are congruent. This leads to a tiling equivalent to the square tiling.

2. There are points A, B, C, D, E, F in order on the polygon boundary, such that the boundary pairs AB and ED, BC and FE, CD and AF are congruent. This leads to a tiling equivalent to the hexagon tiling.

Input

The input contains the descriptions of several polygons, each description consisting of one input line. Each description begins with an integer n ($4 \leq n \leq 50$) that represents the number of sides of the polygon. This number is followed by descriptions of n line segments which (taken in order) form a counterclockwise traversal of the perimeter of the polygon. Each line segment description consists of a letter followed by an integer. The letter is 'N', 'E', 'S', or 'W', representing the direction of the line segment as North, East, South, or West, respectively. The integer represents the length of the line segment as a multiple of the unit length. The described polygon will not touch or intersect itself.

The input is terminated by a line consisting of the integer zero.

Output

For each polygon in the input, print one output line. Print the number of the polygon in the input, followed by the word 'Possible' if it is possible to tile the plane with the test polygon, or 'Impossible' otherwise. Follow the format of the sample output.

Sample Input

```
6 N 3 W 1 S 4 E 4 N 1 W 3
8 E 5 N 1 W 3 N 3 E 2 N 1 W 4 S 5
0
```

Sample Output

```
Polygon 1: Possible
Polygon 2: Impossible
```

H The Great Wall Game

Hua and Shen have invented a simple solitaire board game that they call "The Great Wall Game." The game is played with n stones on an $n \times n$ grid. The stones are placed at random in the squares of the grid, at most one stone per square. In a single move, any single stone can move into an unoccupied location one unit horizontally or vertically in the grid. The goal of the puzzle is to create a "wall," i.e., to line up all n stones in a straight line either horizontally, vertically, or diagonally using the fewest number of moves. An example for the case $n = 5$ is shown in Figure 1(a). In Figure 1(b) it is shown that with six moves we can line all the stones up diagonally. No smaller number of moves suffices to create a line of five stones. (However, there are other solutions using six moves, e.g., we can line up all five stones in the third column using six moves.)

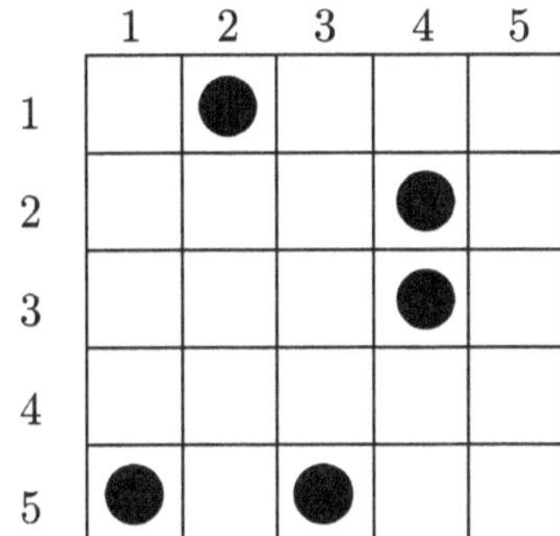
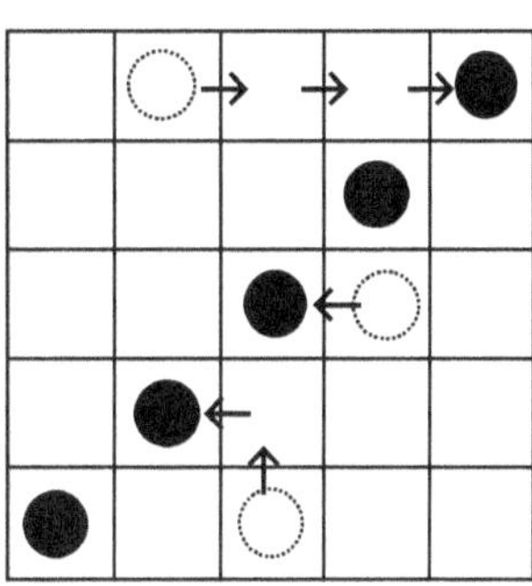

Figure 1. Starting board (a) and a 6-move solution (b) for $n = 5$

There is just one problem – Hua and Shen have no idea what the minimum number of moves is for any given starting board. They would like you to write a program that can take any starting configuration and determine the fewest number of moves needed to create a wall.

Input

The input consists of multiple cases. Each case begins with a line containing an integer n, $1 \le n \le$ 15. The next line contains the row and column numbers of the first stone, followed by the row and column numbers of the second stone, and so on. Rows and columns are numbered as in the above diagram. The input data for the last case will be followed by a line containing a single zero.

Output

For each input case, display the case number $(1, 2, \ldots)$ followed by the minimum number of moves needed to line up the n stones into a straight-line wall. Follow the format shown in the sample output.

Sample Input

```
5
1 2 2 4 3 4 5 1 5 3
2
1 1 1 2
3
3 1 1 2 2 2
0
```

Sample Output

```
Board 1: 6 moves required.

Board 2: 0 moves required.

Board 3: 1 moves required.
```

I Workshops

The first Californian Conference on Holism took place back in 1979 in San Francisco. The term
"Californian" was a slight exaggeration, as all 23 participants actually lived in San Francisco.
Several years later, in 1987, the conference was truly Californian, with 337 participants from all over
the state. Since then, the number of participants has been growing like the size of memory chips. In
1993 the conference was renamed the American Conference on Holism (2,549 participants), and a
second renaming (World Conference on Holism) followed in 1997, when the number of participants
from all over the world had grown to 9,973. The conference obtained its present name (Galactic
Conference on Holism) in 2003 after some discussion as to whether or not the word Galactic was
intended to exclude extragalactic life forms. Still the next year, all registered participants were
terrestrial-though a few participants positively reported to have sensed extraterrestrial presence.

The number of workshops grew with the number of participants. For the upcoming conference,
the organization has to face some down to earth but very nasty scheduling problems. For the 2005
conference the board has decided to have no more than 1,000 workshops concurrently. Nevertheless
they had to rent every hall or classroom they could lay their hands on. Some of these rooms are
available for a restricted time only.

In the morning of the first day the opening meeting takes place in a football stadium, and in
the afternoon the participants attend workshops. Before lunch each participant has to indicate
which workshop he or she wants to join that afternoon. The organizing staff then has a list of
all workshops, including the duration and the number of participants for each workshop. They
also have a list of all available rooms, with the capacity of each room, and the time this specific
room must be cleared. With this information the staff must schedule each workshop in a room of
sufficient capacity and sufficient availability in time. As this problem is not necessarily solvable,
some overflow capacity is supplied by tents in the football stadium. These tents have plenty of
capacity, but they are unpleasantly warm and noisy. So the organizing staff wants the schedule
to minimize the number of tent workshops-that is, workshops that are not assigned to a room.
If there are multiple solutions that minimize the number of tent workshops, the staff wants to
minimize the number of participants attending tent workshops.

We ask you to supply such a schedule (preferably before lunch is over).

Input

The input file contains several trials. Each trial consists of two parts: the list of workshops, and
the list of rented rooms.

The list of workshops starts with a line containing the number of workshops w ($0 < w \leq 1000$).
Each of the next w lines contains two numbers, describing a workshop. The first number is the
number p of participants ($0 < p \leq 100$), and the second number is the duration d of the workshop
in minutes ($0 < d \leq 300$). For your convenience, other details of the workshops are omitted. All
workshops start at 14:00.

The list of rented rooms starts with a line containing the number of rented rooms r ($0 < r \leq$
1000). Each of the following r lines contains the description of a rented room. A line describing
a rented room contains the number s of seats in the room ($0 < s \leq 100$), followed by the time
when the room must be cleared, in the format $hh : mm$ where hh represents the hour and mm
represents the minute, using a 24-hour clock. All the rooms are available starting at 14:00. All
times when rooms must be cleared are between 14:01 and 23:59, inclusive.

The input is terminated by a line consisting of the integer zero.

Output

For each trial in the input file the output must contain a line consisting of the trial number, the number of tent workshops, and the number of participants attending tent workshops. Follow the format shown in the sample output.

Sample Input

```
1
20 60
1
30 16:00
2
20 60
50 30
1
30 14:50
0
```

Sample Output

```
Trial 1:  0 0

Trial 2:  2 70
```

J Zones

Telephone poles are part of an outdated technology. Cell phones nowadays allow us to call whoever we want, wherever we want, independent of any wire. There is one problem - without a service tower nearby a cell phone is useless.

In the absence of hills and mountains, a service tower will provide coverage for a circular area. Instead of planning where to place the wires, a wireless telephone company has to plan where to build its service towers. Building the towers too far apart causes holes in the coverage and increases complaints. Building the towers too close to each other results in large areas covered by more than one service tower, which is redundant and inofficient.

International Cell Phone Company is developing a network strategy to determine the optimal placement of service towers. Since most customers have replaced their old wired home phones by cell phones, the strategy for planning service towers is therefore to cover as many homes of customers as possible.

The figure below shows the service areas for the five towers ICPC's strategic department planned to build this year. Tower 5 will serve 24 customers, 6 of which are also served by tower 4. Towers 1, 2 and 3 have a common service area containing 3 customers.

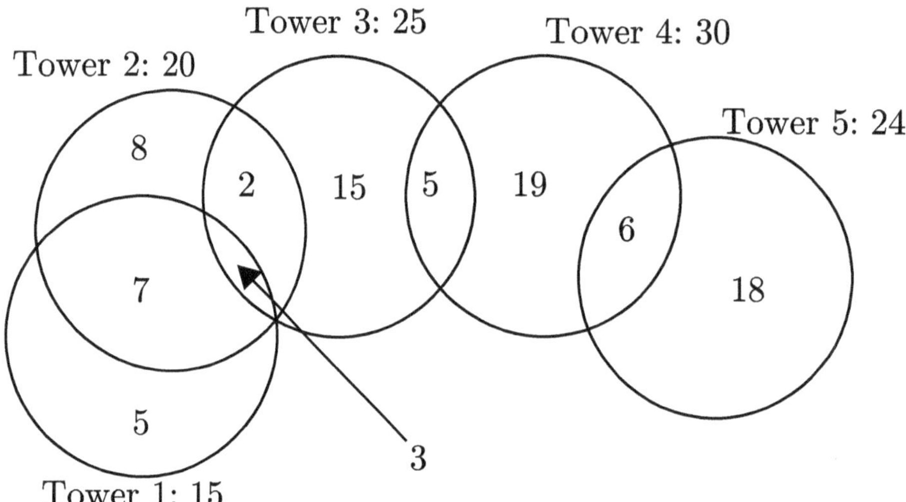

Shortly after the plans for these five towers had been published, higher management issued a stop on all tower building. Protesting customers forced them to weaken this decree, and allow the building of three towers out of the five planned. These three towers should serve as many customers as possible, of course. Finding the best possible choice for the towers to build is not trivial (the best choice in this case is towers 2, 4 and 5, serving 68 customers).

You must write a program to help ICPC choose which towers to build in cases like these. If several choices of towers serve the same number of customers, choices including tower 1 are preferable. If this rule still leaves room for more than one solution, solutions including tower 2 are preferable, and so on.

Input

The input file contains several test cases. The first line of each test case contains two positive integers: the number n ($n \leq 20$) of towers planned, and the number of towers to be actually built. The next line contains n numbers, each giving the number of customers served by a planned tower. (The first number refers to the first tower, and so on.) No tower serves more than a million people. The next line contains the number m ($m \leq 10$) of common service areas. Each of the next m lines contains the description of a common service area. Such a line starts with the number t ($t > 1$) of towers for which this is a common service area, followed by the t numbers of the towers. The last number on the line is the number of customers in the common service area. The last line of the input file consists of the two integers '0 0'.

Output

For each test case, display the number of customers served and the best choice for the location of the towers. Follow the format of the sample output.

<table>
<tr><td>

Sample Input

```
5   3
15  20  25  30  24
5
2   1 2       7
3   1 2 3     3
2   2 3       2
2   3 4       5
2   4 5       6
5   3
25  25  25  25  25
4
2   1 2       5
2   2 3       5
2   3 4       5
2   4 5       5
5   3
25  25  25  25  25
0
0 0
```

</td><td>

Sample Output

```
Case Number   1
Number of Customers: 68
Locations recommended: 2 4 5

Case Number   2
Number of Customers: 75
Locations recommended: 1 3 5

Case Number   3
Number of Customers: 75
Locations recommended: 1 2 3
```

</td></tr>
</table>

WORLD FINALS 2006

SAN ANTONIO, TEXAS

World Champion

SARATOV STATE UNIVERSITY

Roman Alekseenkov

Igor Kulkin

Ivan Romanov

Director of Judging
Dick Rinewalt *Texas Christian University*

Chief Judge
Jo Perry *North Carolina State University*

Judges
Osman Ay *Zambak Publishing*
John Bonomo *Westminster College*
Don Chamberlin *IBM Almaden Research Center*
David Elizandro *Tennessee Tech University*
Derek Kisman *Google*
Peter Kluit *Delft University of Technology*
Shahriar Manzoor *Southeast University*
Robert Roos *Allegheny College*
Matthias Ruhl *Google*
Stanley Wileman, Jr. *University of Nebraska at Omaha*

CLI Live Archive problem numbers
3561 A Low Cost Air Travel
3562 B Remember the A La Mode!
3563 C Ars Longa
3564 D Bitpartite Numbers
3565 E Bit Compressor
3566 F Building a Clock
3567 G Pilgrimage
3568 H Pockets
3569 I Degress of Separation
3570 J Routing

A Low Cost Air Travel

Air fares are crazy! The cost of a ticket is determined by numerous factors, and is usually not directly related to the distance traveled. Many travelers try to be creative, sometimes using only parts of tickets with stops in various cities to achieve lower-cost travel. However, the airlines are aware of this behavior, and usually require that the travel covered by a ticket be completed in order and without intervening travel. For example, if you have a ticket for travel from City-1 to City-2 then to City-3, you are not allowed to use only the portion of the ticket for travel from City-2 to City-3. You must always start at the first city on the ticket. In addition, you are not allowed to travel from City-1 to City-2, fly elsewhere and return, and then continue your journey from City-2 to City-3.

Let's consider an example. Suppose you are allowed to purchase three types of tickets:

Ticket #1:	City-1 to City-3 to City-4	$225.00
Ticket #2:	City-1 to City-2	$200.00
Ticket #3:	City-2 to City-3	$50.00

Suppose you wanted to travel from City-1 to City-3. There are two ways to get there using only the available ticket choices:

Purchase Ticket #1 for $225.00 and use only the first leg of the ticket.
Purchase Ticket #2 for $200.00 and Ticket #3 for $50.00.

The first choice is the cheapest.

Given a set of airline ticket offers, and one or more trip itineraries, you must determine how to purchase tickets in order to minimize the cost of travel. Each trip will be possible.

Input

Input consists of multiple test cases, each describing a set of ticket offers and a set of trip itineraries.

Each case begins with a line containing NT, the number of ticket offers, followed by NT offer descriptions, one to a line. Each description consists of a positive integer specifying the price of the ticket, the number of cities in the ticket's route, and then that many cities. Each city in a case has an arbitrary, but unique, integer identification number. Note that several tickets may be purchased from the same offer.

The next line contains NI, the number of trips that are to have their cost minimized. NI lines follow, giving the itineraries for each trip. Each line consists of the number of cities in the itinerary (including the starting city), followed by that many city identification numbers, given in the order they are to be visited.

There will be no more than 20 ticket offers or 20 itineraries in a test case. Each offer and itinerary lists from 2 to 10 cities. No ticket price exceeds $10,000. Adjacent cities in a route or itinerary will be distinct. Tickets and trips are numbered sequentially in each set, starting with 1.

The last case is followed by a line containing a zero.

Output

For each trip, output two lines containing the case number, the trip number, the minimum cost of the trip, and the numbers of the tickets used for the trip, in the order they will be used. Follow the output format shown below. The output will always be unique.

Sample Input

```
3
225 3 1 3 4
200 2 1 2
50 2 2 3
1
2 1 3
3
100 2 2 4
100 3 1 4 3
200 3 1 2 3
2
3 1 4 3
3 1 2 4
0
```

Sample Output

```
Case 1, Trip 1: Cost = 225
  Tickets used: 1
Case 2, Trip 1: Cost = 100
  Tickets used: 2
Case 2, Trip 2: Cost = 300
  Tickets used: 3 1
```

B Remember the A La Mode!

Hugh Samston owns the "You Want It, Hugh Got It" catering service, which has been asked to supply desserts for the participants in this year's ICPC World Finals. Hugh will provide pie slices topped with ice cream at the various social functions scheduled throughout the week. As with any other dedicated entrepreneur, Hugh would like to offer the best service possible, so he has ordered a wide variety of pies and ice creams to satisfy even the most eclectic tastes.

Hugh plans to serve each pie slice with a single scoop of ice cream, leaving the exact combination up to the whim of the customer. But of course, as with any other dedicated entrepreneur, Hugh would also like to make as much profit as possible from this enterprise. He knows ahead of time how much profit he can make on each combination of pie slice and ice cream scoop, as well as which combinations of pie and ice cream should never be put together (example: Peppermint Banana Chunk ice cream on Key Lime pie).

Given this information, along with the number of slices and scoops he has of each variety of pie and ice cream, Hugh figures he can determine both the minimum and maximum profits he can expect. Since he hopes to be the caterer at subsequent World Finals, he would like a general program to solve this and future problems.

Input

Input will consist of multiple problem instances. Each problem instance will start with a line containing two integers P ($P \leq 50$) and I ($I \leq 50$), indicating the number of types of pie and ice cream, respectively. The next line will contain P integers indicating the number of slices available for each of the pie types. The line after that will contain I integers indicating the number of scoops available for each of the ice cream types. The total number of pie slices will always equal the total number of ice cream scoops available, and it is assumed that all pie slices and ice cream scoops will be used.

Each problem instance will end with P lines each containing I floating point numbers indicating the profit for each pie/ice cream combination: the first value indicates the profit if a slice of pie type 0 is topped with a scoop of ice cream type 0; the next value indicates the profit if a slice of pie type 0 is topped with a scoop of ice cream type 1, and so on. A profit value of '-1' indicates that no combinations of that pie type and ice cream type should ever be sold. All other integers (number of slices for each type of pie and number of scoops for each type of ice cream) will be less than or equal to 100 and the profit on each one of the pie/ice cream combinations (other than '-1') will be larger than 0 and less than or equal to 10, with at most two digits after the decimal point.

The last problem instance is followed by a line containing two zeroes.

Output

For each problem instance, output the problem number (starting at 1) followed by the minimum and maximum profits, using the format shown in the sample output. Display all numbers with two fractional digits. All problem instances are guaranteed to have at least one solution using all of the pie slices and ice cream scoops.

Sample Input

```
2 3
40 50
27 30 33
1.11 1.27 0.70
-1 2 0.34
4 4
10 10 10 10
10 10 10 10
1.01 -1 -1 -1
-1 1.01 -1 -1
-1 -1 1.01 -1
-1 -1 -1 1.01
0 0
```

Sample Output

```
Problem 1: 91.70 to 105.87
Problem 2: 40.40 to 40.40
```

C Ars Longa

You have been struck with inspiration, and are designing a beautiful new art sculpture for the foyer of your local museum. For highly important artistic reasons, you are designing it using very specific materials. However, you are not sure if physics is on your side. Will your sculpture actually stand up?

The sculpture will be composed of various ball joints weighing 1 kilogram each, and various rods (of negligible weight) connecting the joints. Rods cannot be stretched or compressed, and they can never detach from a joint. However, they are free to rotate around the joints in any direction. The joints that lie on the ground are glued in place; all others are free to move. For simplicity, you may ignore the effects of intersections of rods; each rod exerts force only on the 2 joints connected to it. Also, any joint that is in the air will have at least one rod coming out that is not parallel to the ground. This prevents the degenerate case where a ball is supported only horizontally by a rigid structure. In real life, it would sag just a little.

Write a program to determine whether your structure is static (that is, will not immediately move from the effects of gravity). Note that each rod can transmit an arbitrarily large tensional force along its length, and that "being static" means that the tensional forces at each joint balance the weight of the joint.

If the structure is static, you must also determine whether it is stable (that is, will not move if perturbed slightly by pulling its joints).

Input

The input contains several sculpture descriptions. Every description begins with a line containing integers J and R, the number of joints and rods in the structure, respectively. Joints are numbered from 1 to J. The description continues with J lines, one per joint, each containing 3 floating point numbers giving the x, y, z coordinates of that joint. Following are R lines, one per rod, with 2 distinct integers indicating the joints connected by that rod.

Each rod is exactly the right length to connect its joints. The z coordinates will always be non-negative; a z coordinate of 0 indicates that the joint is on the ground and fixed in place. There are at most 100 joints and 100 rods.

The last description is followed by a line containing two zeroes.

Output

For each sculpture description, output 'NON-STATIC', 'UNSTABLE', or 'STABLE', as shown in the sample output.

Sample Input

```
4 3
0 0 0
-1.0 -0.5 1.0
1.0 -0.5 1.0
0 1.0 1.0
1 2
1 3
1 4
4 6
0 0 0
-1.0 -0.5 1.0
1.0 -0.5 1.0
0 1.0 1.0
1 2
1 3
1 4
2 3
2 4
3 4
7 9
0 0 0
-1.0 -0.5 1.0
1.0 -0.5 1.0
0 1.0 1.0
-1.0 -0.5 0
1.0 0.5 0
0 1.0 0
1 2
1 3
1 4
2 3
2 4
3 4
2 5
3 6
4 7
0 0
```

Sample Output

```
Sculpture 1: NON-STATIC
Sculpture 2: UNSTABLE
Sculpture 3: STABLE
```

D Bipartite Numbers

The executive officers of the company where you work want to send each other encrypted messages. Rather than use off-the-shelf encryption software such as PGP, they have tasked the IT staff with handling the encryption problem. The IT staff decided on a solution that requires "public" and "private" integer keys. The idea is that everyone can see your public key, but only you know your private key.

Your best friend in the company is a wonderful person but a not-so-wonderful programmer. He has created a publicprivate key scheme as follows. A public key can be any positive integer. The corresponding private key is the smallest bipartite number that is greater than and a multiple of the public key.

A bipartite number is any positive integer that contains exactly 2 distinct decimal digits s and t such that s is not 0 and all occurrences of s precede all occurrences of t. For example 44444411 is bipartite (s is 4 and t is 1), So are 41, 10000000, and 5555556. However, neither 4444114 nor 44444 are bipartite.

Notice that the large bipartite number 88888888888800000 can be nicely described as 12 8's followed by 5 0's. You can express any bipartite number using four numbers: m s n t. The numbers s and t are the leading and trailing digits as described above, m is the number of times the digit s appears in the bipartite number, and n is the number of times the digit t appears.

The trouble with your friend's scheme is that it is not too difficult to compute a private key if you know the public key. You need to convince your friend that his public-private key scheme is inadequate before he loses his job over his bad decision! You must write a program that takes public keys as input and displays the corresponding private keys.

Input

The input consists of several test cases. Each test case is on a separate line, and it consists of a single public key in the range $1 \ldots 99999$.

The last case is followed by a line containing the integer zero.

Output

For each test case, display a line consisting of the public key, a colon, then 4 integers m s n t where m, n, s, and t are as described above.

Sample Input

```
125
17502
2005
0
```

Sample Output

```
125: 1 5 2 0
17502: 4 7 4 8
2005: 3 2 3 5
```

E   Bit Compressor

The aim of data compression is to reduce redundancy in stored or communicated data. This increases effective data density and speeds up data transfer rates. One possible method to compress any binary message is the following:

> Replace any maximal sequence of n 1's with the binary version of n whenever it shortens the length of the message.

For example, the compressed form of the data **111111110010011111111111111110011** becomes **10000010011110011**. The original data is 32 bits long while the compressed data is only 17 bits long.

The drawback of this method is that sometimes the decompression process yields more than one result for the original message, making it impossible to obtain the original message. Write a program that determines if the original message can be obtained from the compressed data when the length of the original message (L), the number of 1's in the original message (N) and the compressed data are given. The original message will be no longer than 16 Kbytes and the compressed data will be no longer than 40 bits.

Input

The input file contains several test cases. Each test case has two lines. The first line contains L and N and the second line contains the compressed data.

The last case is followed by a line containing two zeroes.

Output

For each test case, output a line containing the case number (starting with 1) and a message 'YES', 'NO' or 'NOT UNIQUE'. 'YES' means that the original message can be obtained. 'NO' means that the compressed data has been corrupted and the original message cannot be obtained. 'NOT UNIQUE' means that more than one message could have been the original message. Follow the format shown in the sample output.

Sample Input

```
32 26
10000010011110011
9 7
1010101
14 14
111111
00
```

Sample Output

```
Case #1: YES
Case #2: NOT UNIQUE
Case #3: NO
```

F   Building a Clock

In Old Town Square in the city of Prague, there is a beautiful Astronomical Clock, constructed in the year 1410. For centuries, the clockmaker's art consisted of using gears to connect a shaft, turning at a known rate, to other shafts until, by the proper combination of gears, two shafts could be made to turn at the correct rates to represent minutes and hours.

You must write a program that, given an input shaft speed and a collection of gears, computes how the gears can be connected to create a clock with an hour hand and a minute hand. You may use as many shafts as you like, but each shaft may have a maximum of three gears. All the gears on a shaft turn at the same rate. If a gear having $T1$ teeth turning at a rate $R1$ is engaged with another gear having $T2$ teeth, the turning rate of the second gear is $-R1(T1/T2)$. Your solution must include two shafts, a minute shaft that turns clockwise at the rate of one revolution per hour, and an hour shaft that turns clockwise at the rate of one revolution per twelve hours. Your solution is not required to use all the available gears.

Input

The input consists of several trials, each described by one line of input. Each input line begins with an integer N ($3 \le N \le 6$), the number of gears available for building a clock. N is followed by another integer R ($-3600 \le R \le 3600, R \ne 0$), the turning rate of the input shaft, which is the number of revolutions made by the shaft in 24 hours. (A positive number represents clockwise rotation, and a negative number represents counter-clockwise rotation.) R is followed by N gear descriptions. Each gear description is a pair: a one-character name that identifies the gear, followed by an integer T ($6 \le T \le 120$), that is the number of teeth on the gear. The names and numbers on each input line are separated by spaces, as shown in the sample input.

The last trial is followed by a line containing a single zero.

Output

For each trial, print a line containing the trial number, as shown in the sample output. If it is possible to construct a clock using the given set of gears, the line containing the trial number must be followed by two more output lines, one for the minute hand and one for the hour hand.

Otherwise, the line containing the trial number must end with the words 'IS IMPOSSIBLE' as shown in the sample output.

The line for the minute hand starts with 'Minutes:' followed by a plan that shows how the input shaft is connected by a sequence of gears to the minute shaft. The plan consists of a sequence of shafts, separated by hyphens. Each shaft is represented by one or two characters. The first character is the name of the driven gear—the gear on the shaft that is engaged with a gear on the previous shaft. For the input shaft, use an asterisk (*) to represent the absence of a driven gear. The second character describing a shaft is the name of the driving gear—the gear on the shaft that is engaged with a gear on the next shaft. The driven gear and the driving gear can be the same gear, in which case the shaft is described by a single character which is the name of this gear. The last shaft in the plan is the minute shaft, described by a single letter which is the name of its driven gear.

The line for the hour hand starts with 'Hours:' followed by a plan for connecting the input shaft to the hour shaft. Use the same format as the minute plan.

Each gear may occur only once in the clock. The minute plan and the hour plan may have an initial part in common, however. A gear in a common initial part will occur both in the minute plan and the hour plan. For the same reason, a given shaft can be used in both the hour plan and the minute plan. If a shaft is used in both plans, it may or may not have the same description in both plans. For example, a shaft containing a single gear named A will be represented as A in both plans. On the other hand, a shaft containing three gears named A, B, and C might be represented as AB in the minute plan (if B is the driving gear in that plan) and as AC in the hour plan (if C is the driving gear in that plan). The following lines represent valid output lines:

Hours: *A-BC-D   An input shaft having one gear, engaged with an interme-
                       diate shaft having two gears, engaged with an hour shaft
                       having one gear.

Minutes: *A-B-C   An input shaft having one gear, engaged with an interme-
                       diate shaft having one gear, engaged with a minute shaft
                       having one gear.

Minutes: *   A plan in which no gears are needed because the input
                       shaft is turning at the correct rate for the minute shaft.

If there are multiple ways to build a clock using the given gears, print the solution that uses the minimum number of shafts. In case of a tie for the minimum number of shafts, print the solution that uses the minimum number of gears. In case of a tie for both the minimum numbers of shafts and gears, print the solution whose string description is alphabetically first. The string description of a solution is its minute plan, followed by its hour plan, concatenated together with asterisks and hyphens removed. For example, a solution in which the minute plan is '*A-B' and the hour plan is '*A-BC-D-E' has the string description 'ABABCDE'.

Print one blank line between trials.

Sample Input

```
6 40 P 7 Q 84 R 50 A 40 B 30 C 14
6 40 P 7 Q 84 R 45 A 40 B 30 C 14
0
```

Sample Output

```
Trial 1
Minutes: *B-A-R
Hours:   *B-A-RP-C-Q

Trial 2 IS IMPOSSIBLE
```

G   Pilgrimage

Jack is making a long distance walk with some friends along the old pilgrim road from Vézelay
to Santiago de Compostela. Jack administers money for the group. His administration is quite
simple. Whenever an amount (60€, say) has to be paid for the common good he will pay it, and
write in his booklet: `PAY 60`.

When needed, Jack will ask every member of the group, including himself, to pay an amount
(50€, say) to the collective purse, and write in his booklet: `COLLECT 50`. If the group size is 7, he
collects 350€ in total.

Unfortunately some of the group members cannot participate in the full walk. So sometimes
the group will grow, sometimes it will shrink. How does Jack handle these comings and goings of
group members in terms of collective money? Suppose, for example, the group size is 7, and that
Jack has 140€ in cash, which is 20€ for every group member. If two group members leave, each
will receive 20€, and Jack will write in his booklet: `OUT 2`. If under the same circumstances three
new group members arrive, they will each have to pay 20€, and Jack will write: `IN 3`.

In these cases the amount in cash could easily be divided, without fractions. As a strange
coincidence, this happened during the whole trip. Jack never had to make calculations with
fractional numbers of euros.

Near the end of the trip, Jack was joined by all his fellow travelers. Nobody was willing to miss
the glorious finale of the trip. It was then that Jack tried to remember what the group size had
been during each part of the trip. He could not remember.

Given a page of Jack's booklet, could you figure out the size of the group at the beginning of
that page?

Input

The input file contains several test cases. Each test case is a sequence of lines in Jack's booklet.
The first line of each test case will give the number N ($0 < N \leq 50$) of lines to follow. The next
N lines have the format: $< keyword > < num >$, where

$< keyword > = $ `PAY` | `COLLECT` | `IN` | `OUT`

and $< num >$ is a positive integer, with the following restrictions:

`IN` k	$k \leq 20$
`OUT` k	$k \leq 20$
`COLLECT` k	$k \leq 200$
`PAY` k	$k \leq 2000$

The last case is followed by a line containing a single zero.

Output

For each test case, print a single line describing the size of the group at the beginning of the part
of the trip described in the test case. This line contains:

- The word 'IMPOSSIBLE', if the data are inconsistent.

- A single number giving the size of the group just prior to the sequence of lines in Jack's
  booklet, if this size is uniquely determined by the data.

- Several numbers, in increasing order, separated by spaces, giving the possible sizes of the group, in case the number of solutions is finite, but the solution is not unique.

- A statement in the format: 'SIZE >= N', giving a lower bound for the size of the group, in case the number of solutions is infinite. Observe that the inequality SIZE >= 1 always applies, since at least Jack himself did the whole trip.

Sample Input

```
5
IN 1
PAY 7
IN 1
PAY 7
IN 1
7
IN 1
COLLECT 20
PAY 30
PAY 12
IN 2
PAY 30
OUT 3
3
IN 1
PAY 8
OUT 3
1
OUT 5
0
```

Sample Output

```
IMPOSSIBLE
2
3 7
SIZE >= 6
```

H Pockets

Origami, or the art of paper folding, often makes use of "pockets" of paper, particularly in complicated models made from multiple pieces of paper where a tab on one piece of paper needs to fit into a pocket in another piece of paper. In this problem you must count pockets in a flat folded square of paper. A pocket is defined as any opening (lying between two surfaces of paper) that is accessible from the boundary of the folded piece of paper. Note that one accessible opening can account for several pockets since each open side contributes one pocket. Figure 1 shows an example. Observe that the "middle" opening (between the second and third layers of paper) contributes 3 to the total pocket count.

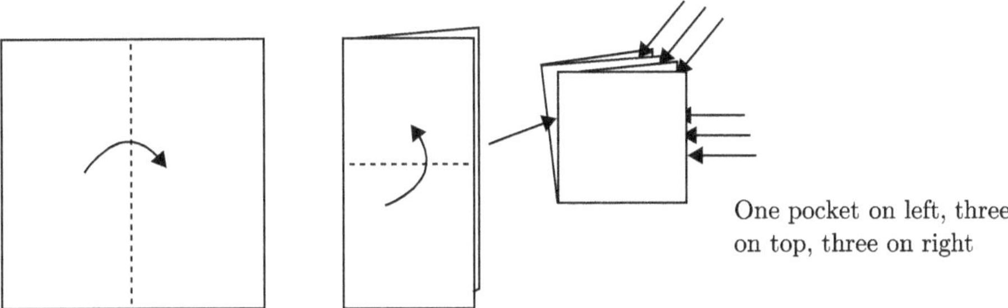

Figure 1: Pockets

Assume the paper is initially lying on a flat surface and is never completely lifted from the surface. All folds will be horizontal or vertical. Fold lines will fall only along equally-spaced crease lines, N in each direction. On the original unfolded square, creases and edges are numbered from top to bottom and from left to right as shown in Figure 2. Each fold reduces the boundary of the folded piece of paper to a smaller rectangle; the final fold results in a square one unit in each direction. Folds are described using a crease line and a direction. For instance, '2 U' means to fold the bottom edge up using horizontal crease 2; '1 L' means to fold the right edge to the left using crease 1. (See Figure 2.) After several folds, creases may be aligned (for instance, creases 1 and 3 in Figure 2). Either number may be used to specify a fold along that line (so, in Figure 2, '1 D' and '3 D' are equivalent instructions after the first fold). Pockets are to be counted for the boundary of the final one-unit square. Once a crease is made it cannot be undone. All creases go through every layer of paper from top to bottom; disregard paper thickness.

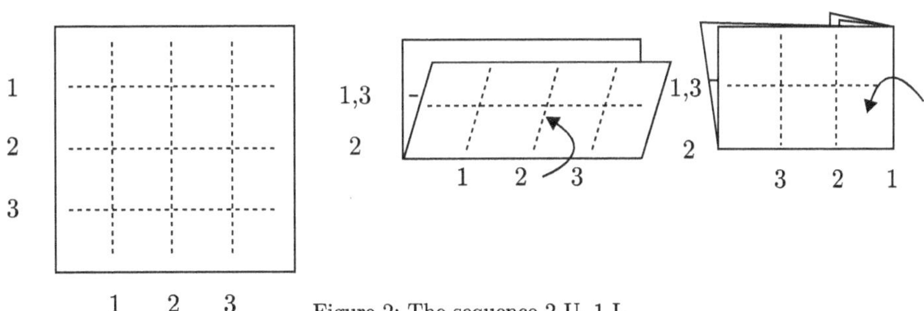

Figure 2: The sequence 2 U, 1 L.

Input

Input is a sequence of test cases. Each test case begins with a line containing two integers, N and K. N is the number of horizontal crease lines (the same as the number of vertical crease lines) of the square. Creases are numbered $1, 2, \ldots, N$ from top to bottom and from left to right. K is the number of folds to be made. N and K are each less than or equal to 64.

Following N and K are K fold descriptions. Each fold description consists of an integer crease number C and a direction, either U, D, L, or R (for up, down, left or right) separated by whitespace. Whitespace also precedes and follows each fold description.

The final result for each test case will be a square one unit in size.

The final test case is followed by a line containing two zeroes.

Output

For each input case, display the case number followed by the number of pockets in the final one-unit square. Use the format shown in the sample output.

Sample Input

```
1 2
1 R 1 U
3 5
2 U 1 L
   3   D
3 R 2 L
0 0
```

Sample Output

```
Case 1: 7 pockets
Case 2: 17 pockets
```

I Degrees of Separation

In our increasingly interconnected world, it has been speculated that everyone on Earth is related to everyone else by no more than six degrees of separation. In this problem, you must write a program to find the maximum degree of separation for a network of people.

For any two people, the degree of separation is the minimum number of relationships that must be traversed to connect the two people. For a network, the maximum degree of separation is the largest degree of separation between any two people in the network. If there is a pair of people in the network who are not connected by a chain of relationships, the network is disconnected.

As shown below, a network can be described as a set of symmetric relationships each of which connects two people. A line represents a relationship between two people. Network A illustrates a network with 2 as the maximum degree of separation. Network B is disconnected.

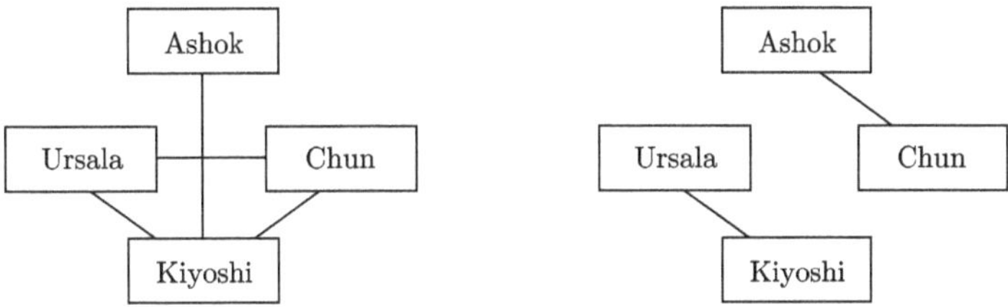

Network A: Max. degree of separation = 2   **Network B:** Disconnected

Input

The input consists of data sets that describe networks of people. For each data set, the first line has two integers: P ($2 \leq P \leq 50$), the number of people in the network, and R ($R \geq 1$), the number of network relationships. Following that first line are R relationships. Each relationship consists of two strings that are names of people in the network who are related. Names are unique and contain no blank spaces. Because a person may be related to more than one other person, a name may appear multiple times in a data set. The final test case is followed by a line containing two zeroes.

Output

For each network, display the network number followed by the maximum degree of separation. If the network is disconnected, display 'DISCONNECTED'. Display a blank line after the output for each network. Use the format illustrated in the sample output.

Sample Input

```
4  4
Ashok  Kiyoshi   Ursala  Chun   Ursala  Kiyoshi
Kiyoshi  Chun
4  2
Ashok  Chun   Ursala  Kiyoshi
6 5
Bubba  Cooter   Ashok  Kiyoshi   Ursala  Chun
Ursala  Kiyoshi   Kiyoshi  Chun
0  0
```

Sample Output

```
Network 1: 2

Network 2: DISCONNECTED

Network 3: DISCONNECTED
```

J Routing

As more and more transactions between companies and people are being carried out electronically over the Internet, secure communications have become an important concern. The Internet Cryptographic Protocol Company (ICPC) specializes in secure business-to-business transactions carried out over a network. The system developed by ICPC is peculiar in the way it is deployed in the network.

A network like the Internet can be modeled as a directed graph: nodes represent machines or routers, and edges correspond to direct connections, where data can be transmitted along the direction of an edge. For two nodes to communicate, they have to transmit their data along directed paths from the first node to the second, and from the second node to the first.

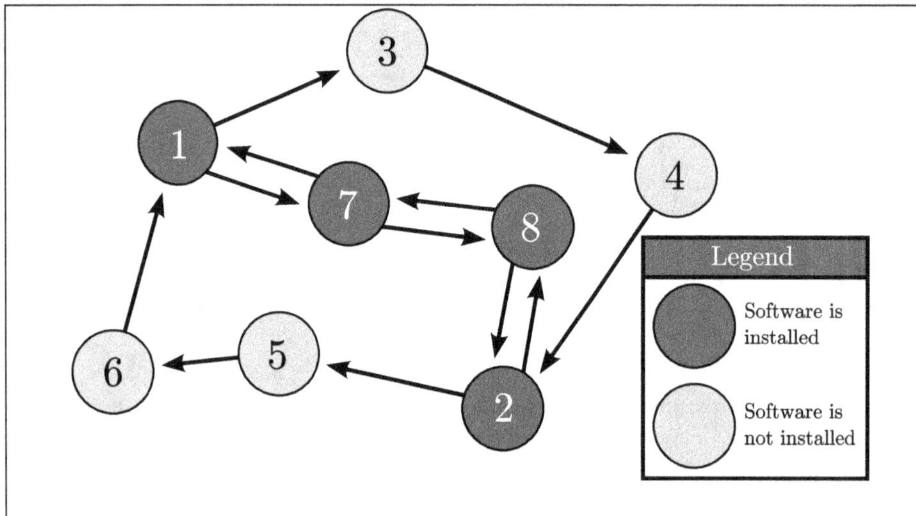

Figure: An arrow from node X to node Y means that it is possible to connect to node Y from node X but not vice versa. If software is installed on nodes 1, 2, 7, and 8, the communication is possible between node 1 and node 2. Other configurations are also possible but this is the minimum cost option. This figure corresponds to the first sample input.

To perform a secure transaction, ICPC's system requires the installation of their software not only on the two endnodes that want to communicate, but also on all intermediate nodes on the two paths connecting the end-nodes. Since ICPC charges customers according to how many copies of their software have to be installed, it would be interesting to have a program that for any network and end-node pair finds the cheapest way to connect the nodes.

Input

The input consists of several descriptions of networks. The first line of each description contains two integers N and M ($2 \le N \le 100$), the number of nodes and edges in the network, respectively. The nodes in the network are labeled $1, 2, \ldots, N$, where nodes 1 and 2 are the ones that want to communicate. The first line of the description is followed by M lines containing two integers X and Y ($1 \le X, Y \le N$), denoting that there is a directed edge from X to Y in the network.

The last description is followed by a line containing two zeroes.

Output

For each network description in the input, display its number in the sequence of descriptions. Then display the minimum number of nodes on which the software has to be installed, such that there is a directed path from node 1 to node 2 using only the nodes with the software, and also a path from node 2 to node 1 with the same property. (Note that a node can be on both paths but a path need not contain all the nodes.) The count should include nodes 1 and 2.

If node 1 and 2 cannot communicate, display 'IMPOSSIBLE' instead.

Follow the format in the sample given below, and display a blank line after each test case.

Sample Input

```
8 12
1 3
3 4
4 2
2 5
5 6
6 1
1 7
7 1
8 7
7 8
8 2
2 8
2 1
1 2
0 0
```

Sample Output

```
Network 1
Minimum number of nodes = 4

Network 2
IMPOSSIBLE
```